For Positivist Organization Theory

For Positivist Organization Theory

Proving the Hard Core

Lex Donaldson

SAGE Publications
London • Thousand Oaks • New Delhi

SAGE Publications Ltd
6 Bonhill Street
London EC2A 4PU

SAGE Publications Inc
2455 Teller Road
Thousand Oaks, California 91320

SAGE Publications India Pvt Ltd
32, M-Block Market
Greater Kailash – I
New Delhi 110 048

British Library Cataloguing in Publication data

A catalogue record for this book is
available from the British Library

    ISBN 0-7619-5226 8
    ISBN 0-7619-5227 6 (pbk)

Library of Congress catalog card number 96–069549

Typeset by M Rules
Printed in Great Britain by The Cromwell Press Ltd,
Broughton Gifford, Melksham, Wiltshire

When we run over libraries, persuaded of these principles, what havoc must we make? If we take in our hand any volume – of divinity or school metaphysics, for instance – let us ask, *Does it contain any abstract reasoning concerning quantity or number?* No. *Does it contain any experimental reasoning concerning matter of fact and existence?* No. Commit it then to the flames, for it can contain nothing but sophistry and illusion.

David Hume

In memoriam

Richard Alex Lewis
(1945–93)

Contents

List of illustrations

Acknowledgements

This book has had a long genesis. The vision of a science of organizations was first conveyed to me by my teachers at the University of Aston: John Child, Jerald Hage and David Hickson. While there, Ron Amey also provided me with a valuable introduction to statistical methods.

It has been my privilege not only to have been taught by John Child but also to have been a researcher with him in the Organization Behaviour Research Group of the London Graduate School of Business Studies. John Child is a model of scholarly conscientiousness and thoroughness. I should particularly like to record my appreciation to John Child for his careful teaching and then forbearance of my gradual dissension as a colleague. If I at all see clearly it is because I have stood on his shoulders. Since I work on the rich legacy of research ideas and materials that John generated I have sometimes come to see some issues a little differently, while continuing to work in his tradition. It has been a great comfort to me that whatever our differences of intellectual opinion, we have nevertheless been able to maintain our friendship, thanks to John's generosity of spirit.

Jerald Hage inspired me with his conviction that it is possible to find general theories of a functionalist kind that illuminate widely differing kinds of organizations. For me he personified the quest for theory as being primary relative to data.

David Hickson combines a remarkable record of achievement with astounding humility. He demonstrated to me that the key to understanding was to allow the data to reveal their patterns.

Derek Pugh headed up the Organization Behaviour Research Group of the London Graduate School of Business Studies. His vision of a science of organizations informed all of our work there, as it had earlier at Aston. For Derek, good research is like good music, there is an elegant mathematical structure beneath both. In my work at the OBRG I was ably and cheerfully supported by Malcolm Warner, who manifests a real capacity for broad understanding of ideas and people. Roger Mansfield was another able colleague at OBRG, who helped me form many views about organizational research, not least an awareness of the hazards of sticking too closely to small sample results when searching for scientific laws.

More recently, my friendship with Frank Schmidt of the University of Iowa reinvigorated the sense that a scientific mission is desirable and possible in organizational matters. He provided the role model that robust general patterns can be found that underlie the results of many researchers, if one avoids the traps to which data are liable. This really inspired the present book. Clyde Caulfield, a doctoral student at Iowa, applying these ideas, joined with me in the analysis of the administrative intensity literature. Sadly he has not lived to see this book.

June Ohlson provided much feedback on the manuscript to make it as clear as possible to the reader. She has also continued her warm support for my efforts, for which I gratefully thank her.

1

Positivist Organization Theory

This book asserts the validity of the positivist theory of organizations. That theory holds that organizations are to be explained by scientific laws in which the shape taken by organizations is determined by material factors such as their size. These laws hold generally across organizations of all types and national cultures. The organization adopts a structure that is required by the imperatives of its situation. Thus, structures are seen as functional. In this way positivist organization theory embraces functionalism. Hence positivist organization theory is determinist, generalizing, functionalist and explains organizations by material factors.

Positivism in organization theory has been opposed by anti-positivism (Burrell and Morgan, 1979). Anti-positivism rejects each of the central tenets of positivism and argues instead for an approach that is the opposite – namely, voluntarist, specific to industries or locales and which explains organizations by complex accounts such as an emphasis on political factors. Pioneering work in organization theory showed that a positivist approach could be fruitful. However, subsequent scholars turned against positivism and embraced more anti-positivist approaches. Their views have become the present-day accepted theory. Nevertheless, a deeper analysis reveals that their positions are flawed. A more in-depth consideration shows that the positivist theory is valid. Accordingly, much contemporary theorizing is founded on error.

Today organizations are often presented as shaped by complex processes produced by struggles between actors whose interests conflict. The resulting accounts of organizations are of subtle, intricate and idiosyncratic causal processes, with much hanging on the choices made by each of the contending parties. However, this view is more myth than substance. While often repeated and enjoying a wide following, it is at odds with the truth. The task of this volume is to sweep away the illusions and show the solid bedrock. Positivist theory explains organizations, and with a strength and robustness that is impressive to behold.

Positivist Organization Theory

The origins of modern-day positivist organization theory lie in the contingency research into organizational structure. This was developed during the 1960s in a series of works by Burns and Stalker (1961), Chandler (1962), Woodward (1965), Lawrence and Lorsch (1967), Thompson (1967), Pugh et al. (1969a), Blau (1970) and others. In each case they showed an empirical connection between some aspect of organizational structure and some aspect of the situation. Burns and Stalker (1961), Lawrence and Lorsch (1967) and also Thompson (1967) showed that the environment determines the required organizational structure. For example, Burns and Stalker (1961) showed that a stable environment requires a mechanistic organizational structure while a changing, innovatory environment required an organic organizational structure. Woodward (1965) and Thompson (1967) showed that the internal technology of the organization is a situational factor that determines the required organizational structure. Blau (1970) and Pugh et al. (1969a) showed that the size of the organization determines its required organizational structure. Chandler (1962) showed that the strategy of the organization determines its required organizational structure.

These situational factors of environmental instability, technology, size and strategy came to be called contingency factors. Likewise, this body of work came to be called contingency theory. This raises the question, what exactly is contingency theory? What is the common theory that connects these researches and underlies their various empirical findings across so many different aspects of structure and situation?

While each of these pioneering works in structural contingency theory emphasized their own contingency factor and their own aspects of organizational structure, nevertheless a commonality may be identified. By going up a level of abstraction so that one considers contingencies in general and structure in general it becomes possible to construct a more general theory. Each of the specific relationships between a particular contingency and a particular aspect of structure can be subsumed under this more general theory. This more abstract formulation may be termed a meta-contingency theory of organizational structure because it transcends any one pair of contingency and associated structure variables. In this way we can create the contingency theory that is missing from the more specific writings of the pioneers.

The organization is seen as existing in an environment that shapes its strategy, technology, size and required innovation rate. These contingency factors in turn determine the required structure; that is, the structure that the organization needs to adopt if it is to operate effectively. The effectiveness of the organization is affected by the fit between the organizational structure and the contingencies. This leads the organization to adapt its organizational structure so that it moves into fit with the contingency factors. In this way organizational structure is determined by the contingencies. We can call this the theory of structural adaptation to regain fit with the contingencies (Donaldson, 1987). Empirical research shows that this models the effects of fit on performance and the dynamics of organizational change (Donaldson, 1987). Thus the general contingency theory has now been developed. It is a theory of a functionalist and positivist type.

This meta-contingency theory of organizational structure is a *functionalist theory* in sociological terms. The organizational structure produces certain functional outcomes such as effectiveness, innovation and so on. The organization moves over time to adopt the organizational structure that is required in order to fit the contingency factors and so be effective. Hence the organizational structure is explained by its consequences for effectiveness. Organizational structure and organizational structural change are seen as results of functional adaptation. The managers of the organization are seen as making organizational structural decisions that are in the interests of the organization to heighten its effectiveness, as the pioneering researchers suggested (Chandler, 1962; Woodward, 1965; Blau, 1970).

The theory is also *positivist* in sociological terms (Burrell and Morgan, 1979). It is positivist in all of six senses:

1 It is *nomothetic*, meaning that the phenomena are analysed using a general framework with factors that apply to all organizations, both for the contingency factors (such as size and strategy) and for the organizational structure (like specialization and centralization). General causal relationships in the form of law-like regularities are sought between contingency and structural factors.

2 The research associated with the theory is *methodologically positivist* in that there is much use of comparative empirical research, often with the measurement of variables and statistical analysis of data.

3 The theory explains organizational structure by *material factors* such as size, technology and so on, rather than by ideationalist factors such as ideas, ideologies, perceptions, norms and the like. (Even in the work of Chandler the 'strategy' that affects structure refers to the degree of diversification and vertical integration existing in the organization; a mere plan or intention of diversifying that was not implemented would not require a change of structure.)

4 The theory is *determinist* in that managers are seen as having to adopt the organizational structure that is required by the contingency factors, in order to gain organizational effectiveness.

5 The theory is closely *informed by empirical research* rather than arm-chair speculation or extended theorizing prior to empirical data collection. It is built upon the data patterns and arguments of the pioneering works.

6 The theory is consciously scientific in style, with *the aim being to produce scientific knowledge of the type achieved in the natural sciences.*

The period of the 1960s was an era of increasing success and acceptance for structural contingency theory. Subsequently the structural contingency theory research was replicated and extended (for example, Blau, 1972; Goldman, 1973; Beyer and Trice, 1979; Lenz, 1980; Blau et al., 1976; Lorsch and Allen, 1973; Pitts, 1976; Pugh and Hinings, 1976). Researchers worked in the paradigm to extend and consolidate it, and to resolve anomalies (for instance, Pugh and Hinings, 1976; Hickson et al., 1979; Routamaa, 1985; Miller, 1987). It was synthesized into multivariate models of how the various dimensions of organizational structure were each shaped by the various contingency factors (for example, Price and Mueller, 1986; Gerwin, 1979; Reimann and Inzerilli, 1979; Pugh and Hinings, 1976). Textbooks on organizational structure and design take the contingency approach as central (such as Khandwalla, 1977;

Daft, 1986; Bedeian and Zammuto, 1991). However, a critical reaction against positivist organization theory has also occurred.

Critical Reactions to Positivist Organization Theory

Burrell and Morgan (1979) have charted how positivism is opposed by anti-positivism within sociology and, more specifically, in organization theory. There are three broad reactions against positivist structural contingency theory.

The strongest reaction rejected the whole positivist organization theory paradigm as inherently flawed and ideologically unsound (for example, Silverman, 1970). This was the tack taken by critical and radical organization theorists who abhorred functionalism and positivism (such as Clegg and Dunkerley, 1977, 1980). They sought to replace structural contingency theory with theoretical approaches that focused often on individual perception, belief and choice, and often on conflict and power struggles between classes or groups (Silverman, 1970; Clegg and Dunkerley, 1980; Benson, 1977). These critics relied heavily on a priori philosophical arguments and theoretical arguments of a sociological kind. They tended to reject also the use of quantitative methods, dismissing much of the empirical evidence out of hand (such as Clegg and Dunkerley, 1977, 1980). Thus they eschewed the quantitative evidence rather than seeking to use quantitative evidence against the positivist theory. Elsewhere, I have rebutted their critiques of positivism, functionalism, structural contingency theory and quantitative methods (Donaldson, 1985).

The second reaction, popular in many parts of the United States, was also to critique structural contingency theory and move away from it, but towards not one but many different organization theory paradigms. Thus the United States, especially from about the mid-1970s onwards, was host to a proliferation of new organization theory paradigms that differed sharply among themselves (though with some commonalities also). These included population-ecology theory, institutional theory, resource dependence theory, agency theory and transactions costs theory (Hannan and Freeman, 1989; Powell and DiMaggio, 1991; Pfeffer and Salancik, 1978; Jensen and Meckling, 1976; Williamson, 1985). These newer US organization theories took among them a variety of stances on the issues of positivism and functionalism, thus overall making their rejection of structural contingency theory complex and multidimensional. These newer US organization theory paradigms are reviewed elsewhere (Donaldson, 1995). Their rejection of structural contingency theory is rebutted and the paradigms are themselves critiqued as having problems of theory and empirical validity (Donaldson, 1995). The continuing cogency and validity of the structural contingency theory approach is asserted (Donaldson, 1995). Thus the first and second reactions to structural contingency theory have significantly rejected the contingency theory explanation of organizational structure.

However, there has been a third reaction to positivist organization theory. This third group is composed of scholars who reject one or other of the central tenets such as determinism, functionalism or generalization. Those opposed to determinism argue that people exercise choice rather than bowing to situational dictates. Those who reject functionalism argue that much of organizational structure is counter-productive and arises to serve the interests of certain organizational members such as managers. A unifying theme here is a tendency to argue that organizations are shaped by actors who pursue their own interests, consciously choose stratagems, and engage in a process of conflict with others so that causal processes are complex and unpredictable. Thus organization studies moves towards accounts that see reality as politically constructed and uncertain, defying simple general laws, or as specific to a certain industry. In place of material factors as the causes of organization, ideas are given more prominence in the anti-positivist organization theory. These ideas include perceptions, beliefs and ideologies. Anti-positivism extends also to arguing that real organizations conform to a few ideal-types. The simplified models of organizations found in textbooks are held actually to constitute the empirical world.

Although many of these scholars reject positivist theory, they embrace its methods. They make use of quantitative methods and empirical data to prove their point. Moreover, they often use data similar to those used by the positivists to prove their theories. Hence they have engaged with positivist research on its home turf. This has made their attacks devastating. Accordingly, their critiques have been telling, and command respect among even the more methodologically sophisticated and positivistically inclined scholars. Thus the views of the critics have become highly influential among organizational scholars and they constitute much of the received view today in the community of researchers and teachers.

Anti-positivist organization theories include: the strategic choice theory; the political theory of organizational structure; organizational typologies; and organizational systematics. The task of this book is to review critically each of these and seek to show that they are flawed, and to prove that positivist organization theory is sound theoretically and empirically. Let us now acquaint ourselves with these anti-positivist theories.

Anti-positivist Organization Theories

We will now briefly outline each of the major anti-positivist theories to be considered here in turn: strategic choice, the political explanation of organizational structure, organizational typologies and organizational systematics.

Strategic Choice

The anti-positivists include those who express reservations about the determinism of positivist organization theory and would wish to assert in its place voluntarism – that is, a role for human choice. The most extreme voluntarists reject completely the proposition that the managers running organizations are determined in the strategies and structures that they choose for their organizations. Whittington (1989) argues that managers make free choices about the conduct of their companies and that they should therefore be held ethically accountable for those choices, with no blurring by talk of situational determinants.

In mainstream organization theory, such an extreme view has not as yet been popular. More influential has been the notion that structural contingency theory has over-stated the degree of determinism of structure by contingencies and that there is a greater degree of choice – that is, a partial voluntarism. A major development was the strategic choice approach (Child, 1972a; Bourgeois, 1984). In the matter of organization structure, this argued against the idea that structure is determined by contingency or context or situational variables such as size. It asserted that the coupling between structure and contingency is loose. There is some tendency for structure to be associated with the contingency factors, but the actual structure adopted depends on managerial decision and is therefore affected by managerial perceptions, values, beliefs, interests, politics and so on. These factors intercede between contingency and structure so that the structure is only weakly determined by the contingency. For the given contingency, the management of an organization may select a range of structures to accommodate their preferences. There is some credence given to the structural contingency theory notion that organizations need to maintain fit between their structure and the contingency factors to avoid performance losses, but structural contingency theory is seen as over-stating the degree of compulsion. Child (1972a) and Bourgeois (1984) have advanced these arguments at some length.

In formal terms, the strategic choice view argues that the influence of contingency on structure is mediated by several intervening factors reflecting the presence of human actors. Moreover, structure can affect contingency in that a misfit between structure and contingency can be rectified by changing the contingency to produce a new fit. Further, the presence of slack can permit the organization to retain a misfitting structure for a long time. The result is that management does not have to adopt a certain structure when the organization has attained a certain contingency factor. Thus determinism is often, and to a considerable extent, avoided and is, overall, muted.

Determinism is felt to be undesirable in value terms because it denies human beings their freedom to decide their own destinies. The idea of structural determinism is felt to be lamentable because it means that certain structures will have to be adopted and these will be traditional, established management structures which are undesirable because they preclude the adoption of radical, humanistic, democratic, alternative structures. Thus the strategic choice thesis connects with ideologies which would aim to assert the necessity for new organizational structures of the industrial democratic type. Moreover, under such a political programme, a central task of the leftist sociologist is to critique the rightist ideology of the inevitability of certain organization structures (Clegg and Dunkerley, 1980). Hence, for such sociologists the ideological battle is joined when they critique management school theories, about the structures adopted by corporations being the required ones.

In bringing the human actor back into organization theory, the choice theorists also bring back in the factors that directly shape human choice, such as ideas and interests. Ideas include here the perceptions, beliefs, theories and values of the human actors. Thus strategic choice down-plays the importance of material, objective causes of organizational structure and thus to a degree breaks away from the materialism of positivism. The ideas may extend also to ideologies that are ideas moulded by interests. Reference to interests brings in the way each individual actor, and their group or class, win or lose according to which decision option is taken up. This focus on the consequences for each individual differs from functionalism, where the focus is on the benefit to the organization as a whole. Thus the analysis of organizational decisions in individual interest terms challenges the functionalism of structural contingency theory. The strategic choice formulation (Child, 1972a) retains some degree of functionalism, modifying it to incorporate a recognition of political factors. Child (1984) calls for the addition of political factors to the structural contingency theory model and refers to these factors as political contingencies.

In the case of Bourgeois (1984) there is an affinity with the idea of free choice for managers and the central presupposition in the subjects of Business Policy and Business Strategy, as taught in business schools. These subjects presuppose that top managers are free to choose among a wide range of alternatives. The concern is that positivist structural contingency theory gives insufficient recognition to the role of management in making structural decisions. More generally in the community, there is some affinity also between the notion of free will and religious views.

The Political Explanation of Organizational Structure

In rejecting the functionalism in positivist organization theory, either wholly or partially, there is often a move towards a political model of organization theory. The political model holds that individual interests are pursued in organizational life through the exercise of power and influence. Thus the analysis would shift to the power resources possessed by different groups in the organization and the way that they use these resources in actual power plays to shape the organizational structure. At the extreme, in the writings of Parkinson, the growth of administrators in the organization is held to be completely unrelated to the work to be done and to be caused totally by the political pursuit of self-interest. Though populist and satirical, the Parkinson thesis has been advocated by serious researchers in the most serious of journals – for example, Child (1973a) in the *Administrative Science Quarterly*. This demonstrates the degree to which functionalism has been, at times on certain topics, replaced by the political model in organization theory. On the specific topic of the growth of administrators, Child (1973a) has opted more strongly for the political theory than in his more programmatic statements about structure more widely construed, where he argues the need to combine the political and functionalist theories by including a set of political contingencies on the list of contingency factors (Child, 1984).

While the political theory of organizations rejects functionalism, it has been pursued on occasions in the organizational theory literature in ways that use positivist methods. Research approaches, such as comparative methods, contingency and structural variables, measurement and statistical data analyses that are similar to those which have been used in positivist research have been deployed to attack functionalist structural contingency theory (for instance, by Freeman and Hannan, 1975; Montanari and Adelman, 1987; Marsh and Mannari, 1989). This has frequently involved damaging criticisms and the replacement of the simple, general models of structural contingency theory by more complex political models (Child, 1973a; Reimann, 1979; Lioukas and Xerokostas, 1982; Smith, 1978). This constitutes a rejection of the positivist ambition to discover highly general causal laws in which material factors such as size are major causes.

Organizational Typologies

The organizational typology school accepts the functionalism of structural contingency theory. More specifically, this school holds on to the notion that there is a fit between the organization and its environment that leads to effectiveness. Indeed, the organizational types or configurations or Gestalts are the fits (Mintzberg, 1979; Miller, 1986). However, it rejects the Cartesian approach that is integral to the contingency theory view.

The original structural contingency theory view is that organizational structure is composed of variables such as specialization and centralization. Each variable is a quantitative scale with many points on it varying from low to high. An organization may score at any point on the variable. These structural variables are independent dimensions, such as bureaucratic structuring (specialization, formalization and so on) and centralization, that form a conceptual space, with the place of any one organization being defined through Cartesian coordinates. For example, organization A is 71 out of 100 on bureaucratic structuring and 36 out of 100 on centralization, while organization B is 39 out of 100 on bureaucratic structuring and 82 out of 100 on centralization. Similarly, the contingency factors such as size and strategy form a set of independent dimensions, so that any organization has a set of scores on those dimensions. Thus the analysis conceives of a set of Cartesian dimensions of contingencies and structure. The position of an organization on the structural dimensions is related to its position on the contingency dimensions. The phenomena of organizations are modelled by this underlying multidimensional space and system of coordinates within it. This is referred to hereafter as Cartesianism.

This Cartesianism pervades the whole analysis of contingency theory. Not only are the contingency and structure factors defined as continuous variables, but the fits between them are also continua, there being many points of fit. This structural contingency theory view, in turn, allows frequent, small movements by organizations from one fit to an adjacent fit, producing incremental change over time. However, the organizational typology or configuration school implicitly rejects this incrementalism. In its place, the organizational typology or configuration school holds that there are few fits between contingency and structure (Miller, 1986). These fits are separated in conceptual space, with organizations having to make 'quantum' jumps from one fit to another (Miller, 1986: 237), because the intermediary positions are implicitly all misfits. The quantum jumps are infrequent (Miller, 1986: 237). Thus change is occasional and sharply discontinuous according to the typology theory.

Structural contingency theory often uses typologies to describe the fits between contingencies and structures (Burns and Stalker, 1961; Pugh et al. 1969b). For example, Burns and Stalker (1961) write that the mechanistic structure fits a stable environment and the organic structure fits an unstable environment. Typologizers seize on these types and assert that they are the only fits. They invoke arguments about the types being internally consistent, such as each type reflecting a single coordination mode (Mintzberg, 1979). For the original structural contingency theories the types are extreme end-points on continua with many organizations lying at intermediary points. There are fits along these continua so that the degree of the structural variable fits the degree of the contingency variable. For example, an organization in an environment of a middle degree of stability would require a structure of a middle degree of organicness to be in fit (Burns and Stalker, 1961). Thus positivist organization theory places emphasis on quantification, not just as measures in empirical research, but substantively, arguing that organizations actually vary from one to another so that they are distributed at many points along quantitative dimensions.

There is, however, an increasing tendency in the writings of some of the typologizers to lose this subtlety. The types become not end-points on continua of many fits but the *only* viable fits. The intermediary space along the continua tends to fall out of view and any point not a type is seen as not viable. Therefore the organization cannot dwell there. Thus the organization has few possibilities: it stays as one type or leaps to one of the few other types. This is dramatic and happens infrequently. In this way the quantitative world-view of modern structural contingency theory is replaced by a simpler, qualitative one. The Cartesianism and incrementalism of modern structural contingency theory is replaced by a model of sharp discontinuities. Instead of treating types as ideal-types to structure a discussion, the ideal-types become the only actual organizations in the world. This is a triumph of ideas over material factors. It sits well with the programme of anti-positivism.

Organizational Systematics

Positivism entails a belief in generalization, yet this also has been called into question – by the organizational systematics approach. This again retains the functionalist aspect of structural contingency theory that organizations need to fit their environment to be effective.

Structural contingency theory argues that organizational structure is shaped by the situation of the organization, including its environment. Population-ecology theory builds on this to argue that the environment is a series of ecological niches (Hannan and Freeman, 1989). These provide resources required by the organization and will sustain those organizations that fit one or other of the ecological niches. One variant or off-shoot of population ecology theory is organizational systematics. This holds that if the organization is to fit its niche then it must develop competencies that are highly specific to that niche and that allow superior performance in that niche. McKelvey and Aldrich (1983) illustrate this by saying that the competences required in the airline industry are highly specific to the industry and differ from those in other industries – that is, other niches. They criticize earlier attempts in organization theory to find general relationships between contingencies and structural factors and see these as having been unsuccessful. Such efforts are flawed at the outset for McKelvey and Aldrich, who view as naïve the presumption that general relationships exist or can be identified in organization theory.

Instead, McKelvey and Aldrich (1983) argue that research should proceed by studying each niche or industry and identifying the characteristic competences of each. The results for each niche are then compared across niches to discover empirically which elements are held in common between which niches. This in turn will form the basis for a taxonomy of organizations that identifies phylogenic trees of similarities and differences across organizations in the manner of a taxonomy in biology. Such an approach to the study of organizations would be highly gradual, cautious and empirically grounded. There would not be the a priori postulation of general theories of the structural contingency theory type such as 'strategy leads to structure' or 'size causes bureaucracy'. Such generalizations are seen by McKelvey and Aldrich (1983) as being invalid.

Thus here the nomothetic aspect of positivism is being questioned, in that generalizations of broad scope are denied in favour of generalizations of narrow scope that apply only to one or a few taxonomically adjacent niches. There is some role for general concepts, but this is checked by the injunction to understand exactly and concretely the distinctive competences which exist and are important in each situation. Such a process of examining the ingredients of success in each specific situation moves away from the nomothetic pole and begins to move towards the ideographic pole of analysis; that is, of comprehending the organization in its own terms and in its own unique situation (Burrell and Morgan, 1979).

The organizational systematics approach has some points of agreement with the structural contingency approach, both being environmentally deter- minist and scientific in aspiration. However, the implicit role model of the structural contingency approach is physics with its wide-ranging general laws. The role model of organizational systematics is biology, and consequently the scope of generalization sought is considerably smaller.

In summary, each of these anti-positivist organization theories can be understood by seeing how it departs from the original structural contingency theory with its positivism and functionalism. The positivism has been rejected in several different ways. Strategic choice theorists partially reject determin- ism and assert more of a role for voluntarism. Strategic choice theory leads away from explanation by objective, material factors and emphasizes instead subjective factors such as ideas, perceptions, beliefs, values and ideologies. Organizational typologies reject the quantitative framework used in structural contingency theory, a framework that sees the contingency and structural fac- tors as variables and the fit between them as continua. This in turn leads to a rejection of the incrementalist view of structural change held in structural contingency theory, in favour of a model of stasis punctuated by occasional quantum leaps between types. Finally, the nomothetic, generalizing aspects of structural contingency theory are rejected to a great degree by the organiza- tional systematics approach. The functionalism has been rejected by the political theory of organizations that explains organization structure by inter- ests and the power of different organizational members.

Much hangs on the question of the explanatory power of the model which seeks to explain organizational structure by contingency factors, such as size and strategy. Contingency theory holds that much of organizational structure can be explained by a few such contingency factors and that this model gen- eralizes across many different types of organizations and national settings. Thus contingency theory holds that its core model features high explanatory power by the contingencies and enjoys robust generalizability. Many of the critics considered herein work by seeking to show this claim to be false. For strategic choice theorists the contingencies only loosely determine organiza- tional structure and so their explanatory power is weak, with ideational factors making up a substantial part of the explanation. For political theo- rists, size and like contingencies are not the true causes, which lie in the pursuit of self-interest through political manoeuvering, so contingency expla- nations must be shown to be invalid, with true causation being much more complex. Similarly, political theorists contest the functional patterns that contingency theorists claim to find in their data. Again, typologizers reject the continuous variables that are the fundamental dimensions of contingency theory, and seek to replace them with a few organizational types. Further, the organizational systematicists reject the claims that contingency theory can find general patterns that are robust across organizations of all types. Thus all the critics discussed in this book take the view that the contingency theory is false in its claim that its simple models are valid, robustly general and of high explanatory power. Thus the theme of this book is to show that contingency theory models of a simple kind are valid, robustly general and of high explanatory power. Many of the critics seek to make their case by offering supposedly damaging criticisms based upon positivist research evidence; accordingly, we shall seek to refute them by offering a more penetrating analysis of such evidence. In this way we will prove the hard core of positivist organization theory.

Overview

The body of this volume will consider each of these lines of objection to positivist organization theory. This involves the examination of four issues.

The first issue is the issue of *determinism*. Are criticisms of determinism in structural contingency theory correct? We will argue that these criticisms are largely in error and will re-assert the validity of a deterministic theory of organizational structure. In Chapter 2 we consider criticisms of the contingency theory which claims that the objective contingency factors determine organizational structure. We rebut these criticisms and argue on behalf of the contingency explanation. Some research has sought to show that subjective factors play a role in influencing organizational structure; in Chapter 3 we show that these studies provide little support for strategic choice, thereby further buttressing the theory of objective determination.

The second issue is the issue of *functionalism*. Political theory holds that organizational structure is determined not by functional necessity and the drive for organizational effectiveness, but by the political process of organizational members maximizing their personal interest to the cost of the organization. Therefore political theorists hold that simple general models of structure, caused by material factors like size, have to be replaced by more complex interpretations that defy the positivist program of finding general laws. Against this view, we will argue that the political theory is flawed theoretically and empirically invalid, and re-assert instead in Chapters 4 and 5 the view that organizational structures result from functionalist adaptation to produce economically effective structures. This in turn allows explanation by simple causal laws that generalize.

The third issue is the issue of *Cartesianism*. Should we really reject the analytic framework of contingency theory that deals in organizations taking many different positions in a multidimensional space and replace it by a few types? Likewise, should we reject incremental change, and instead hold that organizations change by making quantum jumps between widely differing types? Is the mode of analysis used in organizational typologies theoretically and empirically sound? We will argue in Chapter 6 that it is not, and that such typologies are not only erroneous but constitute an unfortunate regression in organization theory that reverses prior progress and prevents future progress.

The fourth issue is the issue of *generalization*. Can one generalize in organizational structure, or is generalization best avoided at present in favour of a gradually emerging taxonomy as advocated by the organizational systematics approach? We will argue in Chapter 7 that generalization is possible and can be demonstrated for organizational structure. Even the concept of a generalizable contingency dimension of organizational size has been challenged. This will be examined critically, and generalization of organizational size asserted (in Chapter 8).

Throughout this volume, the cogency and validity of positivist organization theory will be asserted regarding many of its core features: determinism, functionalism, Cartesianism and generalization. The final chapter (Chapter 9) will summarize the positivist contingency model of organizational structure.

2

For Determinism: Against Strategic Choice

The tension between determinism and choice is perhaps the most central, and least resolved, issue in the social sciences (Burrell and Morgan, 1979). It is central to debate in organization theory (Warner, 1977; Astley and Van de Ven, 1983; Hrebiniak and Joyce, 1985; Whittington, 1988, 1989; Mahoney, 1993). Rejection of determinism is seen as one of the main elements of anti-positivism (Burrell and Morgan, 1979). In contrast, positivist structural contingency theory holds that structure is determined by the contingency variables. It sees little discretion in the selection of structures by management. This is often seen as a very negative view of management in structural contingency theory. Thus the idea of structure being determined by objective contingency factors has come under attack.

This chapter will consider these criticisms of determinism and argue that they are ill-founded and incorrect. It will argue for the view that contingencies determine structure, and show that this view is far more coherent and empirically valid than the critics hold. The focus will be upon the adequacy of objective factors in explaining organizational structure. The ensuing chapter will consider evidence that subjective factors explain organizational structure. And it will also show that structural determinism, far from implying a negative view of management, actually implies a very positive view of management. Thus the present chapter is mainly a defence of the claim that contingencies determine organizational structure, whereas the ensuing chapter is a critique of claims about subjective factors.

The most widely received attack on determinism in organization theory has come from John Child (1972a). In place of determinism he argues for 'strategic choice'. This latter concept has been almost universally applauded and has become a central idea in organization theory world-wide. Probably most scholars today accept its thesis as being both important and valid. We also were influenced by these ideas at an earlier time (Donaldson, 1982a). However, continued study of this issue has led us to grow dissatisfied with the strategic choice idea and to move towards determinism. Since the issue is a central one we must lay out the grounds for now seeing strategic choice as deficient and for our belief in determinism. Because the issue is major and involves so many facets we must devote considerable space to it in order to deal adequately with all of the facts. Thus while we take the liberty of dissenting from the strategic choice view we accord it its rightful status as a major theory. John Child made a key contribution by raising the issue of determinism and by offering a resolution in his strategic choice concept. If our discussion enables us to make any headway on this vexing topic it will be because of the force and thoroughness with which he expounded the issue. Thus if our present critique should lead scholars away from the strategic choice idea it will only be because John Child's masterful statement of that position allows it to be transcended.

The criticisms of the idea of the determinism of structure by contingencies come from two main directions. The first is from sociologists who have argued that contingencies only determine structure to a limited degree and that management exercises considerable strategic choice. They wish to reveal the arbitrary nature of selected structures (Child, 1972a; Whittington, 1989). Some criticisms of the idea of structural determinism by contingency arise from the same radical sociological movement which has led to the political analysis of organizations (Schreyögg, 1980; Whitley, 1977). The second is from management theorists who also argue that contingencies determine structure, and other organizational features, only to a limited degree, and that managers exercise considerable discretion guided by their beliefs and perceptions (Anderson and Paine, 1975; Bourgeois, 1984; Weick, 1987). The aim of these scholars is to recognize the frailty of present managerial judgements so that they may be enhanced through various interventions. Critics of structural determinism tend to emphasize that true causation is in the managerial mind and so stress perceptual, cognitive and ideological causal factors. This emphasis on ideational explanations by strategic choice theorists is part of their anti-positivist quality. The two schools of criticism concur in seeing many defects in the argument and evidence that contingencies cause organizational structure.

Whittington (1989) rejects determinism and argues that managers exercise a free choice over the fate of their organizations. Other writers are less extreme, and argue that there is some degree of choice coexisting alongside of some degree of determinism by the environment and contingency factors (Child, 1972a; Bourgeois, 1984). This more moderate argument has probably received more attention to date in the organizations theory literature, so we will focus on it herein. However, in arguing that contingency determinism is stronger than its moderate critics assert we are also necessarily replying to the extremists who deny any contingency determinism.

Bourgeois is another organizational theorist who has mounted a trenchant attack on the idea of structural determinism by contingencies. This critique has been widely received in management theory circles. The criticisms advanced by Bourgeois (1984) draw on the critique made earlier by Child (1972a) in his seminal article on 'strategic choice', but several further criticisms are added. Accordingly, in this chapter the criticisms of both Child (1972a) and Bourgeois (1984) will be considered together.

The Contested Terrain

The strategic choice theory of Child (1972a) states that organizational structure is partly determined by the contingencies and partly also results from managerial choices. Child (1972a) argues against the idea that structure is determined by contingencies to the high degree asserted in traditional structural contingency theory in the 1960s (for example Pugh et al., 1969a). He allows some determination of structure by contingency, but to limited degree, with a considerable magnitude of managerial discretion in the selection of structures, which he termed 'strategic choice'. This term and its associated argument has become a central part of the modern organization theory literature.

The term 'strategic choice' refers not to choice of strategy (such as plans for diversification), which the words themselves might be taken to mean, but to the choice of structure. A more apt term might have been 'structural choice'. There is an ambiguity in the term 'strategic choice' which might have made it more persuasive, since many management theorists believe that corporate strategy is freely chosen even if they might have been willing to entertain the idea that contingencies determine structure. Moreover, the word strategic in 'strategic choice' may be also taken to mean strategic in the sense of calculating or deliberative. Confusion may be avoided here so long as we are clear that strategic choice is being used in its original meaning of structural choice. Likewise, clarity may be attained if the reader understands the phrase 'structural determinism', as used here, to be a short-hand for determinism of structure by contingencies.

Bourgeois (1984), following Child (1972a), offers a stimulating and provocative attack on the role of determinism in strategic management. He makes the argument for the centrality of strategic choice in this subject and for a better articulation of this concept in research. In so doing, he draws heavily on a relatively negative evaluation of the potentiality and achievements of deterministic approaches in strategic management in general, and in organization theory, specifically. He argues that deterministic models, allied to a narrow approach to the study of strategic management, have led to an unsatisfactory state of affairs. He states that the literature is focused too much on static, correlational studies which allow little scope for management to inaugurate change in either strategy formulation or implementation. This results in a discipline which provides little useful knowledge. The solution is seen in the adoption of the postulate of managerial free will allied to research approaches which feature reciprocal causation and which combine quantitative with qualitative approaches (Bourgeois, 1984). While Bourgeois discusses strategic management, which includes not only organizational structure but also other aspects such as strategy formulation, the focus herein will be on organizational structure – as in the rest of this volume. The view taken in this chapter is that organizational structure is, in some aspects, quite highly determined. Accordingly, prescriptive interventions based on the idea of free will run the risk of being seriously in error and therefore of confusing the search for more effective practice.

Determinism in Organizational Structure

How much choice is there over organizational structure? Similarly, Schreyögg (1980) writes of the scope of choice, but is this large or small? Is organizational structure largely determined? We would submit that there is substantial determinism in organizational structure and that recent research does not support the kind of strategic choice model which some might wish. Thus a fuller appreciation of the achievements of organizational structure research provides evidence of determinacy and suggests that this is proving a fruitful line of approach.

Strategic Choice

Those cautioning against what are seen as theories of organizational structure that are too deterministic have given currency to the concept of strategic choice (Child, 1972a; Bobbitt and Ford, 1980; Bourgeois, 1984). This refers to the substantial zone of choice that exists in the way management, especially the dominant coalition, selects the structure of the organization. Earlier contingency theories (Chandler, 1962; Woodward, 1965; Burns and Stalker, 1961; Lawrence and Lorsch, 1967) have stressed the imperative of adjusting the structure to the contingencies in order to maintain fit and hence high performance. They postulate a set of states of equilibrium in each of which the structure is appropriate to a particular value of the contingency variable – for example, in an uncertain environment an organic structure fits. The theories also posit a dynamic process whereby there is a shift in the contingency variable bringing the organization into disequilibrium or misfit with resulting reduced performance, so then the structure is adjusted to a new value to regain fit and higher performance. Thus the structure is essentially chosen by the state of the contingencies. Also the management is reactive rather than proactive. This structural contingency theory has been formalized into the structural adaptation to regain fit model (SARFIT). It postulates the following cycle: fit – high performance – change in contingency – misfit – reduced performance – structural adaptation – new fit – regained performance (Donaldson, 1987).

   In contrast, the strategic choice thesis (Bourgeois, 1984; Child, 1972a) asserts that there is more scope of choice by management which does exercise discretion over the choice of structure, with structural change being a more complex phenomenon than contingency theory allows. This choice arises in several ways. Management can regain fit by adjusting the contingency to the structure. Also, in conditions of environmentally induced slack, organizations may persist with sub-optimal structures for considerable periods of time. Thus organizations need not in fact adjust their structures to their contingencies and this allows influence by managerial value preferences, perceptions, beliefs, ideologies and power. In these ways, there is a considerable scope for choice of structure (Bourgeois, 1984; Child, 1972a; Bobbitt and Ford, 1980). This is indicated by the failure of contingency variables to explain much more than half of the variation in structure (Child, 1972a:12; Bobbitt and Ford, 1980). This strategic choice model is widely received. However, recent research on organizational structure challenges the validity of this view.

Proponents of strategic choice theory argue that real causation lies in the mind of the manager, yet they present little evidence for this assertion. Their method of argument is rather to seek to show defects in the view that contingencies – such as size, technology and so on – determine structure. Thereby, the strategic choice theorists argue that contingencies only weakly cause structure thus leaving room for managerial choice. It is therefore appropriate to assess the validity of strategic choice theory primarily through an examination of its critique of structural determinism, that is, by considering the defects in structural contingency theory as alleged by strategic choice theorists. This is the task of the present chapter. It will show that the idea of objective determinants of structure is more cogent than its critics allow. In particular, the determination of organizational structure by objective contingency factors is stronger and more robust than the critics assert.

A more direct examination of strategic choice theory would proceed by examining the positive evidence supporting this theory. A critical review of such studies will be presented in the next chapter, which focuses on subjective factors affecting organizational structure. This will lead into a closing discussion of the implications of determinism for values and applications.

The Earlier Debate

Previously we have argued against the strategic choice theory so we need to make explicit why we need to offer another statement, that is, what is different in our present statement? Our earlier criticism was that strategic choice was a good idea that failed to go far enough in asserting the role for choice. Now, in contrast, we are arguing that there is less choice than strategic choice theory holds. Thus our position has shifted appreciably, in the light of new evidence and reasoning, to become more positivist.

Child (1972a) and Schreyögg (1980) criticized the theory that contingencies determine organizational structure. Earlier, we replied to both (Donaldson, 1982a, 1985; see also Schreyögg, 1982) in terms of deficiencies in their theoretical logic. The discussion led us to doubt that their positions were well founded in sociology and internally coherent (Donaldson, 1985). We pointed out that structural contingency theory is not completely deterministic in that a role has long been seen for managers to select the organizational structure required by the contingencies (Woodward, 1965; Blau, 1970). Child (1972a) and Schreyögg (1980) call for more explanation of organizational structure by reference to elements such as the values, perceptions, ideologies and power of the decision-makers. However, since these factors are themselves widely held to be situationally shaped, Child (1972a) and Schreyögg (1980) are not thereby escaping determinism, but rather embracing sociological determinism. Thus their programme will not produce its avowed end of revealing greater choice and facilitating more socially desirable decisions about organizational structure. Such choices, to the degree that they are possible, could only be facilitated by decision-makers exercising greater reflexiveness through better information about the objective outcomes of different organizational structures. This would require pursuing the organizational design agenda of identifying fits between contingency and structure and their consequent outcomes.

Thus our earlier critiques of Child (1972a) and Schreyögg (1980) were not disputing their rejections of contingency determinism, but rather argued that their criticisms are misplaced and that their alternative programme is self-defeating. The present exercise, in contrast, is more substantive. We argue that structure is determined by the contingency factors with little room for managerial choice. Much of the work we draw on has been done since we wrote our earlier publication (Donaldson, 1985). Evidence is accumulating which supports the proposition that the contingencies quite closely determine organizational structure. Child (1984) criticizes an earlier statement by us (Donaldson, 1983) of structural determinism. In the present chapter we will draw on new material to make good deficiencies in the earlier statement and assert the validity of structural determinism.

Contingencies as Determinants of Structure

Against the strategic choice view, we wish to argue for the much more deterministic model that structure, in major aspects, is principally driven by the contingencies. As organizations make strategic moves and so alter their portfolio of activities, so the structure necessary to implement that strategy alters. An increase in scale of operations, in so far as it leads to an increase in the number of employees, promotes a more differentiated structure (vertically and horizontally), greater specialization, more formalization and more decentralization (Blau, 1972; Pugh and Hickson, 1976). An increase in the strategy of diversification leads to greater decentralization and to more use of multidivisional forms (Chandler, 1962). Higher rates of innovation lead to less formally structured roles, more use of occupational specialists and professionals and more organic, project-based forms of organization (Galbraith, 1973; Hage, 1980).

Once changes have been made to shift the corporate activity portfolio appreciably in either scale, diversification or innovation, structures will change according to the contingency systems' imperative to avoid the performance loss which results from misfit. There may be a lag of some time before the appropriate structure is attained (Chandler, 1962). This will lead to lower performance during the interim. This process may be hastened in harsher environments in which organizational slack is not present (Child, 1972a; Williamson, 1971). While this moderates the impact of the contingencies on structure, it too is an environmental force to which management are subject, reflecting the level of competition and so on.

Contrary to the advocates of strategic choice, this chapter asserts that structural adaptation to contingencies is a valid account of the organizational structure. The theory advanced here is deterministic. The model predicts that contingency variables account for most of the variation in structure, substantially more than half, and that the value preferences and choices of the managerial actors make little independent contribution to an explanation. A consideration of the evidence provides a defence of the deterministic view.

Rebutting Strategic Choice

Let us now review the more specific criticisms of Child (1972a), Bourgeois (1984) and Whittington (1989) against the contingency approach. They hold that:

- organizational slack avoids the need for structural adaptation in misfit;
- re-engineering the environment generates such organizational slack;
- time lags in structural adaptation indicate the exercise of choice;
- fit may often be attained by adjusting the contingency to the structure;
- a broad range of structures with equal results allows much choice in selecting a fitting structure;
- the structure selected is the least expensive one rather than the most effective;
- deterministic models have limited explanatory power;
- reciprocal causation is a neglected source of choice;
- reductionism in contingency research makes its models too narrow;
- hypercontingency in contingency research makes its models bewilderingly broad;
- qualitative methods are needed in research.

These will be discussed in sequence below.

Organizational Slack Avoids Structural Adaptation

The argument here is that an organization in misfit can avoid re-organizing into fit if it has sufficient slack (that is, excess performance) to absorb the performance loss from misfit. However, this is fallacious, for slack might lead managers to preserve many forms of maladaptation other than structural misfit. Further, there is empirical evidence against the idea that misfit can be tolerated for too long, even among large, wealthy corporations.

The strategic choice theory implies that slack will prevent structural adaptation because structural misfit has little effect upon performance and can therefore be tolerated easily. Structure has little effect upon performance because other factors affect organizational performance. These other factors are presumed to be large in their effects upon performance and so collectively dwarf the effect of structure upon performance (Child, 1972a). Thus a maladapted structure has a small effect upon performance. Hence only in an environment in which performance pressures were extreme, such as under perfect competition, would the decrease in performance resulting from a maladapted structure create pressure upon management to adapt the structure. By implication, an environment in which competition was less than perfect – that is, one in which there was any degree of slack – could tolerate in existence an organization with a maladapted structure. Because the performance lost through the maladapted structure would be small, the management would be under no imperative to adjust their structure to bring it into fit with the contingency factors, and thus the management could exercise strategic choice over their organizational structure. This idea has proved highly persuasive and is widely received. However, there are several major problems with it.

Problems with the Organizational Slack Argument   One problem is that the argument implies that organizational slack, and hence freedom not to be completely adapted, is always consumed by organizational management first and foremost in a maladapted structure. However, if an organization is a bundle of attributes which affect performance, slack could be consumed through any maladapted attribute, for example, it could be consumed by retaining, or adopting, a maladapted marketing strategy, product, production process or pricing policy and so on, or any combination thereof up to the total value of the organizational slack. Moreover, if management use slack to indulge themselves and to avoid efficiency reforms that they find personally distasteful, why would this always be primarily in their organizational structure? Why not take it out in expense-account living, stock bonuses, pensions or on-the-job-leisure (Jensen and Meckling, 1976)? Surely, if management are out to maximize their personal welfare these are more direct pay-offs than sticking with inefficient structures. Thus there appears to be no good theoretical reason to believe that organizational slack will always be consumed first and foremost by retaining a maladapted organizational structure.

For a company which can afford a slack of, say, 10 per cent less than optimal potential performance, and if there were 10 alternative ways of consuming this slack (such as organizational structure, marketing strategy, production process, product, industrial relations, human resource policy), then by chance one would expect organizational structure to be selected as the alternate way to consume the slack only in one organization in 10. Hence under this scenario, even with a 10 per cent slack, 9 out of 10 organizations would not retain a maladapted structure. Of course in reality there may be many more than 10 factors which affect organizational performance, in which case the scenario above overstates the number of organizations in which slack would be consumed by having a maladapted structure.

On a basis of chance, the probability that organizational structure will be selected as a way to consume slack will be higher only if the amount of slack is greater. Suppose that organization slack is now so large that half of the maximum potential organizational performance is being sacrificed by management. Now 5 out of the 10 ways to consume slack can be indulged by management. Thus on a chance basis there is a 1 in 2 chance that a maladapted structure will be selected by management. On a random basis, 5 out of every 10 organizations which have 50 per-cent slack levels will retain a maladapted structure. Thus, retaining a maladapted structure will only be a frequent event among organizations if levels of slack are high. Yet a 50 per-cent level of slack means that the organization is very inefficient and the pressure on the organization to perform, whether through competition or for some other reason, is very weak. Thus a maladapted structure persisting for some time because of slack is likely only when the level of slack is high, which is itself unlikely and therefore the scenario of a slack-permitted maladapted structure persisting is improbable.

A proponent of strategic choice theory might respond by saying that management tend to choose organizational structures first as the way to consume organizational slack because of the intense political forces affecting organizational structure. This makes the retention of a maladapted structure top management's preferred form of slack consumption. The argument is that major re-organizations affect the positions of senior managers who are powerful players in the political process and will thereby prevent the top managers from launching changes in the organizational structure. However, top management are the bosses of the other senior managers and so can force them to comply. Moreover, in most re-organizations there are some winners among the senior managers who can form a winning coalition with top management over the recalcitrant senior managers. Thus the structural change towards a more adapted structure can go through. Hence internal political forces resisting change are not automatically decisive in ensuring that slack is consumed by retaining a maladapted structure.

Further, while political factors may promote a degree of inertia in regard to organizational structural change, they are present also in regard to other factors which affect performance, such as marketing strategy, product, production process and so on. Changes in any of these are also liable to run into vested interests and hence political opposition to change. Thus the political dimension of organizational life does not constitute a reason why a maladapted organizational structure should be retained. Thus organizational politics cannot be used as a theoretical reason for managers always consuming slack first and foremost through retaining a maladapted structure.

Again, proponents of the strategic choice thesis might respond that such decisions by managers about organizational structure are made imponderable by the subjectivity in the process: that is, subjective perceptions of the existing structure and ensuing problems, and subjective theories about which structures are better. While this may be true, such subjectivity is surely no less present in decisions about marketing strategy, human resource policy and many other organizational attributes which affect performance. Again, considerations of subjectivity seem to constitute no argument for holding that slack will be consumed first and foremost by retaining a maladapted organizational structure.

Thus the existence of a moderate degree of organizational slack will not always result in management electing to consume slack by retaining a maladapted structure rather than by retaining some other maladapted feature or by indulging in perquisites.

Empirical Evidence Against the Slack Argument   The strategic choice argument about slack rests on the presumption that the effect of performance is weak relative to other causes of performance. Therefore the other factors can buoy up performance so that the negative effects of structural misfit can be offset, allowing retention of the misfitting structure.

A study of New Zealand companies by Hamilton and Shergill (1992) assesses the impact of structural misfit on financial performance. They also assess the impact on financial performance of a factor often held to be the dominating cause of performance, the degree of concentration in the industry; that is, an index of oligopolization. They then compare the effects on performance of structural misfit and concentration of industry, so that relative effects of each can be ascertained. The results show that the magnitudes of the effects on performance of structural misfit and industry concentration are about the same order; industry concentration does *not* dwarf structural misfit. Structural misfit explains 23 per cent of the variance in growth in earnings per share, dividends, sales and assets, while industry concentration explains only a little more, at 27 per cent. As for profit, structural misfit explains 16 per cent and industry concentration more at 28 per cent, so here concentration is greater but structural misfit is still not trivial relative to it (Hamilton and Shergill, 1992: 108). Thus, even in a noncompetitive industry, structural misfit is serious. It is *not* the case that in a concentrated industry the slack greatly exceeds the performance loss from structural misfit so as to render the latter trivial. Thus industry concentration does not supply sufficient slack that structural misfit can easily be carried with impunity for the performance of the firm. The idea of slack shielding corporations from the necessity of structural adjustment is overstated.

If the theory that slack prevents structural adaptation were valid, then it would apply most strongly to large corporations, as the monopolists and oligopolists are among their ranks. Yet the studies which show that organizations adapt their structure to their strategy have been conducted on the US Fortune 500 companies which are among the largest corporations in the world and the pillars of 'American capitalism' (Chandler, 1962; Rumelt, 1974; Donaldson, 1987) and also on the largest companies in Britain, France, Germany and Japan (Channon, 1973; Dyas and Thanheiser, 1976; Suzuki, 1980). Thus the largest corporations, including very wealthy corporations, and therefore the firms most likely to enjoy substantial slack, adapt their structure to the contingency of strategy. Consistent with the slack idea, however, these corporations often remain in misfit until their financial performance drops, which would mean that the slack was used up, and only then structurally adapt (Donaldson, 1987). Thus there is a medium-term delaying effect of slack but in the longer run even these giant firms adapt structure to strategy. This argues against the proposition that misfit between contingency and structure can be avoided because of the presence of slack.

In the early 1990s a number of the very largest corporations, usually considered to epitomize the dominant, powerful corporation, have suffered poor performance due to competition; these include GM, IBM and ICI. This had led them to re-organize. Moreover, most organizations in the world are smaller and poorer so their levels of slack would be expected to be less and therefore they could tolerate misfit for a shorter period than the Fortune 500 giants. Thus contemporary international competition has become so strong in many industries that the proposition that slack delays structural adaptation may be becoming increasingly less applicable.

Since the publication of Child's strategic choice article in 1972 there have been many mergers as companies have been taken over in the 'market for corporate control' (Davis and Stout, 1992). This is seen as providing incumbent management who wish to avoid take-over with an incentive to increase profits and dividends rather than maintaining high levels of slack by unnecessarily high costs. This forces adoption of efficient internal practices, which would include the structures that fit the contingencies. Further, when a company is absorbed into a larger parent company, the head office of the parent may provide a discipline for each subsidiary, forcing subsidiary management to reduce slack (Williamson, 1970).

Again, leveraged buy-outs (LBOs) in the 1980s also added to the take-overs and threats of take-overs. The rise of corporate raiders has increased the perception that take-over is possible. Some corporations that have avoided being taken over through paying greenmail are poorer in consequence and so have less slack (Kosnik, 1987). LBOs often occurred where there was a perception that company performance could be improved through buy-out and elimination of slack. New types of companies, such as Kohlberg, Kravis, Roberts and Company, pursued buy-outs and sought to eliminate slack from these investments (Jensen, 1989). Corporations have increased their leverage, through LBO or otherwise; this is also seen as a discipline on management, reducing free cash-flow and thus reducing slack (Jensen, 1989). Greater activism by investors, including institutional investors and 'relational investors', has been widely canvassed in the early 1990s. Public sector organizations, including state monopolies, have been privatized, commercialized or forced to pay dividends to government – all of which may reduce their slack. Governments have also deregulated private sector industries, increasing competition and reducing slack. All of these devices are intended to eliminate slack. The significance and effects of some of these changes may be debatable, but they are all part of a contemporary trend that seeks to curb organizational slack and force management to be more effective. To the degree that any of these devices attain their objectives, then there will today be less slack and so less opportunity for management to retain misfitting organizational structures.

Re-engineering the Environment

The argument here is that organizational slack can be increased by re-engineering the environment to make it more benign and profitable, and so support the retention of misfitting structures. However, it is unlikely that most organizations can appreciably re-engineer their environment to be more benign.

Bourgeois (1984), Child (1972a) and Williamson (1971) recognize that the opportunity to exercise managerial discretion in favour of sub-optimal structures is more prevalent where slack permits performance to be sub-optimal and yet still be acceptable. Under this condition the organization can avoid adjustment of its structure to its contingency. The level of slack in performance enjoyed by an organization is affected by factors such as competition, absence of tariff protection, regulation by government and so on. Many of these are environmental factors largely outside the influence of the organization and its management. Thus the argument for the role of slack is one which gives causal significance to the situation rather than to the free will of management (Franko, 1974; Pfeffer and Salancik, 1978).

Nevertheless, some theorists suggest that the profitability allowed by the environment may be altered by managerial action; for example, by mergers or lobbying the government for changes in industry regulation (Bourgeois, 1984; Perrow, 1979). While there may be some scope in this regard it seems likely that the potential influence of managerial elites on their environment is limited. For example, mergers between rival companies to reduce competition are restricted in a number of countries by governments. If managerial elites in all organizations can manipulate the environment in their favour to make it more benign and promote more slack, why are there industries which are competitive (Lawrence and Dyer, 1983) and bereft of highly benign government regulation (for instance, the textile, steel and automobile industries)? Does one infer that these industrial environments are competitive because the managerial elites in those industries have chosen such stringency of their own free will?

Hirsch (1975) has shown that pharmaceutical firms attain superior profits to phonographic record firms in part because of the greater degree of government regulation which restricts competitive entry more in pharmaceuticals than in phonography. Yet, presumably, managers of phonographic corporations did not volunteer for an open industry. Governments regulate pharmaceuticals because of the concern for potential harm and the lack of expertise among the public. These conditions do not hold for phonographic records and so that industry remains unregulated and thus more competitive. The underlying causal factors are not those which organizational managers control. In practice there seem to be limits to the extent to which environments can be engineered in their own favour by managements. Thus the presence or absence of environmentally induced slack is in considerable measure an externally imposed constraint limiting the exercise of managerial discretion.

Pfeffer and Salancik (1978: 267) have analysed attempts by organizations to render their environment benign and conclude that only a few, large organizations can do so: 'For millions of small business organizations, voluntary associations, and nonprofit organizations, such change of the environment is virtually out of the question.'

As we saw in the previous section, even the largest corporations, the Fortune 500, have adapted their structures to their strategies. Most organizations in most sectors and industries are unable to re-engineer their environment to be more benign and so they cannot avoid adapting their structures.

Time Lags as Choice

Whittington (1989) argues that the delays in structural adaptation to strategy, which can last for decades (Donaldson, 1987), show that managers exercise a considerable degree of choice. However, these delays are themselves determined by performance and structure. They result from the causality of the contingency theory.

At the most, any such choice would be restricted to the timing of the inevitable structural change. However, the timing is actually controlled to a degree by the financial performance of the firm (Donaldson, 1987). This will reflect external competitive pressure and other factors not wholly under management control. Moreover, other internal factors have to be present before the new structure can be adopted, such as management capable of handling increased delegation (Child, 1984; for a discussion, see Donaldson, 1985), and this may have to await retirement, recruitment, training and so on. Again, support systems need to be put in place for new structures to operate; for example, multidivisional structures require the installation of multiple profit-centre accounting systems, while matrix structures may require the installation of dual reporting systems (Davis and Lawrence, 1977). Thus the lack of the other ingredients needed for the new fit can delay adaptation.

Further, the misfitted structure will itself render decision-making ineffective, producing delays in structural re-organization. For example, retaining a functional structure when the firm has diversified is a misfit that overloads top management. This prevents them from giving sufficient attention to the need to re-organize. Hence much of the delay in structural adaptation arises for reasons other than managerial choice. These delays cannot with any certainty be attributed to managerial choice without some evidence that they result from managerial choice, rather than from the other factors such as financial performance for which evidence exists (Donaldson, 1987).

Fitting Contingency to Structure

The argument here is that an organization in misfit can regain fit by adjusting its contingency to its structure, thereby avoiding having to adopt a new structure. However, organizations do not in practice attain fit in this way, for sound reasons, and so there is no alternative but to attain fit by adapting the structure to the contingencies.

Another of the major criticisms of contingency theory (Bobbitt and Ford, 1980; Bourgeois, 1984; Child, 1972a) in the strategic choice thesis is that the fit of structure with contingency may be regained through adjustment of contingency to structure, rather than through the adjustment of structure to contingency postulated by contingency determinism. Hence for an organiza-tion in misfit there is no imperative for the organization and its management to adjust the structure into fit with the contingency, because they can escape from misfit by adjusting the contingency while retaining the existing struc-ture. They may prefer the existing structure on value grounds. In this way strategic choice enters the picture again.

If this argument is true, then regaining fit by adjusting the contingency to the structure will be a frequent occurrence among organizations. Only if this alternative route to fit is actually used in practice is the imperative of struc-tural adaptation to contingency avoided. An examination of organizations in misfit should show that a high percentage regain fit by adjusting their con-tingency to their structure. If both approaches carry roughly equal costs and benefits and if elites are free in their choice, then each route will be chosen with approximately equal frequency.

In the case of strategy and structure, however, corporations in misfit regain fit by structural change in over 95 per cent of cases. In less than 5 per cent of cases is fit regained by the alteration of strategy alone without modifying structure (Donaldson, 1987). Thus strategy is the primary step, and structure is secondary, which is taken subsequently as part of implementation. The traditional business policy model (Christensen et al., 1978) is supported by empirical research. Selection of strategy is the major commitment of organi-zational resources (for example, acquiring a company in order to diversify) and the costs of a new structure are less (for instance, creating a corporate head office to control the original and newly acquired businesses). Therefore strategy takes precedence over structure (Chandler, 1962). Thus there is no readily available, frequently used alternative to structural adjustment. Organizations do not regain fit by adjusting contingency to structure, there-fore fit has to be attained through structural adaptation.

Moreover, even among the 5 per cent of corporations that attain fit by changing the strategy contingency rather than their structure, this may be the result of extreme circumstances forcing this move, not free choice between alternatives. For example, when corporations regain fit by retaining a func-tional structure and de-diversifying, this may be caused by disastrous financial performance (worse than that which causes structural adaptation). This forces a sell-off of peripheral business units and so is motivated by finan-cial plight rather than by the search for fit. Hence even among the 5 per cent of organizations that regain fit after changing their contingency this should not necessarily be interpreted as caused by the search for fit. It is sometimes more an unwanted down-scoping forced by disastrous performance. Thus the idea of an alternative route to regain fit is not supported empirically for the strategy contingency.

Child (1972a) discusses the idea of altering the contingencies to fit the structure with reference to the size contingency in the size–bureaucracy rela-tionship. He considers the case of a management wishing to limit the bureaucratization of their organizational structure in a corporation which has grown large enough for substantial bureaucracy to result (Child, 1972a).

Since size generates the degree of bureaucracy, smaller units will be less bureaucratic. Therefore the suggestion is that breaking the whole organization into a number of sub-units of limited size will create a set of miniature companies each of which has little bureaucracy. Although this logic is appealing, it falls foul of a troubling fact.

This logic works best if the size–bureaucracy relationship is linear, for then splitting the company into 10 smaller sub-units each of one-tenth the original size would likewise decimate the degree of internal bureaucracy in each. However, a reliable finding of the empirical research on size and bureaucracy is that the relationship is curvilinear (Blau and Schoenherr, 1971; Blau, 1972; Child, 1973b). In other words, the bureaucracy–size gradient is shallower at larger size than at smaller. Therefore, a reduction in size of, say, 100 employees, produces less decrease in bureaucracy in larger than in smaller organizations. For instance, reducing the size of the focal organization from 10,000 to 1,000 employees, that is, to one-tenth the size – decreases the degree of functional specialization from 14.8 to 11.6 – that is, by only under one-quarter – a 90 per-cent size reduction reduces specialization by only 25 per cent. (The foregoing is based upon interpolation from the manufacturing sub-sample data of Child (1973b) from the Aston Program data-bank.) Similar results hold for other aspects of bureaucratic structure because of the curvilinearity of the relationship of each with size (for graphs, see Child, 1973b).

Thus it is impossible to reduce substantially the level of bureaucracy of large corporations by any split-up short of that which fragments it into tiny parts. (Greater proportionate gains can be obtained from splitting up small companies, but their level of bureaucracy is not high, so their case is not relevant.) Management of a large corporation is not able to exercise a choice preference for a less bureaucratic form of structure by splitting it up into smaller sub-units. A preferred degree of bureaucracy cannot be selected at will by selecting some feasible level of the size contingency.

Attaining fit by manipulation of the contingency to match the structure is not feasible with either the strategy–structure or the size–bureaucracy relationships. This is cold comfort for the hypothesis that adjusting the contingency allows a dimension of freedom of manoeuvre away from the determination of structure by contingency.

Equifinality in Organizational Structure

One of the arguments used to support strategic choice is the idea that there is a broad range of equally viable structures. This idea is often expressed through the term 'equifinality', meaning equal outcomes, referring to equal performance outcomes from a range of structures and each therefore being an equal fit and thus constituting an alternative. However, the evidence points away from the idea of equifinality.

Traditionally, structural contingency held that for any one given value of the contingency factor there was one value of the structural variable or one type of structure which produced the maximum organizational performance and which therefore constituted a fit (Chandler, 1962; Burns and Stalker, 1961; Woodward, 1965). Thus organizations had an imperative to adopt that one structure for the given contingency. However, the argument has been made that, on the contrary, for any one contingency situation there is a broad range of organizational structures which fit and which produce maximum performance (Child, 1972a). Therefore there is a range of alternative equally viable structures in any contingency situation and so there is a wide choice available without sacrificing organizational performance. This idea of equifinality is widely received in the literature as though the existence of equifinality in organizational structures were an established fact.

However, the empirical basis of the idea of equifinality is open to doubt. The notion of equifinality implies that for any contingency situation there is a large range of values of the corresponding structural variable which are in fit and which display maximum performance. As an example, the fit between the contingency variable of size and the structural variable of role specialization would be such that for any one size value there would be a range of, say, 30 per cent of the role specialization variable which is in fit; namely, an equifinality of 30 per cent of structure. However, an inspection of the empirical data of Child (1975) shows no evidence of this broad band of equifinal (equally fitting) structures which enjoy equal performance. The graph of total role specialization on size shows the regression lines of the organizations in fit and of those that are in misfit. These regression lines can be seen by visual inspection to be quite close together (see Child, 1975: 21, Fig. 1). In fact they are so close that they intersect – that is, cross over each other. Fit is a line – that is, a narrow line, not a broad band. Thus the Child (1975) data provide no evidence of a broad range of fit and hence no evidence of equifinality.

Equifinality is an idea which enjoys currency and a term that, once introduced into the literature, attained the status of uncritical acceptance as a key theoretical insight. Yet the whole idea is questionable theoretically, for it implies that any structure is as equally effective as any other structure in the same situation. Since organizational structures vary markedly there must be some reason. If structures were all equally effective then there would be no reason to have so much variation in structures across organizations. The organizations and their managers would have had no stimulus to make investments in often complex structures, nor motivation to bother to go through the difficult processes of creating the elaborate structures which are visible in our larger organizations – for instance, multidivisional or matrix structures. For example, in the large Australian insurance company, AMP, the organization chart is over 100 pages in length. Equifinality is a theoretically naïve idea. Unsurprisingly, when it is tested by examining data on real organizations it is disproved.

Structural Choice is not Cost-minimizing

In his strategic choice thesis, Child (1972a) argues that low organizational performance, below the level deemed satisfactory, leads to adoption of an organizational structure which requires fewer economic resources. This is essentially a cost-minimizing perspective. By implication, organizations enjoying financial slack will be able to afford more luxurious, expensive structures relative to economically impoverished organizations. However, the evidence is that organizations adopt the structures required to fit with their contingencies even where those structures are more expensive than the structures they replace; hence the cost-minimizing argument is false.

The cost-minimizing perspective yields opposite predictions to structural contingency theory, which argues that poor performance forces an organization in misfit to adapt the structure that fits the contingency factors. This adaptation might involve adopting a more costly form of organizational structure. Thus structural contingency theory predicts that in response to poor performance, firms make additional investments in better-fitting structures. Since misfitting structures are seen as causes of poor performance and fitting structures are seen as causes of good performance, redesigning the structure is seen as producing economic benefits which more than offset any greater costs. In contrast, a perspective which sees structures as not affecting performance, or only weakly so, is less appreciative of the benefit flowing from structural re-organization as an investment and is therefore more likely to dwell on its costs. Hence the more costly structure is seen as a burden to be indulged only under conditions of organizational slack. The evidence, however, supports the contingency theory, not the cost-minimizing view.

For instance, poorly performing corporations which are in misfit, through having diversified and yet retained a functional structure, regain fit through adopting a divisional structure (Chandler, 1962; Channon, 1973; Rumelt, 1974; Dyas and Thanheiser, 1976; Donaldson, 1987). A multidivisional structure is usually considered to be an inherently costlier form than a functional structure. Relative to the functional structure, a multidivisional structure has additional costs through duplication of functional specialists across the divisions. Also there would be expected to be higher remuneration for the new divisional heads relative to the erstwhile functional chiefs. Again, there are costs of the additional financial control systems to report on the new divisional profit centres.

The Child (1972a) thesis would yield the hypothesis that diversified firms in misfit, and thereby suffering reduced performance, would be more likely to retain or adopt a functional rather than a multidivisional structure, because the functional structure is cheaper than the multidivisional structure. However, diversified corporations in misfit tend to adopt the multidivisional structure (Donaldson, 1987). Hence the present empirical evidence fails to confirm the hypothesis from Child that firms in performance difficulties react by choosing cheaper structures. Firms resolve structural misfit by adopting a structure which will yield better performance even though this involves some additional costs. The firm is seeking not to minimize costs but rather to max-imize the benefit to cost ratio (as functionalist theory holds).

Limited Validity of Deterministic Explanation of Structure

Bourgeois (1984) and others (Child, 1972a; Bobbitt and Ford, 1980) argue that the idea of situational determinants is deficient empirically. Child (1972a:12) points to the limited explanatory power of contingency variables in the Aston (Pugh et al., 1968) and similar studies, as providing not much more than about half the variance in structure. However, the actual magni-tude is greater, so that contingencies explain more of organizational structure than is generally appreciated.

Magnitude of Correlations   The true, general relationship between size and any structural variable is best estimated by the average correlation. A meta-analysis of studies using Aston measures of structure calculated the average correlations between each main variable of bureaucratic structuring and organizational size. The average correlations were: functional specialization, +.61, overall standardization, +.55, and overall formalization, +.51 (Donaldson, 1986: 86). However, these correlations between size and the variables of bureaucratic structure will understate the true correlations because measurement errors in both size and structure variables will mask the true magnitudes of the correlations.

A better estimate is obtained by correcting for measurement error in each of the size–structure correlations. The degree of measurement error may be assessed by the reliability coefficient for each scale and these reliability coef-ficients have been calculated for each of the structural scales (Donaldson, 1986: 90). The observed correlations may be corrected to remove the attenu-ation (reduction in magnitude) due to unreliability by use of the correction formula in Hunter et al. (1982). Correcting just for measurement error in the structural scales, the average correlations increase. For the relationship between size and functional specialization, the average correlation rises to +.82. Thus 67 per cent of the variation in functional specialization is accounted for by size alone. For the relationships between size and overall standardization, the correlation rises to +.69; and for the relationship between size and overall formalization, it rises to +.59.

The prevailing explanatory causal model of structure, advanced by Child (1973b), posits that size leads to functional specialization which in turn leads to overall standardization and overall formalization. The theory is that larger organizations have more highly specialized and qualified administrative experts who in turn bring in more standard procedures, rules and documents (Child, 1973b) which are required to manage the larger number of employees effectively. Since the degree of functional specialization is highly determined by size, standardization and formalization are in turn highly determined by size through the intervening variable of functional specialization. Hence the true degree of determination of standardization and formalization by size is understated by their correlation with size. Thus these three major structural variables, aspects of bureaucratic structuring, are all closely determined by size.

Moreover, other artefacts may be present which serve to attenuate the correlation – that is, to understate its true magnitude. Full correlation between contingency and structure will only be revealed in a population if the full range of variation is attained on the structural variable and in all the contingency factors of that structural variable. Yet it is quite common in comparative studies of organizational structure for the sample to be drawn in such a way that the range of variation on a contingency factor is less than the range in the population. For instance, both the study by Woodward (1965) and the Aston study (Pugh et al., 1969a) excluded small-sized organizations and would thus understate the true correlation between size and structure in the universe in general. Again, many samples of organizations do not include the largest organizations in the world, such as US Fortune 500 companies, because of the way the sample is framed geographically; for instance, the Aston study which was a sample restricted to work organizations in Birmingham, England (Pugh et al., 1969a). Thus organizational studies may omit both the smallest and the largest organizations from their samples and in this way, unintentionally, restrict range and so attenuate correlations between size and structure, leading to an underestimate of size–structure correlations.

The structural contingency theory, in its SARFIT form, argues that changes in contingency cause a change in structure only after a time lag (Chandler, 1962; Woodward, 1965; Donaldson, 1987). Thus in any sample of organizations some will still be adjusting their structure to the previous change in the contingency. That is, they will still be in the intermediary stage of misfit, and this will reduce the correlation between contingency and structure below the long-run or equilibrium level. Thus even the true correlation between size and structure in the population of organizations understates the real long-run association. The correlation contains variation in the structural variable which is unattributed in a statistical sense to the size variable, but which is in reality just the temporary lag before structure adjusts to the new size level. Hence, the true corrected size–structure correlation understates the actual degree of connection between size and structure and gives an exaggerated picture of the degree of indeterminacy.

Further, some structural contingency theories hold that organizations remain in the misfitted state until performance has deteriorated sufficiently to impel structural change (Chandler, 1962; Child, 1972a; Williamson, 1971; Donaldson, 1987). Thus organizational performance is an explanatory variable of organizational structure in addition to the contingency variables. The variance in structure explained by structural contingency theory is incomplete until performance is added to the contingency variables. Therefore, prevailing contingency models that explain structure but that fail to include performance (for example Pugh et al., 1969a) understate the explanatory power of structural contingency theory.

A limitation in the amount of variance explained in any one structural variable by any one contingency variable may also arise because the structural variable is determined by more than one contingency variable. There is evidence that the bureaucratic structuring variables are affected not only by organizational size, but also by other contingency factors such as the size of any parent organization (Pugh et al., 1969a). Thus a structural variable may be statistically explained by two or more contingency variables. The multiple correlation coefficient is often used to capture the degree of explanation of the structural variable by the contingency factors. As further contingency factors of each variable of organizational structure are discovered, so they need to be added to the model in order to achieve the full explanatory power of structural contingency theory. It may be premature to conclude that all contingencies have yet been discovered, and so models understate the amount of variance in structure that contingencies can explain.

In summary, to suggest that there is an in-built limit to the extent to which structure can be explained by situational constraint is premature. The true magnitude of the correlation between a structural variable and its contingency variable will only be revealed when all variables are measured without error and over their full range. Observed correlations need to be corrected for measurement error and range restriction to obtain a better estimate of the true correlation. Even then the contingencies–structure correlation will understate the full extent of the explanation of structure by structural contingency theory because of the time lags of adjustment of structure to contingency and the way this is affected by organizational performance. As contingency research continues, the variance in structure which is at present unexplained by the contingency variables will diminish as the full contingency model is brought into play through including more contingency variables plus performance, and measuring variables with less error and less range restriction. Only when this programme is complete will the variance left unexplained in structure be able to be considered as indeterminacy in structure which is available to be attributed to strategic choice – that is, choice over structure which reflects voluntaristic processes such as managerial preferences, beliefs, values and so on.

Lack of Support from Longitudinal Studies   The argument that structure is determined by contingencies is more compelling if longitudinal enquiries into changes over time support this theory. However, diachronic enquiries into size–bureaucracy and strategy–structure relationships (Inkson et al., 1970; Dyas and Thanheiser, 1976; Dewar and Hage, 1978; Meyer, 1979) have failed to produce much evidence in favour of this model, although true effects have been obscured because of problems in these analyses.

In the case of the strategy–structure studies, the problem is that there has been a tendency to operationalize contingency theory in these enquiries by the notion that a change in the contingency variable (namely, increasing diversification) should lead to, or be accompanied by, a change in the structural variable (the shift from functional to divisional structure) (Dyas and

Thanheiser, 1976). This ignores the point that misfit intervenes between strategic and structural change and so strategic change is not expected to produce structural change immediately. A more adequate hypothesis, springing from contingency thinking, would be that *the direct cause of structural change would be a misfit between structure and strategy*. Changes in the strategy contingency variable will cause structural change only if they lead from fit into misfit. Thus misfit rather than change in the contingency *per se* is the trigger of structural change.

This would mean a sequence of diversifying leading to *misfit* which, in turn, leads to structural reorganization away from functionally based towards divisionally based structures. Research reveals this pattern and shows that it generalizes across five countries (France, the German Federal Republic, Japan, the United Kingdom and the United States of America) (Donaldson, 1987). Contingency determinism, which states that changes in contingency lead to changes in structure, is only broadly correct. The actual process runs through an intermediary stage of misfit, and some organizations stay in this position for decades and hence there are lags in adjustment (Donaldson, 1987). The change in the strategy contingency is only an indirect cause of the change in structure. Thus, when properly done, an analysis of changes over time supports the contingency theory that change in strategy leads to change in structure.

In the case of the studies of the relationship between change in size and change in the degree of elaborateness of structure – that is, in the bureaucratization or structural differentiation – the problem is different. Both studies find strong cross-sectional correlations between size and structure, replicating the Aston and Blau studies (Inkson et al., 1970; Dewar and Hage, 1978, respectively), but fail to find substantial positive, consistent correlations between size change and structural change.

These studies measure organizational structure by scales counting degree of formalization – that is, the number of documents governing organization (Inkson et al., 1970); or structural differentiation – the number of departments (Dewar and Hage, 1978). All such variables have a degree of measurement error. This unreliability in measurement of the dependent variable will result in any true correlation being understated in the observed correlation (Hunter et al., 1982). Moreover, the method of analysis used in both studies was to correlate changes in size with changes in structure. The level of the variable at a later time is deducted from the level of that variable at an earlier time to calculate a change score. Such change scores are much less reliable than the basic variables from which they are derived. Change scores are well understood in psychometrics to be highly unreliable (Nunnally, 1978). Therefore correlating size change with structural change will contain a high degree of white noise which will mask any true relationship between size and structure.

Overall, the lack of support for structural contingency theory from longitudinal studies should not be seen as well established at this time. Technical problems may be obscuring underlying patterns more consistent with that theory. For the strategy–structure phenomena, when correct hypotheses are specified they are confirmed by the data. Other similar improvements in methods in future studies may clarify the real meaning of longitudinal data.

Reciprocal Causation

Another of the difficulties seen in contingency structure research by Bourgeois (1984) is reciprocal causation. He sees that a correlation between X and Y that is interpreted deterministically as X causing Y may mean that X and Y are connected through reciprocal causation. Neglect of this possibility may, thus, lead some analysts falsely to infer determinism where choice is present. The main problem with this reasoning is that reciprocal causality is itself determinism.

Even where reciprocality is established, this is not antithetic to determinism and is not proof of free will. It simply means that X causes Y and that Y also causes X (Blalock, 1961). Instead of somehow nullifying the determinism, it just means that each of X and Y determine the other, as well as being determined by the other. The flow of causation back and forth will produce a tight coalignment of these two variables and not some sort of indeterminacy or freedom.

In the strategy–structure area, against the idea that strategy causes structure the converse has been asserted, that structure causes strategy (Scott, 1971; Hall and Saias, 1980). The argument is made that having a divisional structure is more likely to lead to subsequent diversification than is possessing a functional structure. However, the evidence is that corporations with divisional structures are *no more likely* to diversify subsequently than are those with functional structures (Donaldson, 1982b; Hamilton and Shergill, 1992: 104). Strategy leads to structure, but structure does not lead to strategy. The strategy–structure linkage is not reciprocal on this evidence. Thus, for the strategy–structure relationship, research to date indicates that causation flows from contingency to structure and not vice versa, and hence is not reciprocal.

The point of these comments is not to deny that reciprocal causation may exist in some aspects of organizational structure. And the caution (Bourgeois, 1984), that analysts should enquire into the possibility that any causal connection may be reciprocal, is well taken. The point is that a major linkage in organizational structure is not, on the current available evidence, reciprocal.

In the foregoing sections considerable emphasis has been placed upon two nexuses, the connection between size and bureaucracy and between strategy and structure. It is desirable to know how far the patterns found for these two contingency variables generalize to other relationships such as that between task uncertainty and organic structures (Burns and Stalker, 1961). Although the discussion has not been exhaustive, the relationships of size–bureaucracy and strategy–structure are central to structural contingency theory. Accordingly, their case is highly germane and cannot be considered to be peripheral.

The Problem of Reductionism

The objection to reductionism, as Bourgeois (1984) uses the term, is that great emphasis is given to just one situational explanation of organizational structure – namely, monocausality. The problem here is that organizational structural research is not monocausal.

Several leading pieces of contingency research were monocausal, emphasizing one contingency factor: for example, technology (Burns and Stalker, 1961; Lawrence and Lorsch, 1967; Woodward, 1965). However, these are also early pieces of work in that tradition. Many subsequent enquiries have studied the simultaneous impact on structure of multiple situational factors, such as size, technology, dependence, location, environmental hostility and so on (Pugh et al., 1969a; Blau et al., 1976; Khandwalla, 1977; Grinyer and Yasai-Ardekani, 1981). Thus the contingency stream of research has been operating in a mode which recognizes that there is more than one contingency determinant of structure from at least the late 1960s (Pugh et al., 1963). Determinism does not involve monocausality either as a fundamental axiom or as an aspect of research practice. Therefore deterministic research should not be criticized as monocausal or reductionist.

The Problem of Hypercontingency

The criticism of 'hypercontingency' theory (Bourgeois, 1984) is of the opposite kind. The critique is that contingency thinking leads to the view of a large number of contingency variables which intersect to form many different combinations of circumstance, such that the universe of organizations is fragmented into many different positions in this multidimensional space. While Bourgeois (1984) discusses this problem in research into strategy rather than organizational structure, this difficulty is included as a limitation of deterministic theories in general, so a comment is warranted within a discussion of structure. Research into organizational structure has not degenerated into hypercontingency, because parsimonious models of a few contingency factors have emerged.

While research has canvassed many different contingency variables (see Pugh et al., 1969a; Khandwalla, 1977), many major aspects of organizational structure have been shown to be explained by just a few contingency factors. Size explains much of each – of the number of hierarchical levels, the degree of functional specialization, the degree of overall standardization and the degree of overall formalization (Blau and Schoenherr, 1971; Pugh and Hickson, 1976; Pugh and Hinings, 1976). Diversity and dependence together explain substantial amounts of variation in centralization (Pugh et al., 1969a). Task uncertainty is a contingency that explains much at the level of the individual role, such as the degree of formalization of role definition (Gerwin, 1979; Reimann and Inzerilli, 1979). Diversification strategy explains much of divisionalization (Donaldson, 1982b). Thus research on organizational structure has shown that it can be explained by a few contingency factors, rendering the analysis tractable rather than hypercontingent.

The Need for Qualitative Methods

In calling for a revised form of research that better captures the true extent of choice, Bourgeois (1984) argues for more use of qualitative methods. However, adopting qualitative methods does not mean that choice will be found and determinism avoided.

Galtung (1967) states that in social scientific research, qualitative studies often provide the early theoretical insights which are then validated and refined through quantitative hypothesis testing. This process has already occurred in the topic area of bureaucracy with earlier qualitative case and historical studies (Weber, 1968; Gouldner, 1954; Crozier, 1964; Merton, 1957), giving rise to propositions which were tested in quantitative work (Blau and Schoenherr, 1971; Blau, 1972; Pugh and Hickson, 1976; Pugh and Hinings, 1976). A similar process has occurred in studies of strategy and structure (Chandler, 1962; Channon, 1973; Rumelt, 1974; Dyas and Thanheiser, 1976; Pavan, 1976; Suzuki, 1980). Similar remarks apply to the task uncertainty–organic structure literature (Burns and Stalker, 1961; Gerwin, 1979).

The continued combination of qualitative and quantitative research is desirable, but is not an innovation nor leads to support for free will. The foregoing three research strands, even at their qualitative stage, have always contained strongly deterministic threads. For example, the case histories of Chandler (1962) revealed that structure is determined by situation, as with the case histories of Burns and Stalker (1961) and Woodward (1965). Therefore adoption of qualitative methodology will not necessarily lead to nondeterministic theoretical models.

Summary of Rebuttals of Strategic Choice

In summary, several of the specific objections advanced by Child (1972a), Bourgeois (1984) and others against contingency theories of structure are shown to be empirically or logically tenuous.

Although the presence of organizational slack may delay structural adaptation to the contingencies, it does not typically enable organizations to avoid structural adaptation altogether. The performance loss through structural misfit is large enough that even under weak competition it is still necessary to make structural adaptations. Also, to the degree that there is organizational slack, this may be consumed in other ways, leaving none to sustain structural misfit. Structural adaptation to contingencies is observed among even the largest corporations and industry majors. Organizational slack is conditioned by the degree of environmental profitability, but this is largely outside the control of organizational management. An organization in misfit cannot choose to retain its structure and adjust its contingency as there is no such alternative route to fit that is generally available. Organizations may delay structural adaptation for reasons other than slack or choice; these include the disorganizing effect of the misfitting structure delaying decision-making, and also the need to wait for other elements required to support the new structure to come into place (such as personnel or accounting systems). Organizations have to adopt a new structure to fit their contingencies because there is not typically a range of alternative structures that are equally effective (that is, 'equifinal'). New structures adopted are not those that minimise cost but rather those that maximize the benefit–cost ratio.

Structure is highly explicable by contingencies in empirical terms. Where reciprocal causation may be established this does not imply indeterminacy but, rather, tight determinism. Contingency research is not monocausal. Also, multiple contingency models are only moderately complex and not hyper-contingent. Equally, qualitative methods have already played a useful role in deterministic research and their greater use will not necessarily lead to more choice being revealed.

There is clearly a need for further enquiry to replicate and to establish the generality of the findings drawn upon here. However, these elements hang together to form a model in which structural change is ultimately driven by changes in contingencies. Thus contingency theory is less problematic than its critics assert. Since much of the argument for strategic choice hangs on these criticisms of deterministic contingency theory, their rebuttal undermines the strategic choice theory while strengthening the case for contingency determinism.

Table 2.1 provides a summary of the rebuttal offered to the criticisms of determinism by Child (1972a), Bourgeois (1984) and Whittington (1989).

Conclusions

This chapter has reviewed the criticisms of determinism and rebutted them. They have been shown to be poorly grounded in either logic or fact.

Organizational structure is determined by the need to fit the contingencies in order to avoid performance loss. The presence of a degree of organizational slack does not prevent eventual structural adaptation to the contingencies. It is difficult for the organization to engineer the environment to produce such slack, and structural adaptation occurs in practice among even the largest, most dominant corporations. Delays in structural adaptation are not with any certainty attributable to choice since other reasons exist for organizations to delay these adaptations. Organizations do not in reality avoid structural adaptation by adapting their contingency to the structure. There is no evidence of any substantial degree of equifinality of organizational structures that might enable them to choose between widely differing structures with impunity.

The structures implemented are those which lead to greater effectiveness, rather than being the cheapest. Contingencies explain organizational structure to a high degree. Where reciprocal causation exists this implies determinism, not choice. The model that emerges from structural contingency theory is parsimonious, not bewilderingly complex. Qualitative methods do not imply an

Table 2.1 *Criticisms and defences of determinism in organizational structure*

Criticisms	Defences
Strategic choice	
organizational slack allows retention of contingency–structure misfit	structural adaptation occurs even in large, wealthy corporations
performance loss from misfit is trivial relative to organizational slack	performance loss from misfit is substantial relative to organizational slack
	slack partially caused by environmental profitability, therefore presence of choice only under some circumstances and often externally determined
environment can be re-engineered by organizational management to be more profitable	difficult for organizational management to re-engineer their environment
limited determination of structure by contingencies	for certain key structural variables, much variance explained by even single contingency variable, e.g. size
contingency may be adjusted to fit structure	evidence that this rarely occurs in strategy–structure; not feasible for size–bureaucracy
wide range of equally effective structures (equifinality) allows choice	range of structures to fit contingencies is narrow and precludes much choice
delays in adaptation of structure to contingencies signify choice	delays in adaptation of structure due to structural misfit and wait for elements that support new structure to come into place
structure selected is cheapest one	structure selected maximizes benefit–cost ratio
Reciprocal causation	
need to recognize that X causes Y *and* Y causes X	reciprocal causation means high degree of determinacy, not free choice
Reductionism	
monocausality	determinism does not imply monocausality; some structural variables determined by several variables; e.g. centralization by size and dependence
Hypercontingency	
multiple determinants confusing	contingency models are parsimonious and tractable

Source: Criticisms advanced in Child (1972a), Bourgeois (1984) and Whittington (1989)

absence of determinism. The argument that organizations are forced to adapt their structure to their contingencies is cogent and valid.

Having defended the assertion that objective contingencies determine organizational structure, let us now turn to the assertion that subjective factors play a role, as strategic choice holds.

3

For Determinism: Subjective Factors in Strategic Choice

In the previous chapter we defended the claim that contingencies objectively determine organizational structure. In this chapter we consider claims that subjective factors affect decision-making. We show that such work provides only limited support for strategic choice. Thus the discussion of subjective factors in this chapter supports the conclusion of the previous chapter, that strategic choice is a theory of only limited validity. Accordingly, this strengthens the position of deterministic structural contingency theory.

Strategic Choice and Free Will

As we saw in the previous chapter, contingency factors explain much of the variation in organizational structure. Nevertheless, contingency deterministic models do not at the present time provide complete explanations of organizational structure, though if other, additional situational determinants are identified the degree of indeterminacy will shrink further. Some part of the residual variation may be due to subjective factors such as the value preferences of the managerial actors (Bobbitt and Ford, 1980; Child, 1972a). Strategic choice theory holds that decisions over organizational structure are influenced by managerial perceptions, so that the value preferences, interest and power of managers affect which structure is chosen (Child, 1972a). The managerial effect is independent of, and so additional to, the effect of contingencies upon structure. Thus a direct demonstration of strategic choice theory requires showing empirically that organizational structure is affected by subjective factors in the decision-makers.

An issue for strategic choice theory is whether any subjective influences on decision-making are themselves determined. Our previous discussion pointed out that some subjective factors might be the result of prior social or psychological causes, thereby constituting sociological or psychological determinism (Donaldson, 1985). Thus, while it cannot be classed as contingency determinism, the analysis becomes determinism one step removed. This is a problem for strategic choice theory, because managerial decisions are no longer freely taken nor are they really choices. The manager cannot be held to be responsible because his or her decision is pre-determined. If the decision taken has adverse consequences then the manager cannot be held accountable. Thus the strategic choice theory can fall prey to the pessimism and fatalism from which it sought to escape by rejecting the programme of contingency determinism. Hence the case for strategic choice is best made where the subjective factors that influence decisions are not themselves determined. The manager needs to be shown to be a free and autonomous individual. For this reason strategic choice is discussed by Bourgeois (1984) in terms of the free will of managers. This makes the issue clearer and more pointed.

Bourgeois (1984) postulates managerial free will, thereby rejecting determinism of any kind, so that managerial decisions are free of any cause. Thus a direct demonstration of free will would require it to be shown empirically that organizational structure is affected by subjective factors of the decision-makers that are not determined by some cause. Advocates of free will need to demonstrate both the effects of subjective factors on structure and the lack of determinants of these subjective factors. This is a stringent requirement, but one that follows directly from the concept of free will. It would always be difficult to show empirically absence of prior cause of the subjective factors, for it would be difficult to know that the research had examined all possible causes. The researcher is unlikely to know a priori all possible causes, and it is not feasible that they could show them to be inoperative in any practical piece of research. Unsurprisingly, therefore, protagonists of free will have advanced programmatic statements rather than evidence (Bourgeois, 1984).

Let us now examine research into subjective factors influencing organizational structure and see how far it supports the strategic choice view.

A Critique of Research on Subjective Factors in Strategic Choice

The strategic choice theory argues that organizational structure is substantially affected by subjective factors, independent of the effects of the contingencies. As we have noted, much of the assertion of the strategic choice theory (Child, 1972a; Bourgeois, 1984) has been by a critique of the idea of objective contingency imperatives rather than by offering research evidence that subjective choice processes about structure are strong. However, other, subsequent research has sought to demonstrate a role of subjective choice about structure. Our critical review will reveal that this research provides at best limited and equivocal support for strategic choice.

Subjective Factors and Organizational Structure

Miller and Droge (1986), Miller and Toulouse (1986) and Miller et al. (1988) present empirical evidence that the personality of the executives (their need to achieve) affects the organizational structure that the organization adopts.

While Miller et al. (1988) show that personality affects organizational structure, their findings probably overstate its true effect. The organizations in their sample were small (Miller et al., 1988: 552). This means that decision-making would be highly centralized in the top manager. Thus the personality of the top manager could be given more rein and would have more effect. In a larger organization the influence of the top manager is diluted. There are many layers of management in a large organization, so that many individual managers are involved in decision-making. Moreover, there is more delegation of decision-making authority, reducing the effect of the personality of any one manager, even of the top manger. Miller et al. (1988: 564) accept that the influence of the personality of any one decision-maker will be less in larger organizations because of the greater dispersion of power in large organizations. Again, larger organizations are more bureaucratized in their decision processes so that the individual manager is constrained by pre-existing routines, regulations and policies. Miller et al. (1988: 564) accept that the effect of personality on organizational structure may be less in large organizations because of their bureaucratization. For these reasons the impact of personality of the top manager will be less in larger than in smaller organizations. Because Miller et al. (1988) studied small organizations, the effect of personality on organizational structure found therein would be greater than in medium-sized and larger organizations. Indeed, Miller and Droge (1986: 552) found that there was no significant relationship between CEO personality and organizational structure in large firms.

Miller and Toulouse (1986) investigated the effects of personality on organizational structure; they extended the study of personality to two other aspects of CEO personality: flexibility and locus of control. Again, they found that the effects of personality on organizational structure were more numerous in small than in large organizations (Miller and Toulouse, 1986: 1397). There were some effects of CEO personality variables regarding flexibility and locus of control in large organizations, however. It is not certain that the effects of these two aspects of CEO personality on organizational structure are independent of contingencies such as task uncertainty.

Moreover, in a sample of smaller organizations the variance in both size and the structural variables will be less than in a sample of organizations which range from small to large. Thus the correlation between size and organizational structure in a sample of small organizations (Miller et al., 1988) will understate the true size–structure correlation. Hence the *relative* effect of personality, compared with the effect of size, will be overstated in a sample of small organizations. This will make personality seem a more substantial effect than it is in fact. (Similarly, in a sample of only large-sized organizations, the range of organizational size will be restricted so that the effect of size is understated relative to personality.) For these reasons the finding of Miller et al. (1988) probably overstates the true magnitude of the effect of personality on organizational structure. However, the positive findings in Miller and Toulouse (1986) mean that the role of managerial personality deserves continuing attention for a more complete explanation of organizational structure.

Determinism in Studies   Miller and his colleagues argue that the personality of the executives affects the organizational structure that is adopted. However, this means that organizational structure is determined by personality. This is psychological determinism. It is not free will nor the exercise of choice by the executive, for the decision he or she makes is pre-determined by his or her pre-existing personality. Since personality is usually considered to be a trait that is relatively stable over time, the individual cannot modify their personality at will. Indeed, personality is to a degree set by genetics and up-bringing so that adult managers have little control over their personalities. Thus entering personality into the prediction of organizational structure in contingency theory models is to extend determinism from the immediate, organizational situation back to include the inheritance and early biography of the managers. Hence the findings of Miller and his colleagues are probably an overestimate of the effect of personality on structure and, in any case, should not be seen as proof of indeterminism, free choice or free will of managers.

Fligstein (1985) and Palmer et al. (1993) show that the organizational structure selected in large corporations is determined not only by contin-gency factors such as strategy, but also by the functional background of the CEO. However, this is already set by the time the manager becomes the CEO. He or she cannot unmake their career in order to enter the position of CEO with a different background. Thus the functional background is pre-deter-mined. It is not evidence of free will nor free choice by managers. Moreover, the selection for CEO of an executive with a particular functional back-ground is caused by contingency factors, such as the critical challenge facing the organization (Pfeffer and Salancik, 1978; Fligstein, 1990). Thus the func-tional background of the CEO determines structural choices and is itself determined. It is enmeshed in a causal system that is affected by contingency factors.

While the empirical studies of Miller, Fligstein, Palmer and their colleagues provide evidence of managerial determinants of organizational structure, these managerial factors themselves show that managers are determined and not exercising free will. This illustrates the problem that we raised previously (Donaldson, 1985): attempts to identify managerial factors in decisions on organizational structure would actually often provide evidence of psycholog-ical or sociological determinism by revealing the deeper causation, rather than the realm of choice sought by strategic choice theory.

Managerial Decision-making not Capricious   Again, much of the reason for wanting to show strategic choice is because of its supposed effects. Strategic choice theory seeks to show that managerial decisions are arbitrary, capri-cious or selfish (Child, 1972a; Whittington, 1989). But the research fails to provide support for such views. For instance, Fligstein (1985) shows that the functional background of the CEO is a determinant of the organizational structure and also that the functional background of the CEO is a determi-nant of the strategy (Fligstein, 1991). Thus the influence of CEO functional background on both strategy and structure is the CEO choosing a strategy and then choosing a structure that is compatible with that strategy. For example, CEOs with a sales and marketing functional background are more likely to choose a diversification strategy, reflecting their own strengths and experience, and are also more likely to choose a divisional structure (Fligstein, 1985, 1991). Since a divisional structure fits a diversified strategy, the CEO is selecting a strategy and then aligning the structure. This seems to be reasonable use of power by the CEO, for he or she is selecting a combination of strategy and structure that fits and thereby produces higher performance, including profit, for their organization (Donaldson, 1987; Hamilton and Shergill, 1993). Hence the CEO's decision-making is neither arbitrary, capricious nor selfish – that is, detrimental to the organization and its stakeholders.

Managerial Preferences and Organizational Structure

Montanari (1979) offers a model for researching strategic choice in an article entitled: 'Strategic choice: a theoretical analysis'. He also makes a 'preliminary evaluation' of the validity of this model (1979: 217). The strategic choice theory is operationalized as postulating an effect of managerial preferences for particular structures upon the structure adopted in the organization in which that manager is a senior executive. Empirically, a large number of correlations are shown between this strategic choice variable and the structure of the organization (1979: 218). Managerial power is also shown to correlate with organizational structure. This leads to the conclusion that 'managerial discretion does play an important role in structural determination' (1979: 220). There are, however, a number of problems that caution against accepting this conclusion.

The strategic choice variable measures managerial preferences on which structures to adopt when there is a problem. This is consonant with the idea in strategic choice theory that managerial preferences will influence the form of structural adaptation made. However, difficulties arise with the scale used. Strategic choice was measured by four items, and two are reported as examples:

> (a) The manager's first reaction to a new problem should be to delegate decision-making authority to subordinates with expertise in the problem area, (b) A good method of insuring that new organizational problems are dealt with effectively is to include broad representation of executives and stockholders at *major* policy decision-making sessions. (Montanari, 1979: 217fn, emphasis as in original)

Item (a) measures preference for delegation. However, the main means of having representation of stockholders at major policy-making sessions is through the board of directors by including representatives of stockholders (Tricker, 1984). Since the board is the top hierarchical level in the corporation, item (b) is compatible with a preference for extreme centralization. Thus the consistency of the two items on decentralization versus centralization is jeopardized. Since, apparently, items (a) and (b) are aggregated to form the strategic choice scale score, the meaning of that aggregate score is unclear. (The nature of the other two items composing the balance of the scale is not reported.)

These difficulties with meaning cloud the empirical results obtained from the strategic choice scale. Strategic choice is correlated positively with autonomy and delegation of organizational structure (in organizations with mediating technologies). This might be interpreted as showing that senior managers who prefer delegation are implementing such a structure. However, managers who believed in involving stockholder representatives in decisions would rely upon discussion at the board and this would prevent decisions being taken autonomously at lower levels of the organization. Thus the correlation between structure and strategic choice either confirms or disconfirms the theory, according to which part of the operational definition is focused upon. Thus the correlation is ambiguous and cannot be used to distinguish between the acceptance or rejection of strategic choice theory.

The second scale designed to tap managerial discretion measures the power of the manager (Montanari, 1979: 217). The theoretical point is that, in order to effect decisions, the senior managers require sufficient power if their preferences are to carry weight. A positive correlation was found with the centralization structural scale (in organizations with intensive technology) (1979: 218). This would be expected on the interpretation that, if senior managers are powerful, the decision-making in their organization is centralized in their hands; if the organization was decentralized, the senior managers would not be as powerful. However, other correlations with managerial power were more surprising. Managerial power was also *negatively* correlated with the centralization scale (in organizations with long-linked technology) (1979: 218). Again, managerial power was also positively correlated with the two further structural scales, of autonomy and delegation (1979: 218). These three correlations seem to state that in organizations whose senior managers see themselves as more powerful those senior managers tend to make fewer decisions than in organizations with less powerful senior managers. This seems contradictory. Thus the results obtained on the managerial power scale cast doubts on its meaningfulness. Thus, in the Montanari (1979) study there are problems of meaningfulness in both dimensions of managerial discretion: preferences and power.

As Montanari (1979: 208) notes, the strategic choice theory holds that the determination of organizational structure by contingency factors is incomplete and thus there is an influence also of managerial discretion. An empirical validation of this theory requires demonstration that, after the effect of the contingency factors on structure has been registered, there is an additional causal impact of managerial discretion. This requires a research design in which an effect of discretion on structure is shown to hold when the contingency factors are controlled. An analysis using partial correlations could provide such evidence. However, Montanari (1979: 218) presents only the raw correlations. He shows that both contingency and discretion variables correlate with structure. This leaves unanswered the question of whether discretion affects structure when contingencies are controlled. Only this mode of analysis would show whether discretion makes a contribution to the determination of structure independent of the contingency factors.

The ambiguity of the results is compounded by the cross-sectional, correlational research design, so that causality is not known. The results might be due to a reverse causal effect of structure upon managerial discretion. For example, the positive correlation between preference for delegation and structural delegation (referred to above) could arise through the existence of delegation in the present organizational structure, causing managers to state that this was a sound approach (that is, behaviour driving attitudes).

Thus limitations in measurement, research design and data analysis combine so that the Montanari (1979) study is not a crucial test of the strategic choice theory. The study might be best coded as equivocal and thus the strategic choice theory as unproven by the study.

In a further study, At-Twaijri and Montanari (1987) investigated the role of strategic choice on boundary-spanning activities. They tested for strategic choice in terms of whether the effect of contingencies on boundary-spanning activities was moderated by a variable called 'influence on decisions'. This was a derivation from the managerial discretion scales used in Montanari (1979). It measured the preference of individual purchasing agents in organizations for solving problems through boundary-spanning activities and their power to do so (At-Twaijri and Montanari, 1987: 788). However, the study failed to find a moderating effect of influence on decisions on boundary-spanning activities (1987: 792). This contradicted the theoretical expectation of the study (1987: 794).

However, the study also found a relationship between influence on decisions and one aspect of boundary-spanning activities, 'face' boundary-spanning activities (that is, representing or protecting the focal organization) (1987: 786, 793). This structure was more likely to occur where the purchasing agent involved preferred such boundary-spanning activities and perceived that they had the power to implement this structure. While At-Twaijri and Montanari (1987) interpret their data in causal terms through a path analysis, it is not apparent that the influence-on-decisions variable was measured at an earlier time than face boundary-spanning activities. Therefore the data are correlational and so could equally reflect the effect of face boundary-spanning activities on preferences. Those purchasing agents who represented their organization and defended it often would be more likely in consequence to adopt the view that such boundary-spanning activities were the appropriate solution to problems. Therefore the meaning of this correlational evidence is again ambiguous. The At-Twaijri and Montanari (1987) study should be coded as equivocal like the first study by Montanari (1979). Neither study provides decisive evidence for strategic choice.

As we have seen, Montanari and his colleague examine strategic choice in terms of power and preferences. The power possessed by a manager is determined by the power distribution in the organization. This power distribution is itself determined by contingency factors such as size and environmental uncertainty (Pugh et al., 1969a; Lawrence and Lorsch, 1967). The internal distribution of organizational power is also determined by the critical challenges faced by the organization (Hickson et al., 1971; Hinings et al., 1974;

Pfeffer and Salancik, 1978). Thus the managerial power component of strategic choice is not undetermined nor is it a realm of free choice or free will.

The managerial preferences considered by Montanari, as seen above, are in terms of a single structure as the solution to all problems; for example, delegation. This is a 'one best way' approach that is a universalistic, rather than being a contingency approach. Structural contingency theory would hold such managerial preferences to be counter-productive in many situations, because one uniform structure is being selected rather than a structure to fit the contingencies. Thus Montanari is implicitly looking for inflexible, irrational and arbitrary approaches by managers. As we have seen, the empirical studies produce, at best, uncertain evidence of such effects. However, the Montanari studies have the positive characteristic of examining for an effect of the cognitive schema of the manager.

Managerial Cognition and Structural Contingency Theory

Structural contingency theory implies that the cognitive schema of the manager has an effect on the structures that he or she selects, so that education of managers about contingency-structure research will hasten the adoption of better-fitting structures when organizational contingencies change (Woodward, 1965). Thus it would be quite consistent with structural contingency theory to conduct research which identified the cognitive schemas of managers and showed their effects upon structures. This, in turn, could lead to research showing that education in structural contingency theory improved the cognitive schemas of managers and their decisions about organizational structure.

An empirical study by Palmer et al. (1993: 120) shows that, after controlling for contingencies, US corporations are more likely to adopt the multidivisional structure if their CEO had attended a major US graduate school. Palmer at al. (1993) reason that at such schools these managers would have been exposed to the ideas of Chandler (1962), holding that structure should follow strategy. Therefore they would be more likely to implement the new structure after diversifying, compared with managers unaware of such ideas. This means that knowledge of structural contingency theory increased the probability of making the needed structural adaptation. Hence the study finding is consistent with the proposition that greater managerial knowledge of structural contingency theory promotes organizational adoption of the structures as recommended by that theory. Since the adoption of the multidivisional structure was a move into fit by these diversified corporations, the organizations and their managers were acting rationally rather than simply following a fad (Palmer at al., 1993; Donaldson, 1987, 1995).

Thus research into the subjective dimension of re-organization is to be welcomed, especially if it examines the correspondence between the objective structural contingency theory and the cognitive schemas of managers. The focus is on how far managerial cognition mirrors the objective relationships between the contingencies and organizational structure, rather than approaching managerial cognition as a realm of subjectivity inherently in opposition to objective reality. The former approach will illuminate the clarity of managerial thought about required structures and the role for education. This is preferable to approaching managers with the presumption that managerial cognition is inherently simplistic, irrational or selfish, which can occur under the influence of strategic choice theory. Again, the proposition that better managerial knowledge will improve structural decisions is deterministic and makes no presumption that some realm of free choice or free will exists. Hence the theorizing and research about the subjective processes underlying structural change may be enhanced by not always following the strategic choice theory with its dark imagery of managerial arbitrariness and metaphysical illusions of a realm of free choice.

Conclusions on Subjective Factors

The research on subjective strategic choice provides only narrow support to date. There is evidence that managers' characteristics, such as their personalities or career histories, affect their choices of structures, but this merely adds other determinants alongside the contingencies, rather than being proof of free choice or free will (Fligstein, 1985; Miller and Droge, 1986; Miller and Toulouse, 1986; Miller et al., 1988; Palmer et al., 1993). Studies into the effect of managerial preferences on the organizational structures adopted suffer from ambiguities rendering present results equivocal (Montanari, 1979; At-Twaijri and Montanari, 1987). Hence none of these findings provides decisive evidence for free choice.

There is also evidence from Palmer et al. (1993) indicating that managerial schemas affect structures selected, but this is a rational process in support of structural adaptation to the contingencies, which is amenable to education. The key factor is whether managers have had the opportunity to acquire scientific knowledge, rather than using dysfunctional structures because of ideologies, personal preferences or self-interest. There is little evidence here of managerial influence on structure that runs counter to the contingency imperatives, apart from plain lack of awareness of the structures required by those imperatives. There is considerable scope for future empirical studies of the effects of managerial cognition upon structure, but this is best approached in terms of how far structural contingency theory is reflected in the managerial mind. The issue is how far managerial cognitions reproduce the structural contingency theory model.

Choice and Determinism as Independent

The discussion so far has treated determinism as the opposite of choice. The more the outcome of a decision is determined, then the less choice there is for the decision-maker. The more the outcome is pre-determined, the fewer the options and the less the scope for choice – that is, the less free is the decision-maker. This is the model that informs most discussions of determinism versus

free will and that also underlies the organizational theoretical analyses of Child (1972a), Bourgeois (1984) and Schreyögg (1980). However, this has been challenged by Hrebiniak and Joyce (1985).

They argue that, rather than seeing strategic choice and environmental determinism as opposites, they should really be seen as orthogonal – that is, as two dimensions that are independent of each other (Hrebiniak and Joyce, 1985). Thus it is possible to be simultaneously high on strategic choice and also on determinism (1985). They criticize the prior approach of seeing choice and determinism as opposites and assert the superiority of their view. However, Hrebiniak and Joyce fail to explain how choice and determinism can be anything other than opposites. Choice and determinism are clearly concepts which by definition are opposites – that is, antitheses. They cannot be independent dimensions nor can they both be present together. An organization that is environmentally determined cannot also be held to enjoy strategic choice.

Hrebiniak and Joyce (1985: 340) argue that strategic choice and environmental determinism can both be high simultaneously, because the organization faces an environment that is highly constraining in some aspects and not in others where choice is exercised. This definition means that the environment is not highly determining, since it is only constraining in some aspects but not in others. Thus it is hardly surprising that choice is possible. However, this is no demonstration that high choice and high determinism can occur together.

Hrebiniak and Joyce (1985) specify which strategic types fit with each of the four combinations of strategic choice and environmental determinism. Lawless and Finch (1989) have sought to test this model empirically. They find almost no empirical support for the postulated fit between strategic types and the four combinations. More importantly, they offer no test of the contention of Hrebiniak and Joyce (1985) that strategic choice and environmental determinism are independent dimensions; for further discussion of Lawless and Finch (1989) see also Bedeian (1990) and Lawless and Tegarden (1990).

Often in organizational behaviour a single dimension is taken and then reconceptualized into two or more dimensions; that is, as a multiple dimensional construct (for example, Pugh et al., 1968). Here it appears that Hrebiniak and Joyce (1985) have made the same move, but on an impossible subject. Again, there is some proclivity in American culture for asserting, on many topics, that a broader diversity can be attained; this is felt to be more broad-minded, tolerant and pluralistic. However, on the topic of determinism, the notion that choice and determinism are multidimensional is an inherent impossibility.

Discussion

The Role of Management

There is a difference in explanatory emphasis between Bourgeois (1984) and Child (1972a) which reflects differences in metatheory and values. For

Bourgeois (1984), strategic choice is discretion over structure exercised by management as a positive contribution to organizational effectiveness. This is consistent with a management theory view that if management could be supplied with better information and knowledge then their structural choices would become more effective (Woodward, 1965). The implicit role for management is positive and thus this view is pro-management. For Child (1972a) strategic choice, in contrast, is discretion over structure exercised by management to choose structures which they prefer personally or which grants them more control or which suits their ideology. This leads to the selection of sub-optimal structures and therefore makes strategic choice arbitrary, capricious and thereby anti-social. This is consistent with a radical view in sociological theory that organizations, far from being efficient tools contributing to society, are arenas of domination in an exploitative social order. The aim of such sociological analysis is to make the arbitrariness of managerial choice transparent and thereby to delegitimate the present organizational order and pave the way for radical social change. Thus the radical sociological variant of the strategic choice thesis is a negative view of management and is a type of anti-management organization theory (for others, see Donaldson, 1995).

The view taken in this volume is that managers exercise choice between structural options and actively conduct the formulation and implementation of the new structure. However, the discretion or scope of choice is highly circumscribed by the fact that the organization needs to adopt the structure which is optimal given its contingency factors, in order to avoid performance loss. For example, as an organization grows it must bureaucratize and structurally differentiate. Similarly, as an organization diversifies it must adopt a more decentralized structure, shifting from functional to multidivisional. Organizations are under pressure to perform from several sources: from competitors, from stakeholders such as owners and employees, and from the aspirations of their own managers. Therefore organizations will seek to avoid the performance loss that comes from retaining structures that are in misfit with the contingencies. Thus organizations will move from misfit into fit by adopting the structure which best fits. This will typically be one particular structure, or a narrow band of structural alternatives, out of all the various conceivable types of structure. Hence the discretion exercised will be severely limited.

The situational imperatives mean that there is no real strategic choice. Managers may go through the subjective process of choosing, but the outcome is already largely pre-set by which structure is the objective fit to the particular contingencies. This is not a negative view of the role of management. It says that they typically select the right structure or move towards it over time. Thus managers make a positive contribution by selecting the appropriate structure as set by the contingencies. The contingencies causally determine the structure, but the intervening process is through the activity and choice of managers. The managers are mainly conduits of causation, adding little independently in a causal sense, since the structural outcome has already been shaped by the contingencies. Thus it is simultaneously true that managers are not automata, for they process information and make decisions, but also that contingencies determine structure and thus pre-determine managerial choice. Managers add value to the organization by choosing the structure which is dictated by the contingencies.

Thus the view that structure is rigidly determined by contingencies is pro-management. It is more pro-management than the radical sociological view that managers are arbitrarily selecting structures of an anti-social nature. And it is more pro-management than the view that managers are well-intentioned but so misguided at present by their misperceptions and misbeliefs that they frequently choose structures which are at odds with the contingencies. This would mean that managers were generating wide variance in structures associated with any one contingent circumstance, and exercising a considerable, but often woeful, discretion.

Equally, structural determinism does not require the abrogation of the philosophical principle that managers are responsible morally and ethically for their own decisions, though it weakens it in practice (Whittington, 1989). Managers are not mere automata, and intervene purposefully between the contingencies and the structure they choose. However, they choose the structure in the light of the effectiveness that results. Given the need for most organizations to be effective, especially over the longer-run, it is hard for management to choose a structure other than that required by the contingencies. Thus, while one may hold managers responsible ethically for their organizational structures, as Whittington (1989) wishes, it is unlikely that this in itself will lead them to choose different structures in the future. Since the structures presently chosen are necessitated rather than arbitrary, the scope of choice by managers is restricted.

Potential Applications

If managers use their choice to select a more or less optimal structure, as structural contingency theory shows, then this knowledge has utility in three ways. The first way is that by refining our understanding of what constitutes a fit through research and feeding this back to managers, then managers can be assisted to attain more, rather than less, optimal structures, with consequential gains in organizational performance. Better knowledge may lead also to surer and swifter structural adaptations thus reducing the time spent in misfit, which is sometimes substantial at present (Dyas and Thanheiser, 1976; Donaldson, 1987). Again, publicly shared, scientifically valid knowledge might eventually enable management to make the needed changes in their structure simultaneously with the changes in the contingency, thus avoiding the state of misfit and moving directly from one state of fit to another. This would involve anticipation and planning of organizational change and would make managerial action on structural matters proactive rather than reactive.

The second way in which structural contingency theory can be used is to argue that organizational management, left to their own devices, mostly select appropriate structures and therefore there is no need for intervention from outside. It cautions against interventions by governments, shareholders, institutional investors and citizen bodies who may seek to impose structural change on organizations in the mistaken belief that organizational managements do not make needed structural adaptations. The radical sociological variant of strategic choice theory depicts managerial selection of structures as arbitrary and capricious, thus opening the door to outside intervention. However, studies show managerial decisions about structure to be mainly rational. Therefore interventions are liable to be resisted by incumbent management if they frustrate the on-going adaptation of the organization to the imperatives of its contingent situation. Thus such outside interventions may be a waste of time and energy for the outside reformers and the corporate executives, distracting both parties from more useful activity, such as the managers from dealing with international competition. Worse, outside reform attempts, if backed by sufficient external power, could lead to the imposition of ineffective structures on organizations which are ill-suited to their needs and which upset the on-going internal structural adaptation.

A third way in which structural contingency theory may be used is to predict the structural changes of other organizations. An outside observer in another organization can predict how the focal organization will change structurally over time. As the organization grows, diversifies, innovates, down-sizes, refocuses and so on, the consequential changes can be predicted in degree of structural and bureaucratic elaborateness, dispersion of decision-making authority and so on. An external organization which is trying to sell to the focal organization may use structural contingency theory to predict how the focus of financial decision-making authority will change over time.

Again, an external organization which is a competitor trying to take market share from the focal organization may use structural contingency theory to predict when the focal organization is most vulnerable to attack. This will be when contingencies have changed, producing structural misfit, so that the organization is off-balance, suffering reduced performance, and is disorganized. Then the focal organization is self-obsessed and unable to manage regular operations, let alone to deal with a whole new hostile threat. The competitor organization can strike a blow with devastating effect, taking away customers while the focal organization flounders around unable to respond. Competitors can plan their assault so as to be ready to unleash it when the focal organization is most vulnerable – that is, in misfit.

Thus structural contingency theory, although deterministic, nevertheless yields practical utility. Whatever the attractions of a nondeterministic view, it cannot really yield practical usefulness given that the world is actually deterministic. Its agenda is a mission impossible.

Democratic Values and Structural Determinism

Turning to the political left, their dislike of determinism in structural contingency theory lies in their distaste for the idea that some structures are inevitable given certain contingencies. The left believe that these deterministic ideas provide a justification for managerial choices of certain structures, using the argument that there is an imperative to choose that structure out of respect for efficiency and effectiveness (Schreyögg, 1980). Thus the left see in deterministic structural contingency theory an ideological buttress for structures which are bureaucratic and monolithic, and which focus power in the hands of the managerial elite oppressing the workers (Clegg and Dunkerley, 1980). However, when contingency theory holds that size leads to bureaucracy in the sense of specialization, procedures, rules and paperwork, there is nothing oppressive of the workers in the statement.

Bureaucracy is an impersonal system which diminishes the extent to which managers can exercise discretion and therefore have power over the workers. Trade unions have typically fought to create more bureaucracy in the organizations which employ their members in order to reduce management power and opportunity for managerial caprice (for example, requiring that overtime be offered to each worker in turn by roster rather than selectively at the discretion of the foreperson) (Bain, 1970). Trade unions themselves employ bureaucracy in their internal administration (for instance, in collection of dues, employing head office staff and so on), and they increase in bureaucracy with increase in size, similar to capitalist firms (Donaldson and Warner, 1974a; 1974b). For most people in industrialized capitalist countries, the main alternative to employment in a large bureaucracy is employment in a small firm run by a dominant owner-manager. He or she wields almost all the power and can deal with employees, including supposedly managerial employees, in summary fashion (Pugh et al., 1969a). The scope for domination of one human being by another is much higher in a small firm than in a large, impersonal bureaucracy.

When the left counterpose the established order to the alternative organizational forms they value, they are mainly envisaging industrial democracy. Industrial democracy, as advocated by the European left, typically involves vesting power in a central body which contains elected representatives of the workers. Organizational research indicates that the main influence of such bodies is to centralize decision-making authority so that they can decide matters and thus reduce decentralization of decision-making authority down the managerial hierarchy (Pugh et al., 1969a; Donaldson and Warner, 1974a). These elected enterprise councils and similar bodies create more, rather than less, organizational centralization.

Thus the democratization of organizational structure widely advocated by the left is not endangered by bureaucratic formalization nor by centralization. Statements in deterministic structural contingency theory of the sort that size inevitably leads to bureaucracy are not inimical to industrial democracy and thus are not a threat to the agenda of the left. Bureaucracy is a politically neutral instrument which can be used for many different purposes. It is no more a creature of the right than of the left. Hence deterministic statements about size leading to bureaucracy are neutral statements about bureaucratic administration being necessary in order to resolve the problem of the administrative organization of large numbers of people, whether they be conservatives or progressives.

Thus there is no need to see in deterministic structural contingency theory 'metaphysical pathos', meaning pessimism and fatalism (Child, 1972a). Bureaucratization is inevitable with increase in size. Diversification and size growth lead to delegation of authority. These structural developments are inevitable but they are not negative in terms of human values. Accordingly, there is nothing fatalistic in the sense of standing back passively while something unpleasant happens. Hence our view about the inevitable structural developments as organizations grow and diversify is optimistic.

The final issue requiring comment here is the underlying model of science that is implied by determinism.

The Model of Scientific Endeavour Utilized in Social Science

Bourgeois (1984) sees determinist researchers as modelling their efforts on linear causality as exemplified by Newtonian physics. This is contrasted with modern enquiries as in quantum physics, with concepts such as indeterminacy (1984).

While explanations of fundamentals of matter or of cosmic origin seem to have outgrown simple linear concepts of time and Cartesian geometry, Newtonian physics is still an established body of knowledge which offers reliable explanations of many phenomena such as motion or light. As many schoolchildren still confirm experimentally to this day, the angle of reflection of a ray of light coming from a mirror is determined by the angle at which it falls upon the reflecting surface – the angle of incidence equals the angle of reflection. Similarly, the rate at which steel balls roll down wooden slopes is still predicted by the laws of motion. These scientific laws remain valid and useful knowledge. Relative to modern atomic physics with its complex, multiple particle models, this is, of course, simple science. But the natural sciences have been developing for several hundred years.

Administrative sciences, as taught in management schools, have a research base which is overwhelmingly post-1945. If we are to take the natural sciences as models and exemplars for our endeavours, which is the more sensible point of reference, Western physics in its mature form or that subject in its earlier phase? Surely present attempts at administrative enquiries parallel studies of reflection or falling bodies more than they do the physics of black holes. Bodies of knowledge have to begin with simple, validated models and then proceed to more refined, complex formulations. Thus, in so far as social scientists take natural sciences as an inspiration, Newtonian physics may be more helpful than quantum physics. The associated conceptual building blocks of cause leading to effect, past preceding present and general laws, also command continuing respect (Behling, 1980) – at least until alternative postulates of proven greater explanatory power are available.

Conclusions

Attempts to date to show a substantial effect of managerial choice independent of the contingency imperatives have not been conclusive. Factors other than the contingencies have been shown to play a role in shaping organizational structure, but these factors are determinants, such as managerial personality or career history, that are themselves already fixed at the time they influence structural choice. Hence any evidence for such factors is evidence for determinism, not free choice nor free will.

It is in the nature of social science that it explains things by finding causes and showing that these causes are in turn caused. Hence it is unlikely that social science research will confirm the existence of free will, which would require it to be shown that factors causing the selection of structures were themselves uncaused.

Thus organizational structure is mainly determined by contingency imperatives. There are decisions involved and these may be taken consciously and, in some cases, with consideration of alternatives. Individual characteristics of the managers have some impact, such as their personalities and career histories, but these are determinants which are themselves the results of causes, including contingency factors. The structural option chosen is largely pre-specified by the contingencies. Structural decision-making involves human actors such as organizational managers and other persons. However, they are mainly intervening processes between contingencies and the inevitable structural outcome.

The managers accommodate necessity. This is a positive act, since it produces an adapted structure that facilitates effective management and greater organizational performance. In this way the managers, by bowing to the inevitable, 'add value', for the retention of the misfitted structure would be injurious to the organization. Thus our deterministic view is not fatalistic, for fatalism implies bowing to inevitable outcomes be they good or bad. The managers in our theory work purposefully to correct structural defects and strengthen the organization. The structural adaptation to the contingencies implies bureaucratizing as the organization grows. This is not incompatible with values of democracy and social justice. Equally, recognition of determinism is compatible with the mission of management education. A wider understanding of the need to fit organizational contingencies and of the required structures may speed structural adaptation and make it more complete.

Taking this chapter together with the previous one, we conclude that strategic choice is limited and that the determinism in structural contingency theory is sound.

4

For Functionalism: Against Politics and 'Parkinson's Law'

The anti-positivist and anti-functionalist movements in modern organization theory come together strongly in political explanations of organizations. The political approach paints a dark and cloudy picture of the organization as shaped through the pursuit of self-interest of its managers, in complex swirling political processes that defy parsimonious scientific models. Fortunately, as we shall see, far simpler and more robust explanations are provided by positivist, functionalist organization theory. These reveal that elegant models have great explanatory power and apply very widely. They paint a far brighter picture of the organization and show how material factors propel it towards greater economies. They offer an interpretation of organizations without recourse to political theories.

Politics and Anti-Positivism, Anti-Functionalism

The political explanation of organization holds that its structure is caused by the interests of powerful parties in the organization, rather than being shaped by the requirement to produce operational effectiveness as set by contingency factors. The growth in numbers of managers, administrators and support staff is one aspect of organizational structure that has been the subject of rival interpretations by political and contingency theorists. Contingency theory holds that the number of managers, administrators and support staff is determined by the contingency of organizational size. Thus the explanation is by a material factor, making the theory positivist. Political theory holds that, on the contrary, the numbers of managers, administrators and support staff is determined by the self-interest and political power plays of the managers – that is, by human intentions, not material factors – rendering the theory anti-positivist. Moreover, the contingency theory sees that there are economies of scale in administration that benefit the organization, whereas the political explanation sees that the growth in administrative personnel is counter-productive for the organization. Thus, regarding the administrative component of organization there is a clear divide between the positivist, functionalist view of contingency theory and the anti-positivist and anti-functionalist view of the political theory of organizations.

Political theories of other aspects of organization structure can be offered (Child, 1973b; Pfeffer and Salancik, 1978). However, growth in the numbers of administrators and support staff has attracted the political explanation, in that there could be seen, in tangible form, the build-up of costly managerial empires (Child, 1973a; Reimann, 1979). Hence, supposedly, the operation of naked managerial self-interest is revealed in a clear way. Moreover, this political model easily inclines to the view that the growth of managers and administrators in an organization is uneconomic, dysfunctional and disproportionate to the growth in number of employees. For example, Roy (1990) critiques the functionalist explanation of organizations and advocates an explanation in terms of capitalism. He criticizes Chandler's (1962, 1977) functionalist account of the rise of the corporation and points out negative aspects, stating: 'There is no serious attention given to possible inefficiencies of scale such as the geometric increase in administrative personnel when an organization grows' (Roy, 1990: 28). Such statements paint a picture of the burgeoning, excessive growth of administrators in the modern corporation and treat a geometric increase of administrators as an established fact.

A Positivist, Functionalist Theory of Administrators

In contrast, Blau (1970) has offered a structural contingency theory of the administrative component of organizational structure which is positivist and functionalist. An organization is held to increase its complement of managers, administrators and support staff as it grows in total size (that is, its total employees). But these administrative personnel grow less than the growth in direct production personnel (namely, workers), so that larger organizations have lower proportions of administrative personnel than smaller organizations. In this way, organizational growth in size leads to economies of scale in administration, in other words, it is functional. The ratio of administrative personnel to total employees is termed the administrative intensity of the organization.

Growth in organizational size leads to a decline in administrative intensity (Blau, 1970). This occurs through several intervening variables. The greater internal complexity of large organizations raises their administrative intensity. However, this is more than offset by the greater homogeneity of the more specialized work teams that simplifies management and also by the greater reliance on standard rules and procedures that simplifies management as well. The net effect is less administrative intensity in larger organizations.

Blau's theory is general, applicable across many sorts of organizations. It is presented in the form of a series of propositions similar in style to Newton's laws in physics. Blau and his colleagues offer evidence from a number of quantitative comparisons of organizations (Blau, 1970, 1972; Blau and Schoenherr, 1971). These include graphs and the results of multivariate regressions. Their evidence attests to the validity and generality of the relationship between size and administrative intensity. Thus the theory and research of Blau and his colleagues on this topic is seen as positivist and, indeed, as one of the most positivist branches of structural contingency theory.

An Anti-Positivist, Anti-Functionalist, Political Theory of Administrators

If Blau is the leading structural contingency theorist on administrative intensity and exponent of the view that the growth of administrators is functional and can be studied positivistically, the leader of the political view is Parkinson (1957). He sees the growth of administrators as shamefully irrational and uneconomic. Parkinson (1957) advances a law whereby administrators proliferate in bureaucracy with no relation to the amount of real work and in a way which needlessly accumulates costs and which benefits only the administrators personally through greater status and the like. Parkinson states his thesis in a manner which pokes fun at social science, by means of satire. Such an irrationalist mode of argument sits well with those who would make a counter-cultural critique of rationalism in organizational science and who would embrace the technology of foolishness. Parkinson (1957) wrote satirically but his writings are widely invoked not only by social commentators but also by academic organizational researchers, and have become part of the standard literature on this topic.

Positivist Methodological Support for the Anti-Positivist Theory   Some researchers who have used social scientific methods to investigate the issue of administrative intensity have interpreted their results in a way contrary to the functionalist and positivist theory of Blau and have favoured the political model of Parkinson (Child, 1973a; Reimann, 1979). Thus researchers coming after Blau (1970, 1972) and using similar methods have nevertheless moved away from his theoretical view. These later researchers have called into question both the idea that organizational growth leads to economies of scale in administration and the simple law-like regularities that Blau propounded. In their place, later researchers have been more inclined to see complexity and political processes (Child, 1973a; Reimann, 1979; Lioukas and Xerokostas, 1982; Smith, 1978). Other researchers subsequent to Blau have also concluded against Blau's theory, again favouring a more political interpretation in terms of the self-interest of managers. This has been argued through assertions that the cross-sectional correlational methods of Blau are flawed (Freeman and Kronenfeld, 1973), and conceal dynamic processes that are contrary to his theory (Freeman and Hannan, 1975; Montanari and Adelman, 1987; Marsh and Mannari, 1989).

　　It will be convenient to break the discussion of the political explanation of the administrative component of organization into two parts. In the first part, in this chapter, we will consider Parkinson's thesis that growth in administrative intensity is driven by the political self-interest of managers. This will involve a critique of Parkinson's thesis and also of his academic followers who claim to find evidence in his favour. In the second part, in the next chapter, we will consider Blau's theory. We will argue that many of the criticisms of Blau's theory and methods are erroneous. Our conclusion will be that organizations tend not to display the pathological diseconomies of scale argued by

Parkinson and his academic supporters. We conclude also that simple, positivist models are superior to complex, anti-positivist interpretations. Thus the positivist and functional explanation of administrative intensity is more valid than the political and anti-positivist interpretation.

In the body of this chapter we will first critically examine the inspiration of modern political explanations of the administrative component of organizational structure – the thesis of Parkinson (1957). The discussion will then turn to a critical examination of the social science research that finds in his favour (Child, 1973a; Reimann, 1979). We will next examine other empirical research that supports the explanation of the administrative component of organization as politically driven (Smith, 1978).

A Critique of Parkinson's Law

Both Child (1973a) and Reimann (1979), and indeed others writing in the administrative intensity literature, draw upon Parkinson's Law (Parkinson, 1957). This is contained in a satire by Parkinson of the growth of administrators, and by implication, administrative cost, unrelated to any real need, that is, without benefit for effectiveness. Parkinson (1957: 4) states his two basic propositions:

1   'An official wants to multiply subordinates, not rivals', and
2   'Officials make work for each other.'

Child (1973a) and others invoke this political theory, so brilliantly penned by Parkinson, that administrative hierarchies grow because administrators seek to multiply subordinates and not peers who are career rivals, resulting in vast hierarchies wherein administrators are toiling away, busily administering other administrators, trapped in a situation of their own making and with no productive outcome.

Since Parkinson's Law is a compelling fable with both a note of humour and a literary lightness to relieve the unending seriousness of academic social science, any attempts at critical analyses are liable to be eschewed as boring in the extreme. This is a pity, since otherwise the topic of administrative intensity remains under the spell of popular mythology. The Parkinsonian populist belief powerfully buttresses and sustains those academic analyses that depict growth of administrators as political, uneconomic and organizationally irrational. Yet all beliefs, even populist ones, deserve critical, social scientific scrutiny. Accordingly, we shall offer some criticisms of Parkinson's Law in an effort to approach the truth about administrative intensity.

The evidence which Parkinson, apparently only somewhat tongue in cheek, adduces in support of his theory, concerns the growth in administrators in the British public service, in particular the Royal Navy and the Colonial Office. It is not entirely clear how much of this is fact and how much is whimsy, but because Parkinson presents it as if it is fact, and many subsequent scholars and commentators on organizations have accepted his account as substantially factual, we shall treat his case histories seriously.

The Royal Navy

Parkinson (1957: 8) presents evidence that over the period 1914 to 1928, the number of capital ships in the Royal Navy fell by 68 per cent, the officers and men of the Royal Navy also fell by 32 per cent and yet the number of Admiralty officials (that is, the size of the administrative hub of the Royal Navy) grew by 78 per cent, from 2,000 to 3,569 officials, 'and that this growth was unrelated to any possible increase in their work. The Navy during that period had diminished, in point of fact, by a third in men and two-thirds in ships' (1957: 8).

Since the technology of the Navy was becoming more complex over this period, some part of this increase in administrators might be explained by the increase in administrative work to manage a more capital-intensive Navy. Parkinson allows for some trend of this type but essentially controls for the effects of technology by showing that the increase in naval dockyard personnel, whose work would also increase due to this enhanced technological complexity, was less than the increase in Admiralty officials. In particular, the number of administrators – that is, officials and clerks – in the naval dockyards increased only by 40 per cent (1957: 8), which is half the rate of increase of 78 per cent of the Admiralty officials. Thus the increase in technological complexity failed to account for all the increase in Admiralty officials. However, Parkinson essentially dismisses the caveat regarding technological complexity with the statement that the growth in administrators really is completely unrelated to any operational work done and hence is wholly political and not functional: 'The officials would have multiplied at the same rate had there been no actual seamen at all' (1957: 10). Hence Parkinson sticks to his view that the growth of administrators in organizations is governed by its one logic, the famous law, and that it is a phenomenon of political self-interest, totally irrational from the standpoint of the public goals of the organization of delivering a service in a cost-effective manner. Let us examine these figures about growth in Admiralty officials and see whether there are grounds for a less extreme, less whimsical interpretation.

To begin with technological complexity: clearly, this has been increasing in naval warfare over the last 200 years, and the period 1914 to 1928 was one of continued fast-paced development. As McNeill (1982) perceptively remarks, the naval warship which evolved in the nineteenth century was really the first to possess the modern conception of a weapons system – that is, it contained a series of related devices (including propulsion, gunnery, guidance, fire control, signals), each of which was quite sophisticated technically, was expensive, and which interrelated to destroy the enemy. The period of history through the nineteenth and into the twentieth century saw a continuing arms race between the major powers. In a situation of increasing technological complexity and technological competition, and of increasing expense, modern navies are actively engaged in researching, designing, tendering, contracting, estimating and costing a bewildering array of devices. Many of these are complex and so require additional administration, much of which is done centrally – that is, at the Admiralty. One should recall that even a single naval vessel such as a submarine is in reality a host of devices, or as we would now say, sub-systems. To envisage the scale of naval research, design and procurement activity, this must be multiplied many times across all the submarines, battleships, cruisers, land stations and so on. As all of these assets become more powerful and expensive individually, and more closely interconnected, the implied administrative complexity and workload is increased accordingly.

On top of this complex task must be added the requirement for thrifty and correct public administration of the Navy on behalf of the democratic public. This generates procedures for public tendering of procurement contracts, for costing systems and for procedures for giving preference to domestic manufacturers (for reasons of security and of national economic self-interest). These all require administrative personnel to design, operate, adjudicate and review them. Demands grounded in the democratic nature of public administration would be expected to have led to more rather than fewer controls on navies in our century.

The figures Parkinson himself displays are suggestive here. The growth in dockyard personnel of 40 per cent between 1914 and 1928 suggests that technological complexity of weapons systems and the derived complexity for administration were increasing over this period, as Parkinson himself grants. However, unlike Parkinson, one could take the next step and see that this might logically imply that Admiralty officials would increase by 40 per cent. Thus about 40 of the 78 per-cent increase in Admiralty officials would be expected due to technological complexity. This leaves only the other half of the increase in Admiralty officials, 38 per cent, as requiring explanation.

Another major factor here would be the shift from a wartime to a peacetime Navy. Any military force at cessation of hostilities demobilizes large numbers of front-line personnel and de-activates their equipment. In peacetime, many front-line units of the order of battle are reservists who are not counted in the active service list. There is a tendency to rely on reservists in roles such as infantry, field medical, fighter bomber and mine-sweeping operations. Roles which require fewer militarily specific skills and which often involve less sophisticated equipment (that is, which do not need the latest fighters or tanks or submarines) are assigned to reservists, with the regular, active military personnel in charge of the larger, most sophisticated systems. Thus demobilizations will tend to decrease numbers of armed service personnel and to decrease, to a lesser degree, the number of capital assets in use, as the larger, more sophisticated units are kept in active service with smaller, less sophisticated, more numerous units placed in the reserves. This means that the military in peacetime is proportionately more capital intensive than the same force under war conditions. Thus the decreases in men and equipment (32 per cent in men and 68 per cent in ships) which Parkinson observed over the period 1914 to 1928 are consistent with a military force moving from wartime to peacetime.

As part of this change in status, military forces essentially go into a condition where they are partially ready to be mobilized should war break out again. This means that they are structured for a rapid growth in size should reservists and the general population be mobilized. Therefore their command and control structure is suitable for a larger size than their actual peacetime number suggests. This is part of the reason for the high proportion of generals and admirals to ordinary soldiers and sailors in peacetime, relative to time of war. The headquarters, staff, training, command, communications and other military administrative services are therefore kept disproportionately large in peacetime. Similarly, the administrative centres of the civilian government concerned with the military, such as the Admiralty, have to be kept disproportionately large to provide an administrative apparatus for mobilization and deployment of a larger military force in wartime. Again, the military planners give disproportionate emphasis, relative to wartime, to the 'big ticket items', that is, new weapons systems which are expensive, long in lead-time and indivisible, relative to ordinary volume items, such as ammunition rounds, which can be quickly increased in numbers if the onset of war makes them necessary. This tends to boost the level of technological complexity and capital intensity of the peacetime service, and thus raise the corresponding requirement for central administrators to manage these complex programmes, such as officials at the Admiralty.

For these reasons, the shift from a wartime to a peacetime Royal Navy would be expected to raise the number of Admiralty officials while simultaneously reducing the number of ships and sailors. This effect partly works through technological complexity but has a substantial direct effect independent of technological complexity. Thus the change in status from war to peace over the period 1914 to 1928 must surely have tended to boost the ratio of Admiralty officials to Royal Navy sailors and offers a further explanation of Parkinson's figures which is opposite to his own.

Another explanatory factor can also be invoked here. Parkinson notes that the number of naval ships was limited from 1922 by the Washington Naval Agreement between the major naval powers (1957: 8). He (1957: 8) uses this fact to make the point that, because of this treaty limitation, the number of ships could not be further increased in future despite the employment build-up of administrators. However, this treaty limitation on the number of ships of countries vying for naval supremacy would push competition away from sheer numbers of vessels and into the quality of the vessels – that is, into 'capital ships of real quality', to use a phrase of Winston Churchill. There would be a greater emphasis on the firepower, speed and performance of each capital ship. This in turn throws the emphasis back on to sophistication, technological complexity and to the 'back-room' activities of research design and liaison with contractors – all of which boost the need for central administrators. Thus the treaty further intensifies the competitive race, moving from number of ships in the water to activities which heighten the need for Admiralty officials.

In summary, the decline in the number of ships and sailors in the Royal Navy between 1914 and 1928 and the simultaneous rise in the number of Admiralty officials which Parkinson presents and attributes to office politics is at least equally attributable to four other interconnected factors operating at this time: the increase in technological complexity of naval weapons systems, the demobilization from war to peace, the international treaty limitations on numbers of capital ships and a secular trend towards enhanced accountability. These are explanatory variables which are highly consistent with the facts which Parkinson presents. They provide an alternative plausible explanation. And this alternative explanation is of military administration as a rational activity geared to the changing requirements for the military defence of Britain. Thus, contrary to the Parkinsonian account, which is wholly a theory of self-interested empire-building by bureaucrats and which depicts the British government defence organization as irrational, we would assert an interpretation which is more functionalist. The truth may be some admixture between these two antithetic theories. At the very least, it suggests that academic followers of Parkinson have to make a serious case for why the political view should be seen as more compelling than the functionalist.

The Colonial Office

The second of the two case studies presented as evidence of his law by Parkinson is the British Colonial Office. Over the period 1935 to 1954 this grew in size from a staff of 372 to 1,661 (Parkinson, 1957: 11). Parkinson notes that the geographic area and population of British colonies fell in the middle of this period due to World War II enemy occupation, rose again by 1947, 'but have since then shrunk steadily from year to year as successive colonies achieve self-government' (1957: 11). Despite these fluctuations and the eventual decline, he argues that the Colonial Office staff size simply shows 'an inevitable increase . . . [which] has nothing to do with the size – or even the existence – of the Empire' (1957: 11). On the contrary, the growth in Colonial Office staff is seen by Parkinson as similar to increases in other government departments, the driving force of Colonial Office staff being not operational work but again internal office politics.

Parkinson (1957: 11) presents the Colonial Office staff numbers at five dates, mostly four years apart (1935, 1939, 1943, 1947 and 1954) and they display an increase in size over every period (372, 450, 817, 1,139 and 1,661 staff, respectively), being increases of 21, 82, 39 and 46 per cent, respectively, for each of the periods. Granted that these figures show a continuous increase in staff over an historical period when British colonial territories fell, especially in the final period of decolonialization, but is this proof of bureaucratic excess?

Presumably the loss of territories by enemy occupation during World War II was seen as temporary, and British foreign policy was to regain them (which essentially was achieved later). Therefore, it would be rational to retain structures and staffs with appropriate expertise in anticipation of repossession. Moreover, the war and enemy occupation would both raise new issues of policy and administration of each British colony, adding to pre-war functions and thus requiring additional staff. The increase in size of the Colonial Office staff from 450 to 1,139 between 1939 and 1947 may have been required because of the exigencies of war.

Perhaps the more apparently difficult data are the staff expansion from 1947 to 1954 during a period of British decolonialization. Yet the granting of independence to a former colony causes, short-term, a considerable amount of additional work for the former colonial power if the transition is to be even moderately orderly. The former colony must develop and enhance its capacity for internal political self-government and provision of services formerly provided, to a degree, in one form or another by the colonial power; for example, defence, education, government officials, judiciary. This transmogrification of the administrative apparatus of a former colony requires much administrative work of the former colonizer, in both policy and implementation. Under this scenario the staff of the British Colonial Office might well increase even at the very time when the number of British colonies was declining. Again, it seems that a plausible alternative explanation can be advanced to account for the figures which Parkinson sees as wholly bureaucratic-political. At the very least, the Parkinsonian thesis requires a serious attempt to show that the volume of real work in the British Colonial Office was declining and not rising over this period.

Comparison of Royal Navy and Colonial Office

Parkinson (1957: 12) notes a striking similarity in the annual growth rates of administrative officials in both the Admiralty and Colonial Office cases: they are both close to an average of 5.75 per cent. Again, although he is semi-satiric in his presentation, this concretizes his argument of a constant trend of increase over time in administrative hierarchies quite independent of any real work output (1957: 12). However, Parkinson (1957: 11) ignores the war period in the Colonial Office figures, but includes the war years in the Admiralty case, which is inconsistent. Including the war years in the Colonial Office case, the average annual increase in staff there is 18.23 per cent, which is over triple the figure for the Admiralty, 5.6 per cent (1957: 8). This destroys the notion of a trend which generalizes across these two arms of government.

In summary, Parkinson's claim to have found an annual average increase of about 5.75 per cent per annum across different organizations is not consistent with his own figures. He presents evidence of a trend towards increasing staff in both the Admiralty and Colonial Office at times when the number of persons under their jurisdiction was, by certain indices, declining. However, the actual work being done by these administrators is not empirically studied, and the possibility exists that their load of real administrative work was increasing over the period due to the peculiarities of their differing situations: namely, the onset of peace marked by competition and technological complexity for the Admiralty and the upheaval of decolonialization for the Colonial Office. In both organizations, an at least *prima facie* alternative, plausible explanation can be offered of these organizations as rationally building up their central staff in a manner congruent with their policies and goals and reflecting their changing task contingencies. Thus an interpretation diametrically opposite to Parkinson's model of political self-interest can be made. The rational, functionalist interpretation has the merits of being consistent with known facts about British history and available insights about military organization. The decision between these two rival, opposite theoretical explanations is a matter for future research, through empirical tests of the differing, derived hypotheses. In particular, a crucial variable is the level of productive work of these two organizations. Was productive work static or declining, as under Parkinson's Law, or was it increasing as under the functionalist theory, as staff size increased?

The Rhetoric of Satire

Parkinson's Law is poorly founded in theory and empirical evidence. This conclusion may confound some of its followers. Other admirers of Parkinson's Law will see in this conclusion only further proof of the poor wits of these social scientists silly enough to examine earnestly the exactitude of good satire. Only a fool takes comedy seriously.

This raises an interesting issue of academic process. What, ultimately, is one to make of a contribution such as Parkinson's which is clearly semi-serious. The manner is waggish: a parody of the solemnity of social science, no less. Elements of exaggeration are clear. Therein lies the comedy. Yet the case data of the British Admiralty and Colonial Office are apparently real. And they are a heightened form of exactly the kind of pathological growth in public bureaucracy which many commentators and citizens see as really occurring and as wasteful. Herein lies the serious aspect. Parkinson's Law is almost endlessly cited in speeches, lectures, student texts and the most serious of academic journal articles. Partly Parkinson's Law is invoked for comic relief, but more than that, it is credited with much wiser content as raising a fundamental issue and as pointing the way forward. As Child concludes in the *Administrative Science Quarterly*: 'We still have to pursue Parkinson in order to make progress' (1973a: 347).

By its very simplicity and wit Parkinson's Law becomes a powerful tool of agitation and propaganda. Its self-identification as satire allows the Law to state ideas which are probably untrue. Yet these ideas are already widely believed to be all too true by many citizens and academics: witness the evergreen popularity at electoral hustings of promises to curb government bureaucracy, to cut fat and to save the taxpayers' money. For academics steeped in the world-view that organizations are essentially irrational and driven by the political self-interest of their officials, the Law finds a ready reception. Thus in Parkinson's Law we find a perfect rhetorical weapon (McCloskey, 1983): a persuasive argument which cannot be challenged, because it is a satire. As comedy it is exempt from the tests of truth. Thus critics of bureaucracy can invoke this Parkinson's Law as a potent weapon for their cause, to delight and rally their audience. Those who hold to opposite or just sceptical beliefs are outmanoeuvred. Parkinson may readily fail normal truth tests, but it stands inviolate in a realm separate from ordinary theories and hypotheses, for it is satire, comedy and popular writing. It is therefore 'off limits' to scholarly critique. One may call this the Rhetoric of Satire. Most social scientists are all too grimly aware that their craft often strikes the readers as dull; few among them would have the poor taste to criticize the clown, to risk being unpopular.

Social Scientific Support for Parkinson

Child (1973a) and then Reimann (1979) examined the relationship between organizational size and the size of the administrative support staff in empirical studies of manufacturing organizations (in the United Kingdom and United States respectively). Neither report finds increasing administrative intensity with increasing organizational size, as would be expected from Parkinson's theory. Child (1973a: 340) states that the *proportion* of supportive employees has little relationship to organizational size in his data. Thus there is no evidence here of the administrative intensity (that is, the ratio of administrators to production workers) rising as size increases. On the contrary, both studies found that organizational size and administrative support staff size were highly related to organizational size in a linear, proportional manner; that is, support personnel are added in direct proportion to the growth in production employees. This suggests a balanced and functional approach to the addition of administrators. Moreover, the phenomenon of support staff growth is shown to be amenable to a simple, positivistic modelling approach. Child (1973a) and Reimann (1979) concluded, however, that this seemingly rational pattern was somewhat misleading, masking a real underlying pattern of considerable complexity.

Their approach is to critique the simple, positivistic evidence that the number of support staff is driven by size, which they themselves discover, in order to move towards complex, disaggregated models which they see as more compatible with a political explanation (Child, 1973a; Reimann, 1979). The administrative support staff was shown not to be a homogeneous category but rather a heterogeneous construct, with different types of support staff varying in their relationship to one another. Similarly, causation was more complex, with each of the differing support dimensions being caused by a distinct set of multiple contingencies. Further, the managerial decision processes generating these complex patterns were seen as being similarly complex, reflecting the decisions and interest of dispersed organizational actors. Both articles close with the call to move the study of administrative support staff away from the functionalist, structural contingency theory type of approach towards a political process approach as initiated by Parkinson.

Thus, while the Child (1973a) and Reimann (1979) articles came out of the functionalist, positivist, quantitative comparative approach of the type made

popular by Blau and his colleagues, they use their results to attack that tradition and to question its worth, opening the door to political, processual
approaches. Thus, on the topic of the size of administrative support staff, the
articles of Child and Reimann are important as transitions from positivist,
functionalist to anti-positivist, political approaches. This is the more so in
that both Child and Reimann were already accomplished researchers in the
comparative, quantitative, positivist tradition, each with a string of published
contributions in the tradition of structural contingency theory, so their repu-
diation of that tradition on this topic area was the more compelling.

There can be no doubt that the painstaking and careful analysis that Child
mounts is in the best traditions of scientific exactitude and conscientiousness,
and was guided by the methodological principles of its day. Moreover, his
considerable efforts provided a large-scale field study of real organizations,
which led Child to make important discoveries. These data and discoveries
allow later scholars to build on them and to see larger patterns across the
original and subsequent studies. Similar remarks apply to the other scholars
whose work we will discuss. However, we hold that different methodological
principles should be used today, and that when used in conjunction with a
theoretical commitment to positivism and functionalism, a substantively different interpretation of their data comes into view.

Child's Study

Child (1973a) presents evidence which initially supports an ordered relationship between administrative intensity and size; however, he then focuses in on
parts of the picture to assert a far more complex, if not confusing, pattern, or
indeed lack of a pattern.

Child (1973a: 337, 338) shows that organizational size (total employees), in
his sample of 54 manufacturing organizations, correlates highly with the
administrative component, whether measured as total nonworkflow employees ($r = +.95$), total indirect employment ($r = +.96$) or total line management
(workflow superordinates) ($r = +.89$). These are very high degrees of association by any normal standards of social science. One might conclude that size
dominates growth in the administrative support component, and that there is
little scope for the useful addition of further explanatory variables. There is
little unexplained variance (9 to 20 per cent over the three indices). Some part
of this unexplained variance must be due to errors of measurement in both
size and support component. And some other part would be due to lags in
adjustment of support component to organizational size (that is, being tem-
porarily in misfit as argued in Chapter 2). Thus there is probably very little
real variance left to be explained by some factor other than size.

Going further, the slope coefficient of the regression of total nonworkflow
employees on total employees (size) is .515 (Child, 1973a: 338). Rounding this
figure, one can say that the slope is .5, which means that one nonworkflow
employee is added for every additional two total employees. Total employees
is the sum of total nonworkflow employees and total workflow employees

(which is direct workers and *their* managers). Hence, for every one workflow employee added, one nonworkflow employee is added. This is a simple, elegant and aesthetically pleasing result. Moreover, it suggests that organizational staffing is governed by a managerial rule of thumb that is plausibly simple and robust: add one support staff person for every person added who is a direct worker or one of their managers. Thus the ratio of support employees to direct employees is one to one.

Thus one should conclude that research has shown that the number of support staff is almost wholly driven by size and that the functional form connecting support staff and size is a coefficient of $\frac{1}{2}$. This is a conclusion which is scientifically attractive and would readily allow us to feel that the research was producing positive knowledge. It also would be eminently easy to communicate to managers, government officials and students. However, this was not the interpretation chosen in the study.

The Political Explanation   While acknowledging that the 'high linear relationship displayed in the data between total nonworkflow employment and total organizational employment is too remarkable to be ignored' (Child, 1973a: 346), and seeing that a rule of thumb is used to regulate employment decisions, Child nevertheless calls for more study of the politics of decision-making about administrative staff size. He (1973a) concludes his article by lending credence to the satire by Parkinson. He calls for a greater future attention to the details of decision-making around staffing decisions, seeing these as varying from one organizational setting to another. And he (1973a: 347) also calls for greater attention to political processes *à la* Parkinson and less reliance upon functionalist and contingency theory, summarized in his final sentence: 'We still have to pursue Parkinson in order to make progress.'

Child (1973a: 346) argues that there is some higher-level decision rule connecting organizational size and support staff size in aggregate, but that this is specific to 'organizations of the same broad type or in the same industry'. He holds, furthermore, that, within this broad framework, decisions about staffing the different support specializations are taken at lower organizational levels than top management, so that each component is the product of 'a specific combination of circumstantial factors' (1973a: 346). Child (1973a: 346) also holds that, apart from questions of functionality and effectiveness, there is a need to attend also to 'the political processes which Parkinson touched upon satirically'. And in criticizing the limitations of functionalism, he (1973a: 346, 347) calls strongly for future research on this topic to examine the decisions about employment, the circumstances which affect them and their 'manifest and latent rationales':

> A political approach would in a sense act as a counterbalance to an exclusive reliance on functional or contingency explanations. It should lead us to a study of the decisions which are in practice taken on the permissible sizes of divisions and departments within organizations. These are major issues in the ebb and flow of managerial politics, but they have rarely been studied as such. Possibly the only strategy for further research which offers some hope of disentangling the confusion

about supportive personnel is to focus upon (1) the decisions which are taken in organizations to make changes in the numbers employed in different categories, (2) the circumstances in which they are made, and (3) the manifest and latent rationales of the decision makers. Parkinson made a serious point in drawing attention to such decision making as the nub of his Law. We still have to pursue Parkinson in order to make progress.

Thus the focus is seen as needing to shift from functionalist contingency analyses to political and decisional processes.

There is a theoretical problem here as to how a phenomenon which in aggregate is highly law-like, and governed by one simple variable, organizational size, can be less governed by this same law at the disaggregate level. There is also a problem in how complex causation of the disaggregated parts can coexist with simple causation of the aggregate. If organizational size drives aggregate support staff size almost completely, how can the components of support staff size be driven by several causes which differ from one component to another? Surely this would mean that expansion in one component could go on independent of expansion in other components and of organizational size. But if that is happening how is the close correlation between the total support staff and organizational size brought about? If top management is regulating the addition of total support staff on the 'one for one' rule, how can their subordinate managers be hiring people independent of this rule? In many organizations hiring within divisions and departments requires senior management approval, or is constrained with staffing budgets or establishments, either of which means that the piecemeal hiring by middle managers is constrained within an overall regulating framework approved by senior management. Thus the theoretical formulation of Child (1973a) fails to explain the connection between the two processes which he conjectures, the staffing decisions made at top and lower hierarchical levels of the organization. Until this lacuna is filled the coherence of this theoretical formulation must be in doubt.

Heterogeneity and Complexity   While Child (1973a) finds a simple empirical relationship between organizational size and support staff, he chooses not to stop the analysis at this point, and the research result is dissected to the point where meaningful patterns are no longer visible. He looks for causes of support staff other than size and then argues for the decomposition of total support staff into various specific support staff specialisms. Then he considers the multiple causes of each specific support staff specialism, with the causes differing from one support staff specialism to the next.

Firstly, Child investigates possible causes of support staff other than size. He (1973a: 340) finds total nonworkflow employees to be explained by, apart from size, number of operating sites, lack of workflow rigidity, fewer workflow divisions and larger size of owning group. The addition of these other factors adds little, raising variance explained by only 3 per cent – (from 91 per cent to 94 per cent (Child, 1973a: fig. 1, p. 338, and Table 3, p. 340, respectively). Also, the size of the owning group is conceptually related to organizational size, so this merely rounds out the theme of the importance of size. The introduction of these four other causes of support staff contributes little new to the explanation already provided by size. It runs the risk of complicating and confusing the analysis of how support staff is caused by size. This is only the first step of several in a process that yields increasing complexity, that begins to defy comprehension.

Heterogeneity of the Support Component   The next step in the analysis by Child is to investigate the internal composition of the supportive component and find it to be heterogeneous. Data were collected on numbers of employees in each of 16 functional, nonworkflow specializations which normally account for almost all the nonworkflow employment found in each organization (Child, 1973a: 340). Child (1973a: 343) uses these more detailed data to show that 'it can be concluded that the supportive component is not a homogeneous category'.

Child bases his conclusion about heterogeneity of the support component on a factor analysis of employment in the 16 functional specializations which produces more than one underlying factor. Normally this would be compelling evidence of multidimensionality. However, Child performs the analysis on the number of support staff in each specialization *after* controlling for total organizational size. The support staff specialisms are typically positively, substantially related to organizational size. The average correlations between each support staff specialism size and organizational size is r = +.56 (calculated from Child, 1973a: 341). Hence the control for organizational size has taken out a great deal of common correlation among the size of the support staff specialisms. This unintentionally predisposes the factor analysis results in favour of a finding of multidimensionality of support staff components. Thus the factor analysis results overstate the internal heterogeneity of the support staff construct.

Child (1973a: 341) uses the correlations between organizational size and size of each support staff specialism as part of the case for their multidimensionality. Child notes that for seven out of the 16 specialisms, the covariance of their size with organizational size is less than 20 per cent, and for three of these specialisms the covariance is under 10 per cent. Yet an association always seems smaller if one expresses it as a covariance, or variance explained, which is the correlation squared, rather than the correlation. For example, the correlation between organizational size and size of the legal and insurance specialism is .43, but squared this becomes a variance explained of 18.5 per cent and thus, 'under 20 percent' (Child, 1973a: 341). While the seven lowest correlations between organizational size and size of each specialism are not large, ranging from +.43 to +.18, they are all positive. The use of covariance coefficients means that there is some danger that the full magnitude of the correlations between organizational size and size of specialism may be overlooked.

The size of each specialism is based essentially on a single answer to a single question and is therefore inherently prone to unreliability. Moreover, organizations will be less likely to know and accurately report to researchers the size of a specialism, because much hinges on how each specialism is defined (Child, 1973a). Any single category will be less reliable than a general category like total nonworkflow employees. This is more likely to be assessed from available total and personnel breakdowns by broad organizational categories such as departmental headcounts. The total nonworkflow figure is broader, and while this may at first glance seem less precise than size of an individual specialism, the very process of aggregation probably makes such broad figures more reliable than those of their constituents. Errors in counting one specialism will be counteracted by opposite errors in counting the other specialisms. In contrast, in breaking down total figures into more specific categories errors may occur that can make these finer categorizations actually less precise.

Moreover, any unreliability of measurement will depress the observed correlation below the true correlation. Thus true correlations with organizational size are likely to be more understated for each specific support staff specialism size than for total support staff size. Thus the average correlation between support staff specialisms size and organizational size of $r = +.56$ probably understates the true correlation. And some part of the gap between this correlation ($r = +.56$) and the correlation between organizational size and total nonworkflow employees ($r = +.91$) is due to measurement error and is not real.

Further, since the size of each specialism is affected by unreliability, the correlation between any two of them will understate their true correlation. Thus factor analyses such as that by Child (1973a: 341, 342 and 343) will understate the true degree of commonality and will tend erroneously to ascribe more multidimensionality than is really present, thus overstating the degree of heterogeneity of the support component.

Thus considerations of the reliability of measurement of variables suggest that we should be wary of breaking total support staff down into finer and finer sub-groupings. Much of the resulting dispersion in sub-grouping results may be spurious, giving a misleading impression of greater precision revealing greater complexity.

In summary, there is substantial commonality among the sizes of the supportive components. Their average correlation with organizational size is +.56 and their true, underlying intercorrelation is probably higher because it is being masked by measurement error. The Child (1973a) analysis gives an impression of more heterogeneity than there may actually be, through taking out the organizational size commonality prior to analysing dimensionality, discussing squared correlations and underemphasizing measurement error. Thus part of the apparent heterogeneity of the support component is illusory. There is probably no gain in precision from using specific support staff specialism sizes. It is preferable, rather, to utilize total support staff size as this yields results that are more reliable and meaningful.

Complex Causation of the Support Components The final part of the analysis of Child (1973a) is to treat each of the staff support specialisms separately

Table 4.1 *Correlations between numbers in 16 specialized nonworkflow functions and postulated predictors with total employees partialled out*

		Postulated predictors							
Functions	Functional specialization	Number of workflow divisions	Vertical span	Number of operating sites	Workflow rigidity	Automaticity (mode)	Automaticity (range)	Net assets	Group size
Buying and stock control	22	-21	-21	-33†	-32†	-18	-12	-15	20
Production planning and control	07	-25	27	-46§	-35±	-20	-08	-18	12
Quality control	19	-27	-11	-36±	-21	-17	-07	-16	18
Production methods	48§	01	07	-17	-12	08	15	07	28†
Design and development	36±	-01	07	-39§	-22	12	11	02	29†
Training	44§	04	01	-24	-08	-06	-09	21	23
Employment	50§	24	13	-22	03	09	04	29†	33†
Welfare and security	20	47§	07	-22	16	19	12	48§	18
Legal and insurance	30	15	07	00	00	20	15	42§	23
Maintenance	-03	19	15	14	31†	27	17	26	-04
Finance	29†	25	37§	49§	07	06	22	14	-03
Office services	45§	06	-02	-10	03	-03	-12	09	37§
Market research	43§	11	10	-19	07	13	12	-16	20
Public relations, advertising	06	15	08	-24	10	14	08	19	19
Sales and service	14	08	36±	68§	14	08	15	07	09
Transport and dispatch	-16	07	19	78§	17	12	11	04	-21

Notes:

$N = 51$ organizations ($N = 47$ for net assets)

Decimal points omitted

† $p < .05$
± $p < .02$
§ $p < .01$

Source: Reprinted from 'Parkinson's progress: Accounting for the number of specialists in organizations' by John Child, published in *Administrative Science Quarterly*, 18 (3), by permission of *Administrative Science Quarterly*. Copyright © 1973 Cornell University

and analyse their relations with several contingency factors, after controlling for organizational size. This is presented in a table of 144 correlations (see Table 4.1).

Child (1973a: 344) comments: 'The results are listed in Table [4.1], and they indicate the presence of a considerably more complex set of relationships than could be imagined from the hypotheses and analyses formulated with reference to an aggregative measure of supportive employment.'

Now we have arrived at a set of results and associated interpretation of considerable complexity (see Table 4.1). Thus the research strategy, with the best of intentions, instead of yielding meaningful, intelligible results, seems rather to lead us into a welter of correlations that are very difficult to interpret. However, an inspection of these results reveals that the surface appearance of complexity may mask a deeper simplicity that goes with the earlier argument that administrative component is mainly driven by size.

Of these 144 correlations between the nine contingency factors and the 16 sizes of functional specialisms, eight are statistically significantly different from zero at the one in twenty level. But with 144 correlations one would expect 7.2 significant findings due to chance alone at this significance level, so these eight correlations might best be treated as not really significant. Another four correlations are significant at the one in fifty level, against a chance expectation of 2.88, and so most of these correlations are probably sampling error again. However, there are 15 correlations at the one in a hundred level and the chance expectation would be only 1.44, thus these correlations are not due to chance and so will be examined further.

However, five of these 15 correlations are between size of five support staff specialisms and the Aston scale of degree of functional specialization, which means that organizations with more functional specialization have more people in specialist functions. This bears out that size and specialization are connected. Of the remaining 10 correlations, perhaps six are meaningful while four are apparently not so.

The six meaningful correlations are between the sizes of certain staff specialisms and three contingency factors: number of operating sites, assets and size of owning group. However, all three of these contingency factors (number of sites, assets and size of owning group) are sub-dimensions of the concept of size. Thus these six results also point to the importance of size.

Hence this more finely grained analysis of the relationship between size of support staff specialisms and several contingency factors produces results which are either theoretically uninterpretable or bear out the theme of size.

Conclusions on Child's Study   Our conclusion is that the size of the support staff is overwhelmingly a correlate of organizational size in this study. The correlation between organizational size and the total administrative and support staff is high (+.9 or better). Disaggregation of the support staff specialisms and recourse to multiple contingency factors yields results of bewildering complexity. However, much of this complexity is probably artefactual in origin. Disaggregation of support staff into numerous specialist sub-groups is a laudable but potentially misleading exercise because of a probable increase in measurement error. The 16 functional specialisms into which support staff have been disaggregated here show, in the main, considerable evidence that the support staff may be viewed as a homogeneous construct. There is evidence here that some support staff specialisms are affected by factors additional to organizational size, but these are chiefly just other aspects of size. Organizational size drives the support staff size. The methodological point is that aggregate level analysis is to be preferred in this topic to disaggregated modes of analysis.

The data in this study offer a simple and clear picture of how support staff grows with growth in organizational size. It suggests that this is orderly and not disproportionate, and thus it is not *prima facie* evidence of dysfunctionality. Yet the analysis and interpretation offered in Child (1973a) dispensed with this picture. It sent a message to subsequent researchers about heterogeneity, multidimensionality and complexity which has been echoed since. It raised questions about the cumulativeness and comparability of research which was not disaggregated and complex. And it lent support to the idea that administrative intensity is best explained by a theory of political processes in the manner of Parkinson.

Support of Child by Reimann

Reimann (1979) investigated the same set of questions in a study of American manufacturing companies in Ohio. Again, his focus was on the veracity of Parkinson's satire as pursued through an enquiry into the relationship between organizational size and the size of the support staff, operationalized as the staff in 17 designated nonworkflow functional specialisms (the Aston list of 16 functional specialisms plus the electronic data-processing specialism).

In his concluding remarks, Reimann (1979: 639) notes how his results have replicated those of Child (1973a) in finding 'that the aggregate support staff measure is likely to be a very heterogeneous category, at least in manufacturing organizations'. And he states:

> Therefore, the results of the many previous studies that have focused on the total size of support staff or similar aggregate variables are highly suspect and even misleading.
>
> This study demonstrated that the total support staff was not homogeneous, but composed of at least four relatively independent components – each of which was related in a very different way to a set of organizational and situational 'predictor' variables. That is, an analysis of the various staff components revealed some interesting relationships to such variables as technological change and process technology, where the aggregate support staff was found to be related only to the size of the organization – not a very interesting finding!
>
> In spite of its shortcomings, then, this exploratory study certainly carries an important message for future research in this area. If we want to start making some real progress in our pursuit of Parkinson and his famous law, our first step should be to get away from the traditional use of aggregate measures and focus instead on the relevant individual components or staff specialities. (Reimann, 1979: 639)

Thus Reimann (1979) offers strong endorsement for the position taken by Child (1973a), with both researchers obtaining similar results and asserting the need for disaggregation of support staff and for a multiple contingency approach. And Reimann, like Child, attests to the complexity of the support staff phenomenon and its determination. He expresses some difficulty about interpreting the theoretical meaning of all the findings, as will be seen below. And he recommends that the Parkinson thesis be seriously pursued in future.

Once again Reimann (1979: 631) found that total support staff size was correlated highly with total employment – that is, organizational size ($r = +.90$). And again, an investigation into 10 other possible determinants of support staff size showed that none of them had a significant correlation with support staff size once organizational size was controlled. Thus the Reimann results provide striking confirmation in America of Child's finding in the United Kingdom that support staff size is highly determined by organizational size with little scope for any additional explanatory variables which are not themselves closely related to size. Such evidence of statistical power, simplicity, meaningfulness and general validity should be taken as an encouraging sign about the ability of social science to explain the phenomenon of administrative intensity. Moreover, it confirms that the growth of support staff is rational – that is, closely related to total size and therefore to the growth of direct workflow employees. However, once again, this is not the approach taken by Reimann (1979), who opts for a more complex treatment in the mould of Child (1973a).

Following Child (1973a), Reimann moves to the issue of homogeneity of the support staff. Again, the correlation is presented separately between the size of each support staff specialism and organizational size. This shows correlations which range from +.87 to +.14 (1979: 633). And, once again, the number of correlations having less than 20 per-cent variance in common with organizational size is quoted: 'the sizes of 11 of the 17 functions had less than 20% of their variance explained by variations in total employment' (1979: 632). And the correlations among size of each staff specialism, again with controls for organizational size, are quoted by Reimann (1979: 632) as further evidence of the internal heterogeneity of the support staff construct. Since these results are all somewhat similar to Child (1973a) and utilize similar statistical procedures, they suffer similar limitations as outlined above in our discussion of Child.

A different piece of evidence adduced by Reimann (1979: 632) for his data is the intercorrelation between the 17 staff specialism sizes which range from −.14 to +.96. Negative or low correlations are disquieting here; however, one needs to keep in mind that they can arise for purely technical reasons. Low correlations may reflect just low variation on one or other staff specialism size. Also, any unreliability in measurement of each staff specialism size will further depress their correlation. Any such low correlations will also have sampling error variation, which will be considerable with a small sample of 20 as in this study (Reimann, 1979). Such low positive correlations can turn into low negative correlations by sampling error. Thus some of the range in correlations obtained here will probably be due to these artefacts (Hunter et al., 1982). Thus the heterogeneity of the staff size component would be expected to be overstated in Reimann (1979).

Reimann then proceeds to factor analyses of the support staff specialism size variables, both with and without controls for size. Again, these factor analysis results will be determined by the intercorrelations between the variables, so all the limitations noted above will apply.

Reimann (1979: 636) concludes his analysis with a multiple regression analysis in which each of the four factors of support staff extracted by the factor analysis are regressed separately against several independent variables. Again, these results are somewhat complex (1979: 637). And tellingly there are several findings which are 'more difficult to interpret', 'rather unexpected' or 'another curious result' for the author of the study (1979: 638). The results also yield a specific finding that greater size of maintenance staff specialisms is positively associated with degree of mass production which, as Reimann (1979: 639) notes, accords with the technology thesis of Woodward (1965) – similarly, for the association between technological change and development staff size (1979: 637). Thus this more disaggregated mode of analysis reveals some effects upon specific components of support staff which are other than size effects. However, for the most part the variables revealed as significant predictors of the differing support staff specialism factors are variables such as specialization, vertical span, formalization and delegation. Correlations between support staff specialism size and functional specialization mean that there are more functionally specialized support staff where there are more functional specialities, which bears out the theme that size and specialization are related. For functional specialization, vertical span, formalization and delegation, these variables are so clearly bound to organizational size that this analysis should probably be interpreted as teasing out intervening variables connecting size and support staff rather than identifying causes other than organizational size (Pugh et al., 1969a; Child, 1973b; Donaldson, 1986; Miller, 1987). Once again, this recalls our earlier comments on Child (1973a).

Thus the similarities in results between the Reimann and Child studies stem in part from similar difficulties, particularly in reliance upon disaggregation which is methodologically fraught. In the main, the reliable findings of Reimann are that organizational size strongly affects support staff size, thereby confirming the main finding about the importance of size. Once again, the results from the disaggregated analysis need to be approached cautiously but mainly support the importance of size. Both Child and Reimann concur in breaking the support staff size down into its component specialisms, but a comparison of their studies shows that is hazardous.

Comparison of Results of Child and Reimann

Both Child (1973a) and Reimann (1979) emphasize that there is a wide variation in the correlations between organizational size and the size of each support staff specialism. Our view is that much of this variation is artefactual and hence the correlations have limited real value. If these correlations were meaningful in the way suggested by Child (1973a) and Reimann (1979), then they would be fairly consistent across both studies, both of which only sample manufacturing organizations.

Hence the correlations which are high in Child would be expected to be high also in Reimann (1979), and vice versa for the low correlations. For instance, the highest correlation in Child (1973a) is between organizational size and size of maintenance staff ($r = +.91$). However, the correlation between organizational size and maintenance staff size is only $r = +.14$ in Reimann (1979), which is the *lowest* in his study (see Table 4.2). More generally, the correlation between the 16 correlations (of organizational size and each staff specialism size) of Child (1973a) and Reimann (1979) is virtually zero, at $r = +.02$. Thus there is no correspondence between the degree to which a particular specialism relates to the organizational size in the Child (1973a) study and in the Reimann (1979) study. This lack of association is expected for unreliable data. It bears out the argument that the results involving specific staff specialism sizes are unreliable and not meaningful. Therefore these results that are drawn upon by Child (1973a) and Reimann (1979) to make much of their case are not dependable.

Table 4.2 *Correlations between number of staff in 16 specialized nonwork-flow functions and organizational size (total employees) in Child (1973a) and Reimann (1979)*

Function	Correlation with Total Employees			
	Child (1973a)	Rank	Reimann (1979)	Rank
Maintenance	.91	(1)	.14	(16)
Finance and accounting	.89	(2)	.72	(3)
Sales and service	.86	(3)	.87	(1)
Transport and dispatch	.78	(4)	.45	(6=)
Quality control	.76	(5)	.42	(9=)
Public relations and advertising	.72	(6)	.42	(9=)
Buying stock control	.65	(7=)	.29	(15)
Welfare and security	.65	(7=)	.32	(14)
Production planning and control	.45	(9)	.67	(4)
Legal and insurance	.43	(10)	.75	(2)
Market research	.39	(11)	.45	(6=)
Training	.38	(12)	.41	(11=)
Employment	.32	(13)	.63	(5)
Design and development	.29	(14)	.41	(11=)
Office services	.25	(15)	.43	(8)
Production methods	.18	(16)	.38	(13)
Average correlation	.557		.485	
Correlation of r's		+.022		

Sources: Reprinted from 'Parkinson's progress: Accounting for the number of specialists in organizations' by John Child, published in *Administrative Science Quarterly*, 18 (3), by permission of *Administrative Science Quarterly*. Copyright © 1973 Cornell University. Reimann (1979: 633)

While both Child (1973a) and Reimann (1979) concluded in favour of Parkinson, their results have to be questioned for the reasons shown above. In both studies (Child, 1973a: 337; Reimann, 1979: 631) their data showed strong correlation between total support staff size and organizational size ($r = +.95$ and $+.90$, respectively), indicating that support staff size is almost totally explained by organizational size. However, in both cases this meaningful conclusion was eschewed in favour of disaggregated analysis of components of support staff and multiple causes other than size. The analyses reveal a complex set of findings which strain interpretability and which reflect limitations in method. The impression of bewildering complexity is to a degree an artefact of the analytic approach taken. The influence of Parkinsonian theories of political processes causing administrative intensity has inclined the authors to search for results that transcended the simpler message of their data.

Our view is that a more accurate interpretation, on which greater confidence can be placed, is the aggregate level result, which is also simple and meaningful. Organizations add to their support component in close correspondence to their addition of direct workers. This means that, in consequence, the support component is very highly, positively correlated with organizational size – so highly, that there is little scope for effects of any nonsize variables. This holds in studies of manufacturing organizations in two countries, Britain and the United States, and holds both for nonworkflow support staff (including their managers) and managers of the direct workers.

Thus the research reveals clear findings and order. The addition of support staff is not chaotic but law-like. However, this discovery is in danger of being overlooked in favour of a view which allows more leeway for political and subjective, if not satirical, forces in the determination of support staff levels. In this way erroneous theory may mislead us in the interpretation of empirical evidence.

Corroboration

The results of Child (1973a) and Reimann (1979) have been echoed by Lioukas and Xerokostas (1982) in a study of the organization of Greek retail electricity distribution. Analysing different geographical divisions, Lioukas and Xerokostas (1982: 861) found that the correlation between the number of administrative or support personnel (including their managerial staff) and the number of production or direct personnel was $+.95$. The number of administrators increased proportionately to the number of production workers (1982: 863). Thus the study by Lioukas and Xerokostas confirms the findings of Child (1973a) and Reimann (1979) that the number of administrators is highly correlated with the number of production workers and that the number of administrative personnel increases as the number of production workers increases in a linear, proportionate manner. Hence the growth of administrative personnel is once again revealed to be explained by a parsimonious model with a single explanatory variable – size – and the manner of growth is highly regular and rational. Thus the pattern of growth of admin- istrative personnel with growth in organizational size replicates across the studies of Child (1973a), Reimann (1979) and Lioukas and Xerokostas (1982). The relationship generalizes over three national cultures: the United Kingdom, the United States and Greece, respectively. Further, the results show that administrative personnel increase in proportion to increases in production personnel rather than increasing disproportionately and in exces- sive numbers unrelated to production personnel in the way depicted by Parkinson. Thus, taken together, the three studies support positivist and func- tionalist theories of administrative and support components in organizations.

Profits and Administrative Intensity

An example of anti-functionalist work of the kind within the political inter- est approach advocated by Child (1973a) and Reimann (1979) is the analysis by Smith (1978) of the relationship between profits and administrative inten- sity.

Smith (1978: 510ff) critiques functionalist theories of administrative inten- sity which hold that administrative intensity contributes to organizational performance and hence, for profit-orientated firms, is a cause of their profit level. He draws on the concepts of Simon (1965) and others to argue that the boundedness of rationality makes it difficult for managers to assess the opti- mality for performance of structural elements, and that, in consequence, decisions are open to be shaped by the self-interest of groups such as man- agers. The managers exercise a degree of choice to increase their administrative staffs in the manner which Parkinson (1957) argued – that is, new, subordinate administrators superfluous to functional needs are hired to boost the status and remuneration of senior managers. Smith states:

> The importance of all this for organization research and theory is that it raises the very real possibility that some variations in organizational attributes may, at least some of the time, be explained less in terms of the exigencies of optimization of per- formance than in terms of the interests of groups of organizational decision makers. (1978: 511)

With this as the general theoretical orientation, Smith concludes from his spe- cific empirical analysis :

> Using data on the relations between profits and administrative intensity in U.S. manufacturing industry this paper attempts to show that even within profit-making organizations, there are grounds for thinking that under appropriate conditions, organizational structures that get adopted are likely to deviate significantly from the requirements of optimal performance. (1978: 509)

Similarly, he concludes in his final paragraph:

> More generally, finding a strong positive relationship between profits and growth in administrative intensity for 1963 to 1967 suggests that decisions on hiring may well have coincided with the interests of decision makers as well as with the technical requirements of efficient production. That in turn suggests that even where an organization is profit making there is room for managerial discretion (cf. Pondy, 1969). Moreover, if that can be shown for profit maximizing organizations in more

or less competitive contexts, it is likely to be even more significant in those rapidly growing areas which are either not profit making or not competitive; that is, in areas like government and regulated industry. Equally important, those outcomes of the exercise of managerial discretion are unlikely to be neutral with respect to organization structure. Some organization forms are more likely to provide a situation where the exercise of managerial discretion is feasible than others. That raises the very real possibility that findings on the determinants of administrative intensity and other aspects of organization structure that assume technical optimization will sometimes be confounded with the outcome of discretionary, interested, behaviour. (1978: 520)

Smith analyses the relationship between administrative intensity and profits over a 20 year period: 1947 to 1967. His method makes careful allowance for complexities such as business cycles, but the heart of his analysis is to examine the relative strengths of empirical connections between administrative intensity and profits, each measured at five different time points: 1947, 1954, 1958, 1963 and 1967. The research design is to assess causal influence by seeing which time lag yields the strongest correlations. Also examined is the direction of causality, that is whether the stronger path is administrative intensity causing profits, or profits causing administrative intensity. The functionalist model is that administrative intensity causes profits; that is, that hiring more administrators is an investment that pays off subsequently by boosting profits. In contrast, the political model predicts the opposite, that profits cause administrative intensity – namely, that surplus profits are wasted by managers, through hiring more administrative staff, to boost managerial status and claims to fatter salaries. Thus by seeing which path is stronger, Smith tests the validity of functionalism as opposed to political theory.

In his results, as Smith notes (1978: 518), in general, the stronger paths are those from administrators to profits – the functionalist model – many of which are statistically significant (Smith, 1978: 517, 518), across time lags of various durations. In contrast, the paths from profits to administrators are weaker and in every case, except one, fail to attain statistical significance.

This single exception is in the short time-lag analysis (Smith, 1978: 518). Here the path from profits to administrators is statistically significant in the years 1963 to 1967, though not significant (and often negative) for the three earlier time lags: 1947 to 1954, 1954 to 1958 and 1958 to 1963. (In this short time-lag analysis, the paths from administrators to profits are all statistically significant for each of these four lag periods – though varying in sign.) This correlation supports the political theory that managers spend profits on more administrators, thereby benefiting themselves to the cost of the organization.

On the hypothesis test as constructed by Smith (1978), the evidence overwhelmingly supports the cause–effect pathway or linkage: that administrators affect profits. Yet the interpretation drawn by him and the conclusion which he advances favour the political model. This is done by selectively focusing on the one profit–administrators path which happened to be significant and making its time period the focus of the conclusions ('for 1963 to 1967'). This is a highly selective interpretation of data achieved by ignoring the bulk of his results which overwhelmingly support the functionalist hypothesis.

Such research procedures show the weakness of the support for political theory in Smith's study and the tenacity with which that theory is advanced, on occasions, *despite* the results of empirical tests.

Conclusions

The received literature asserts that study of the administrative component requires highly complex models in order to capture the myriad complexities and subtleties introduced by the political process which are held to be the underlying causes (Child, 1973a; Reimann, 1979). As we have seen, the complexities of the various elements of the administrative support component and their multiple and varying causes are largely chimerical. The complex statistical results arise more out of the artefacts introduced through disaggregation and consequent unreliability than out of the real phenomena. The disaggregation produces effects which fail to replicate from study to study, and this is consistent with the idea that they are spurious artefacts. The research results reveal, rather, the simple model that the administrative component is almost totally determined by a single independent variable – organizational size. This model generalizes across studies conducted by different authors in different countries.

The results from these studies provide evidence that the administrative component grows in a manner which is organizationally rational and functional and does not grow out of proportion to the production personnel in the manner asserted by Parkinson. Given the simple, linear growth in the administrative support component as organizational size increases revealed in the empirical studies, it is hard to see how the size of the administrative component overall in an organization could be shaped by a whole series of complex, subtle, decentralized decisions by managers according to a political logic which is at cross-purposes to rationality and economy at the organizational level.

Nevertheless, the view that organizations proliferate administrators in a way which is counter-productive and according to the self-interests of managers is highly consonant with the political model and anti-functionalist theoretical stance which is found not only in Parkinson but across much of the organizational sociology of the 1970s and 1980s (see, for example, Pfeffer and Salancik, 1978; Meyer and Scott, 1983; and see Donaldson, 1995 for a critique). Thus on the matter of the administrative component, Parkinson was readily taken up by organizational analysts.

In similar vein, Smith (1978), in his examination of the relationship between administrators and profits, clings assiduously to the anti-functionalist interpretation that profits are consumed away in more administrative staff, notwithstanding the overwhelming evidence in his data that administrators caused profits, the antithetical view. The orthodoxy in organizational studies is the anti-functionalist interpretation of the administrative component in organizations and research data are interpreted in that way, notwithstanding the actual patterns in the data.

Our enquiry in this chapter fails to find support for the fashionable view that the growth of the administrative component in organizations is political but rather supports the functionalist interpretation. The Parkinson theory that administrative growth is excessive and uneconomic is not supported. If we are to make progress we must eschew Parkinson.

There remains the issue of whether the opposite view, advanced by Blau, that there are administrative economies of scale, enjoys any validity. The next chapter will examine this issue.

5
For Functionalism: The Validity of Blau's Theory

The political theory of the organization holds that the growth in numbers of managers, administrators and support staff is caused by the pursuit of managerial self-interest and is dysfunctional for the organization. In the previous chapter we examined this theory as advanced by Parkinson (1957) and his followers, and argued that it was mainly false. In the present chapter we turn to one of the principal advocates of the opposite view, Blau (1970). He argued that the administrative component of organizations is functional. Moreover, he states that as organizations grow in size they attain administrative economies of scale. Blau (1970) explains the administrative component of organizations by the material contingency variable of size – in other words, his theory is positivist. Thus Blau's theory is both functionalist and positivist. Nevertheless, later organizational researchers have been highly critical of both the theory and evidence of Blau and his colleagues. In this chapter we will argue for Blau against major criticisms. Our conclusion is that both the functionalism and the positivism of his theory of the administrative component of organizational structure are valid.

Economies of Scale in Administration

The leading advocate of the functionalist view has been Blau. He advanced a general theory of organization in which he argued that increasing organizational size produced increasing economies of scale in administration (Blau, 1970). Thus Blau's theory is the opposite to the political view of the growth of managers and administrators with increasing organizational size, as advocated by Parkinson (1957) and as supported by Child (1973a), Reimann (1979) and Smith (1978).

In Blau's theory (1970), increasing organizational size leads to an increase in the structural differentiation of the organization – that is, to an increasingly elaborate structure both horizontally, as in numbers of divisions and of sections within divisions, and vertically, as in the number of levels in the hierarchy (see Figure 5.1). The greater the number of pieces into which the organization is divided, the more complex is the coordination required, thus raising the requirement for managers and administrators, causing the administrative intensity (that is, the ratio of managers and administrators to total employees) to rise with increasing organizational size (Blau, 1970). However,

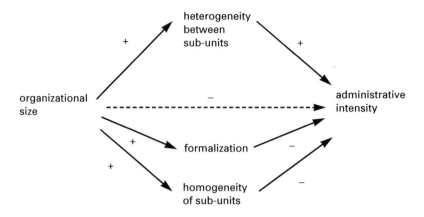

Figure 5.1   *The effect of organizational size on administrative intensity* (adapted from Blau and Schoenherr, 1971: 320)

this is offset by two other causal processes which reduce administrative intensity as organizational size grows.

The first of these offsetting causal processes is that increasing structural differentiation as size grows means that each structural unit is more homogeneous in the work it is performing (Blau, 1970) (see Figure 5.1). This makes supervision easier, which leads to larger spans of control. This, in turn, lowers the ratio of supervisory management to production workers, thus reducing administrative intensity as size grows (Blau, 1970). The second causal process which works to reduce administrative intensity with increasing organization size is the growth of formalization – that is, rules, regulations and standardized programmes to guide decisions – so reducing the number of managers who are required (Blau, 1970) (see Figure 5.1).

Thus, according to Blau (1970), there is one process increasing administrative intensity with size increase, and this is more than offset by the two processes which are decreasing administrative intensity with size increase, thus resulting in a net decrease in administrative intensity with size increase. Thus Blau asserts that administrative intensity declines with increasing organizational size and that therefore there is economy of scale in administration. This is quite the opposite of the disproportionate increase in ratio of administrators to production personnel claimed by Parkinson (1957). Thus Blau (1970) states that size has a negative relationship with administrative intensity.

More particularly, Blau (1970) holds that administrative intensity declines with increase in size but at a decreasing rate with increase in size. Thus increasing organizational size yields increasing economies of administration but the economies no longer increase as much with each unit growth in size when the organization is large as when it is small. Bigger organizations enjoy better scale economies of administration than smaller organizations, but the *increase* in these scale economies is less for each increase of 100 employees for bigger than for smaller organizations. In other words, while these economies of administration grow with increase in size, they taper off as size increases so that initially large increases become smaller increases (see Blau and Schoenherr, 1971).

This curvilinear relationship becomes linear when size is transformed logarithmically, a procedure which is followed customarily in the research of Blau and others on this topic. This greatly simplifies data analysis and discussion, for one can simply state that size leads to a linear decrease in administrative intensity (Blau and Schoenherr, 1971). Thus there is a theoretical reason for transforming size logarithmically in the research on administrative intensity, as this better reflects the underlying phenomenon (cf. Kimberly, 1976).

Blau and his colleagues report finding a negative relationship between size and administrative intensity in several studies of different sorts of organizations: governmental employment security agencies, governmental finance departments, universities, department stores and so on (Blau and Schoenherr, 1971; Blau, 1972). The evidence they present in each study is a negative correlation between organizational size and administrative intensity. The correlation is based on a cross-sectional comparison across organizations that considers size and administrative intensity at the same point in time.

Criticisms of the Blau Thesis

The work by Blau and his colleagues was followed by a series of investigations which purported to damage the Blau thesis in several fundamental regards. Because the administrative staff has been argued to be a bundle composed of disparate types of staff, the administrative component was asserted to be multidimensional and heterogeneous, not unidimensional and homogeneous (Child, 1973a; Reimann, 1979). Further, each different dimension of staff was related to different contingency variables, so in place of a single general contingency of size there were several contingency factors, with a specific combination for each dimension (Child, 1973a; Reimann, 1979). Hence, instead of the pairing of a single contingency factor, size, with a single dimension of administrative intensity, the relationship became multidimensional for both contingency and structure. However, we have considered and rebutted these objections in the previous chapter.

Additionally, the whole methodology of Blau and others who correlated size with the ratio of management and administrators to size has been critiqued as seriously flawed (Freeman and Kronenfeld, 1973). Also, the reliance upon cross-sectional studies by Blau and his colleagues (Blau, 1972; Blau and Schoenherr, 1971) has been questioned by researchers who have used longitudinal methods and obtained different results from those of Blau (Freeman and Hannan, 1975; Marsh and Mannari, 1989). They argue that change in organizational size is a further moderating variable of the size–administrative intensity relationship (Freeman and Hannan, 1975; Marsh and Mannari, 1989). They hold that the dynamic analysis reveals a very different picture from the static cross-sectional view (Freeman and Hannan, 1975; Marsh and Mannari, 1989). Decline differs from growth, so producing asymmetry in the relation of size and administrative intensity. The real causal factors behind growth in administration have been held to be political interests and influences (Freeman and Hannan, 1975). Managers build their administrative staff over the years by adding staff when the organization grows and retaining administrators when the organization declines. Thus the Blau (1970) theory is argued to be naïve, and a political explanation is offered in place of his functional theory.

In this chapter we will consider each of these issues in turn. First, we will attend to the criticism that the correlation between size and administrative intensity is a tautology masking the real empirical relationship. Second, we will consider the criticism that the cross-sectional research designs underlying such correlations produce a static picture that masks the real dynamic processes. We will demonstrate that neither criticism is as damaging as has been claimed. Thus we will assert the continuing validity of correlations drawn from cross-sectional studies of size and administrative intensity. On this basis we will review the results from these studies and see how far they support the Blau theory.

The Methodological Problem of Definitional Dependency

Blau (1972) and others take as given the veracity of the negative correlation between size and administrative intensity. However, the veracity of this negative correlation has been called into question by Freeman and Kronenfeld (1973). They assert that, on the contrary, these negative correlations between size and administrative intensity are tautologies and thus not genuine evidence of a real negative association. The assertion is that the definition of the variables makes each dependent upon the other so that the correlations between size and administrative intensity are spurious.

Freeman and Kronenfeld (1973) argue that there is a tautological connection between size and administrative intensity. This produces a strong, spurious negative association, which offsets and masks any true positive association, so producing the observed negative correlations of the kind seen in the work of Blau. If this is true, then the research findings of Blau and all other studies using similar approaches are masking true positive correlations between size and administrative intensity. Thus, in reality, increasing size leads to increasing ratios of managers and administrators to production personnel – and Parkinson (1957) is right. Hence the critique of Freeman and Kronenfeld merits close attention.

Their critique has been influential and has been seen as damaging to all such evidence. For example, Lioukas and Xerokostas (1982) cite Freeman and

Kronenfeld (1973), accepting their argument that there is an in-built tautology which produces a spurious negative correlation between size and administrative intensity. Lioukas and Xerokostas actually fail to find such a negative correlation in their own data, which is surprising, for a tautology would be expected always to produce the same result – namely, an in-built negative correlation. However, Lioukas and Xerokostas do not comment about their finding as to its implication for the supposedly inevitable tautological negative correlation. Such is the regard in which the Freeman and Kronenfeld (1973) critique is held.

The studies of Blau (1972) and his colleagues place considerable emphasis on variables such as the proportion of supervisors relative to size (that is, all employees) and their relationship with the variable of organizational size. Freeman and Kronenfeld (1973) argue that such relationships may not be true empirical relationships but arise out of the definitions utilized. Thus the relationships are likely to be tautologous, in that they are analytic (that is, definitional) relationships masquerading as synthetic (namely, empirical) relationships. These critics of Blau mount their attack through mathematical and statistical analysis. Indeed, the article by Freeman and Kronenfeld (1973) is both dauntingly esoteric and cryptic.

Freeman and Kronenfeld (1973) see the problem in the definitional dependency between the number of supervisors relative to size. The same variable, size, appears on both sides of the equation. Size is the independent variable, and the dependent variable is supervisors divided by size – that is, size is the denominator. This means that size is being associated with a second variable which contains the mathematical term, one divided by size. Size is bound to be negatively related to one-over-size, so a negative correlation will be present. The observed correlation will be the result of this in-built strong negative correlation (of $r = -1.0$) and whatever is the empirical correlation between size and the numerator, the number of supervisors. Given the strength of the artefactual negative correlation, there is likely to be a resulting correlation which is negative. This would mask any true but weaker positive correlation. Thus the negative correlations of Blau and his colleagues are spurious (Freeman and Kronenfeld, 1973).

Freeman and Kronenfeld (1973: 109) conclude that correlations between size and personnel components divided by size are so potentially misleading that substantive inferences about economies of scale, as drawn by Blau and others, cannot validly be made from these correlations (Freeman and Kronenfeld, 1973: 110). They go on to recommend instead the use of regression between the simple variables, such as the number of supervisors and size. This avoids the use of complex variables which utilize the division by size in the same analyses as those in which size itself is also used. In a subsequent article from the Aston programme of research, Child (1973a) draws on the critique of Freeman and Kronenfeld (1973) and uses their recommended regression analysis of simple variables. Their prescriptions about data analysis have been adopted by other leading researchers.

The critique of Freeman and Kronenfeld (1973) casts doubts on the validity and meaning of the administrative intensity findings of Blau, his colleagues and also of many previous enquiries (see Freeman and Kronenfeld, 1973, for a critical review of studies). From the point of view of science as a cumulative activity, the Freeman and Kronenfield critique suggests that decades of research findings are of little value in contributing to a body of knowledge on this topic. Moreover, previous enquiries are of value only if they report the results of regressions of simple variables, which they mostly do not. Thus arises the spectre which haunts structural contingency theory, that all (or almost all) previous results on a major topic are in error. Here the critique is within the body of positivist methods and from a researcher, John Freeman, who is a leading positivist and went on to become Chief Editor of the *Administrative Science Quarterly*.

In an earlier volume (Donaldson, 1985) defending the paradigm of positivist, functionalist organization theory against attack from rival paradigms, I also discussed with approval the definitional dependency critique of Freeman and Kronenfeld (1973). Now, however, the validity of their critique will be challenged.

Freeman and Kronenfeld (1973) focus their analysis on the relationship between the ratio of administrators to production workers and size – that is, the sum of administrators and production workers. They pursue their critique of the way definitional dependencies upset valid inferences in several arguments. Three will be considered here.

The first critique by Freeman and Kronenfeld (1973) is that, even when administrators and production workers are random variables that are actually unrelated to each other, substantial correlations of the ratio of administrators to workers with size can be produced just by manipulating the variances of administrators or workers (1973: 109). Comparing across organizations, if the number of workers varied across the organizations but the number of administrators was constant for all the organizations, the ratio of administrators to workers would decline with increases in workers. Therefore the ratio of administrators to workers would decline with increases in size (which is defined as administrators plus workers). This would produce a negative correlation between the ratio of administrators to workers and size. From this, Freeman and Kronenfeld conclude that 'The result is that it is improper to test a null hypothesis of "no relationship" by comparing the observed correlation with zero' (1973: 110). In an accompanying footnote, Freeman and Kronenfeld (1973: 110 fn) report that in computer runs using 'quasi-random' variables of administrators and workers, they have yielded correlations from –.999 to +1.00 just by manipulating the variances of these two variables. However, these correlations seem to be accurate summaries of the relationships between size and ratio of administrators to workers.

To appreciate the point, consider an example where the number of administrators is constant and the number of workers varies across organizations – in other words, there is zero variance in administrators and some variance in workers. If in the first organization there are 10 administrators and 10 workers, the ratio of administrators to workers is 1; if in the second organization there are again 10 administrators but 30 workers, the ratio is .33; if in the third organization there are 10 administrators and 50 workers, the ratio is .2. Thus across the three organizations the ratio decreases: 1, .33 and .2, as size increases to 20, 40, 60 total employees, respectively. Moreover, the successive, equal-size increments of 20 employees correspond to decreasing decrements in the ratio of administrative workers ratio of .67 and .13. The relationship between the ratio and size is decreasing with size, but at a decreasing rate with respect to size; we see the familiar Blau curve. Thus there is an actual negative relationship between the ratio and the size that is produced by manipulating the variance of one variable in the ratio relative to another.

A negative correlation would be computed from these data and this would reflect reality. Hence the sensitivity of the correlation between size and the ratio of administrative workers to variations in the variance of the constituent variables is not evidence of a problem. Varying the numbers of workers while keeping the numbers of administrators constant alters the ratio of adminis-trators to workers. This is mathematically correct. The correlation between this ratio and size for these data should be negative. Thus the correlation involving the ratio yields the correct inference about reality. By altering the variance of one variable relative to the other variable the ratio can take many values. Thus the correlation between the ratio and size can swing wildly from high negative to high positive, depending on the variances of the two variables in the ratio. This is all to be expected and no proof that the procedure is invalid.

The second piece of evidence by Freeman and Kronenfeld is also the most dramatic. They present an analysis in which 'randomly distributed points in [the administrators', product workers'] space are mapped onto the [ratio of administrators workers to size] space' (1973: 110). The resulting scattergram shows a negative relationship decelerating with size – that is, like the curves published by Blau (1970; Blau and Schoenherr, 1971). This seems to show that even random data with no real relationship will produce results which misleadingly look like Blau-type findings just because of the tautologous definitions of the complex variables. The Blau-type findings are made to look totally spurious, though Freeman and Kronenfeld (1973: 110) express the point more graciously: 'While the points in Figure 1 [Blau's scatterplot of pro-portion of staff on size] clearly are not the results of points randomly distributed in [administrators, workers] space, the transformation of the data does account for most of the structure noted.'

Third, Freeman and Kronenfeld go on to explain mathematically how the transformation of random data produces spurious negative relationships. They utilize the 'physicist's idea of phase space' (1973: 110). They show that if administrators and workers 'are allowed to vary independently and uni-formly' (1973: 112) then the mapping of this space on to the ratio of size space causes distortions so that a negative relationship appears. They conclude: 'These figures show why almost all such data exhibit the generally "expo-nentially" shaped, decreasing pattern such as in Figure 1. This pattern is primarily the result of the coordinate transformation, and not because of any inherent relationship between A and P.'

However, again their analysis is problematic in that the original distribution of points in the administrator and worker space means that in fact there *is* a tendency for the ratio to decline with size. Thus again the negative correlation between the ratio and size reflects a real negative relationship.

To appreciate this, consider their diagram of the points in the administrator-worker space (Freeman and Kronenfeld, 1973: 112, Fig. 3A). This is a rectangle bounded by (reading from their diagram) a minimum of 10 administrators and a maximum of 50 administrators and a minimum of 10 production workers and a maximum of 300 workers. This means that when there are only 10 workers, the number of administrators is between 10 and 50 – that is, at least the same or greater. When there are 300 workers the number of administrators is between 10 and 50 – that is, fewer. Thus the ratio of administrators to workers declines as size (administrators plus workers) increases. And so the diagram already has the declining ratio of administrators to workers built into it.

Since points are independently and randomly distributed in the administrator-worker space (Freeman and Kronenfeld, 1973: 112), the expected value of administrators is a constant for all values of workers, at about 30 administrators. When there are 10 workers there are 30 administrators, a ratio of 3, at size 40 (= 10 + 30). When there are 155 workers there would also be 30 administrators, a ratio of .19 at size 185. When there are 300 workers and again 30 administrators, the ratio is .1, at size 330. Thus the ratio of administrators to workers actually *declines* with size in the data: 3 at size 40, .19 at size 185 and .1 at size 330. Moreover, the rate of decline is decreasing as size increases, yielding the negative, geometric curve: the two successive, equal increments of 145 employees are associated with a decline in the ratio of 2.81 and .09, respectively. Hence a negative correlation is not invalid, for the independently and uniformly distributed points in the administrative workers' space contain the increasing administrative economies of scale. Thus the negative relationship does not arise as some kind of artefact of transformation but rather from the administrative workers' data used by Freeman and Kronenfeld (1973). They extract the conclusion of a negative relationship because they put a negative relationship into the data.

The fallacy is to suppose that a nil relationship between the ratio and size is based on a random distribution of administrators to size. Actually, a nil relationship between the ratio and size requires that administrators increase proportionately with workers. Thus administrators and workers are not independent quantities. They must co-vary together to produce a nil relationship between the ratio and size.

To understand this point, consider data in which there is *no* relationship between the ratio of administrators to workers and size. For example, suppose that there is one administrator for every worker. This is *not* a random distribution of administrators on workers, for the correlation is one (r = + 1.0). When there is 1 administrator and there is 1 worker, the ratio is 1 and the size is 2. When there are 100 administrators and 100 workers, the ratio is again 1, but the size is 200. Thus the ratio is constant and does not decrease as size increases. There is a nil relationship between the ratio and size (because the ratio is always 1 for increasing values of size). The transformation into the ratio and size space would give a correlation of zero, which yields the correct inference of no relationship.

Where the original administrators–workers data are such that there really is no relationship of administrative intensity to size, then the correlation of the size and the ratio of administrators to workers variables accurately show this. Thus there is nothing inherently wrong in the transformations of administrators and workers into a ratio and the correlation of this ratio with size. This correlation of the ratio and size reports a relationship when one is present and none when a relationship is absent.

Thus we conclude that the critique of definitional dependency by Freeman and Kronenfeld (1973) is without foundation. Their critique is based on a faulty operationalization of the null hypothesis condition in their simulations and analyses. Correlations between size and proportions of size are valid and allow meaningful inference. While size occurs on both sides of the equation, the correlation is computed between size and the resultant of the numerator (for example, number of supervisors) and the denominator of size. The ratio is free to vary between zero (for zero supervisors) and one (for as many supervisors as workers). Thus the ratio is a genuine empirical quantity. There is no in-built restriction on the ratio that produces a tautologous correlation between the ratio and size. Correlations between size and administrative intensity which have been reported in the literature are valid and meaningful (unless there is some other problem) and deserve to be drawn upon to inform the body of knowledge on this topic. These correlational studies are of value and should not be dismissed. They continue to provide a valid source of empirical findings on the issue of administrative economies of scale.

The foregoing re-evaluation of the critique of Freeman and Kronenfeld (1973) has been based on considerations of their argument and data. The conclusion gains support from the empirical analysis by MacMillan and Daft (1979, 1984). They analysed data using the supposedly flawed administrative ratio variables and the supposedly sounder simpler constituent personnel variables recommended by Freeman and Kronenfeld (1973) and found no difference in substantive results. This corroborates our argument that there is no tautology built into the use of administrative ratio variables. Hence correlational results connecting size and administrative intensity are not flawed, and the negative correlations found by Blau (1970, 1972) and others are genuine. In the studies of Blau and others, larger size is associated with lower proportions of managers and administrators, thus signifying increasing economies of scale in administration. There is no true positive correlation between size and administrative intensity *à la* Parkinson which is being masked in these correlational results.

Asymmetry in Organizational Growth and Decline

A problem in the analysis of administrative intensity concerns the symmetry of causal processes. Empirical investigations of change over time in size and administrative intensity found differences between growers and decliners. A 'bumperjack' or ratchet effect has been described whereby once size produces a certain level of administrators, that level will tend to be retained despite subsequent decline in size (Freeman and Hannan, 1975). Thus the causal processes connecting size and administrators are presented as asymmetric, for increasing size leads to an increase whereas decreasing size does not lead to nearly such a decrease.

This is seen as challenging claims about the robustness of structural contingency theory. Further yet, the implication is that structural contingency theories are valid for boom conditions and are invalid in conditions of recession. Thus theories promulgated in the boom times of the sixties may be invalid in the leaner times of the following decades.

As the organization goes through repeated episodes of growth and decline, the ratchet effect means that the administrative intensity rises over time. This, some scholars claim, satisfies managerial self-interest at cost to the organization. Thus the ratchet effect is explained by theories of a political nature which refer to self-interest that contravenes organizational effectiveness and is organizationally dysfunctional.

This political interpretation is propounded in conjunction with a critique of the inadequacies of the cross-sectional, rather than longitudinal research design used by Blau and his colleagues. Longitudinal studies are customarily seen in social science as stronger research designs which allow surer inferences about causality and a truer picture of the real processes than cross-sectional designs which are seen as weaker and allowing for more hazardous inferences (Cook and Campbell, 1979). Findings from cross-sectional studies may give initial support to a theory, but this is viewed as weakly supported until tested by longitudinal research designs. If the later, longitudinal research produces findings contradictory to the earlier cross-sectional results this is viewed as disconfirming both the cross-sectional results and the theory associated with those cross-sectional results.

To many readers of the literature on administrative intensity such a process appeared to have occurred therein. The earlier, methodologically weaker, cross-sectional research of Blau and others (1970, 1972; Blau and Schoenherr, 1971) supported the theory of Blau (1970) on size and administrative intensity. However, the later, methodologically stronger, research produced contradictory findings, especially regarding decline. This is seen by scholars as casting doubts over the meaning of earlier cross-sectional research results and over the generality of Blau's theory (Freeman and Hannan, 1975; Ford, 1980; Montanari and Adelman, 1987; Marsh and Mannari, 1989).

Earlier cross-sectional studies had provided evidence that the proportion of administrations declined as size increased (Blau, 1970, 1972; Blau and Schoenherr, 1971). However, subsequent longitudinal research showed that declining size, such as a reduction in production, did not necessarily produce a reduction in the number of administrators, and thus the proportion of administrators could rise with declining size (Freeman and Hannan, 1975). Further, the number of production workers did rise with an increase in work volume and decline with a decrease in work volume, indicating that rational adaptiveness was undertaken in the direct cost personnel but not in the indirect cost personnel (Freeman and Hannan, 1975). These administrative, indirect cost personnel are closer to management and their presence assists management and boosts managerial status. Having larger numbers of administrators relative to production people was interpreted as a burgeoning of bureaucrats relative to productive workers. Thus increasing administrative intensity with declining size was interpreted politically (Freeman and Hannan, 1975: 218) and as evidence of maladaptive, irrational behaviour. Two major studies of US state school systems revealed this pattern (Freeman and Hannan, 1975; Ford, 1980). A further study by Child of changes in numbers of administrators and of production workers in a British manufacturing company also revealed a ratchet effect on administrators, and a tendency for the administrative intensity to rise when production personnel numbers declined. Child also tends to interpret this trend as evidence of dysfunctional bureaucratization.

The Freeman and Hannan Study   Freeman and Hannan (1975: 227) conclude from their longitudinal study of administrative intensity that:

> growers and decliners will be alike in the relations of size of direct (or production) component to demand for organizational products or services, but that the two [that is, growers and decliners] will differ in the relation of sizes of supportive component size to the direct component size and to demand. This hypothesis is strongly supported in our analysis.

This conclusion has been widely received into the literature. It forms the basis for the view that their study disconfirmed Blau's theory (1970). The associated cross-sectional evidence of Blau and colleagues (Blau, 1970; Blau and Schoenherr, 1971) is held to mask important asymmetries between growth and decline in the effects of size changes on the ratio of administrators to production workers, termed the 'A/P ratio'. As Freeman and Hannan (1975: 227) themselves put it: 'our analysis suggests that A/P ratios are too complex to be useful in many analyses and that cross-sectional analysis of organizational demography may be quite misleading . . . cross-sectional results will not be dependable'.

Freeman and Hannan (1975: 219) consider the effect of size changes on the supportive component, termed 'SUP', that is, the total of administrators (such as principals, superintendents), professional staff (for example, counsellors, librarians) and nonprofessional staff (like janitors, cafeteria workers). They state as their theoretical expectation:

> Our expectation is that a given increment of size . . . will produce a larger increment of SUP [supportive component] in growth than the same change, taken as a

decrement, will decrease SUP. For example, suppose an increase of one hundred teachers yields an increase of twenty SUP. We expect that a decrease of one hundred teachers will tend to produce a decrease of only ten or fifteen SUP. (Freeman and Hannan, 1975: 222)

Freeman and Hannan (1975) summarize the difference they have found between growth and decline in the metaphor of a bumperjack – that is, a ratchet effect. They state:

> When demand is increasing, the size of the direct component increases as does the supportive component. But when demand declines, the loss in direct component is not matched by loss in the supportive component. That is, the supportive component tends to increase on the upswings but decreases less on the downswings. (Freeman and Hannan, 1975: 227)

If the loss of production workers in organizational decline is not matched by the loss of administrators, then the administrative intensity ratio is increasing when the organization declines in size. But this is what would be expected from Blau's proposition (1970) – that size and administrative intensity are negatively related. As organizational size declines, the administrative intensity will rise. It follows from this proposition that in organizational decline the number of administrators will decline less than proportionately to the decline in the number of production personnel. Thus, comparing decliners and growers, the decrease in administrators relative to the decrease in production personnel in decliners would be expected to be less than the rate at which administrators are added relative to increases in production personnel in growth. This is consistent with the example given by Freeman and Hannan (1975: 222) – for an increase of 100 teachers, support staff would increase by 20 and for a decrease of 100 teachers, the support staff would fall by only 10 or 15; the decrease in support staff in decline is less than their increase in growth. The conclusion stated by Freeman and Hannan (1975) is the pattern which would be *expected* from the theory of Blau (1970).

If size and administrative intensity are negatively related, administrative intensity should change in different ways in growth and decline. Administrative intensity should shrink in growers and it should rise in decliners. Thus administrative intensity should show more decrease in growers than in decliners. Hence Blau's theory predicts an asymmetry in effects on administrative intensity between growth and decline. Thus neither the idea of asymmetry nor the stated research conclusions of Freeman and Hannan (1975) challenge the theory of Blau (1970).

Hence it is not the case that later, stronger, longitudinal research design (Freeman and Hannan, 1975) contradicts the results of earlier cross-sectional research. Nor can the results from Freeman and Hannan (1975) be used to argue that longitudinal research produces findings different from, and superior to, cross-sectional methods, so that such cross-sectional methods are inherently unreliable or incapable of producing valid information on the phenomenon of administrative intensity (Blau, 1970, 1972; Blau and Schoenher, 1971).

It follows that the bumperjack or ratchet analogy is incorrect.

Administrative intensity rises with size decline and falls with size growth in the Blau model, and in the results of Freeman and Hannan. There is no need to fear the bumperjack as in the scenario depicted by Freeman and Hannan (1975: 227) in their finale: 'the supportive component tends to increase on the upswings but decreases less on the downswings. Consequently, a turbulent environment producing oscillations in demand for the organization's products or services may produce an increase in administrative intensity even if there is no upward trend in the oscillations.' Here the idea is that every time demand falls, the administrative intensity is ratcheted up, so a series of episodes of growth and decline will produce a cumulative increase, for the ratchet means that administrators tend to be added but not cut. However, while administrators are added in growth and only cut to a lesser degree in decline, the ratio of administrators to production personnel (the administrative intensity) rises in decline but falls in growth. Therefore, in a series of episodes in which growth spurts alternate with declines of equal magnitude, the increases in administrative intensity in the decline episodes will be offset by the decreases in administrative intensity in the growth episodes, producing nil effect on administrative intensity in the long run. If the bumperjack operated, then organizations that had grown over time to become large would have greater administrative intensity than smaller organizations. Yet cross-sectional comparisons find the opposite – namely, that larger organizations have less administrative intensity than smaller organizations (Blau, 1970, 1972; Blau and Schoenherr, 1971). Hence the pessimistic scenario on which Freeman and Hannan close is a spectre of their own imagining. The reality is better captured in the theory of Blau (1970) that in the long run, as organizations increase in size, administrative intensity declines, producing economies of scale in administration.

Nevertheless, the view received in the literature is that Freeman and Hannan have empirically established that administrative intensity tends to rise even where this is dysfunctional because the organization is declining. This is seen as disproving functionalist theories of organization and revealing powerful political forces of self-interested management. Managers are seen as pushing for the relentless addition of administrative staff, unrequired by the volume of work, leading to a creep upwards over time in administrative staff through the bumperjack effect. Since Freeman and Hannan are high-profile and influential scholars publishing in high-status journals such as the *American Sociological Review*, their message is authoritative. The received view becomes the conventional wisdom which later writers strive to fit within, thus reinforcing and enshrining the view of the size of organizational administrative staffs as irrational.

The Montanari and Adelman Simulation   Montanari and Adelman (1987) take up the idea of a ratchet effect on administrative intensity when size declines. They build on the scenario advanced by Freeman and Hannan (1975: 227). They produce a rising administrative ratio through a mathematical model of how administrative and production personnel numbers shift over time as the underlying demand variable cycles through swings of increase and decrease. Their model produces an increasing administrative ratio – to the point where there are more administrators than production people. Montanari and Adelman conclude from their analysis that size cannot be the primary, major cause of administrative intensity and review a host of other factors, such as politics, which they feel should be incorporated in future explanatory endeavours.

While Montanari and Adelman (1987) reach the conclusion endorsed by current academic conventional wisdom, this does not follow at all from their analytic efforts. Their mathematical model is built of equations in which demand causes production personnel which in turn causes administrative personnel. Thus the model has size as the only causal variable. There is no mention in their model of any other factor, political, or cultural or otherwise. At best, such causes other than size would presumably have to figure as more underlying variables that cause the size-based causal processes which are captured in the equations. However, the equations are presented without any such rationale. Essentially, demand causes production personnel, which therefore fluctuates up and down in response to the demand cycle. However, administrative numbers are fixed by an equation in which the number of administrators can increase but never decline. The number of administrators in this period is always equal to the number in the last period and may also increase, depending on whether there is a growth in production personnel. This mathematical model therefore simulates a rising administrative ratio, but is solely based on size and the ratchet concept. Thus the mathematical model reproduces the ratchet findings but does not explain them.

Moreover, the model identifies size as the only causal variable, and certainly does not justify the conclusion that size is not a major cause of administrative intensity. The results of Montanari and Adelman (1987) provide no support whatever for the assertion that growth in administrative intensity is governed in reality by political or cultural factors. Nevertheless, this is the interpretation which they advance in order to be in keeping with the conventional wisdom – namely, 'that it's all politics really', when in the case of their analysis, it's all mathematics, which could hardly be more rational.

The Marsh and Mannari Study

Marsh and Mannari (1989) have also contributed on the issue of administrative intensity and its causation, or not, by size. They utilize a longitudinal research design in a study of Japanese factories at two points in time: 1976 and 1983. They find that the theoretical relationships found by Blau (1970) hold in their data cross-sectionally but that, once again, this pattern breaks down when the organizations are analysed longitudinally. This leads them to express reservations about the validity of Blau's theory about economies of scale in administrative intensity and to call for more research using longitudinal design in order to understand the causal relationships. Their analyses draw on the idea of asymmetries between growth and decline but include other arguments as well, so while echoing Freeman and Hannan (1975), they go beyond them.

Interestingly, while noting the similarities between their own findings and the longitudinal study of Freeman and Hannan (1975) on Californian school systems, Marsh and Mannari (1989) do not embrace the anti-functionalist, political interpretation of Freeman and Hannan. Marsh and Mannari (1989) remain sceptical about the power explanation and continue to see some possible efficiency-orientated reasons for failure to adjust administrative intensity to size changes. These include the discontinuities in structural change with downsizing due to the need to retain separate work units and their supervisory managers for task system reasons, even when direct working subordinates are reduced in numbers in such units, thus swelling the administrative intensity ratio. Another factor preventing smooth, continuous adjustment of administrative intensity to downsizing is that disproportionately more managers may be needed in such circumstances to try and manage an environment which has become less benign, in order to obtain greater resources from it. Marsh and Mannari (1989) call for future research to test between such functionalist efficiency and power political theories.

Thus Marsh and Mannari (1989) are agnostic regarding the theoretical interpretation of their data. However, their conclusion is a firm one about the limitations of Blau's theory, reflecting the limitations of cross-sectional method, revealed by the superior methods of longitudinal research and panel analysis:

> In this paper we have seen that panel analysis of the causal influence of organizational size on several aspects of organizational structure leads to quite different inferences from those made by Blau, the Aston group and others whose data were cross-sectional. Blau's theory is, in important respects, misspecified. On the basis of our Japanese factory findings, as well as longitudinal analyses by Freeman and Hannan, Ford (1980) and others, we concur with Cullen, Anderson and Baker's (1986) conclusion that Blau's theory explains structural differences in size across organizations at one point in time rather than structural change over time within organizations.
>
> In Japanese private manufacturing firms, as in U.S. public school systems, the changes in administrative intensity in declining size organizations are not simply the mirror image of what happens to personnel components in growing organizations. There is what may be called a universal ratchet effect by which managers, supervisors and other support personnel increase more rapidly in growing organizations than they decrease in organizations declining in size; production personnel decrease more rapidly when size declines than they increase when the size of an organization is growing.
>
> Thus, causal inferences about the effect of size on administrative intensity are different when based on data over time than when based on static, cross-sectional data. This is probably true of other organizational relationships as well. It would be advantageous, therefore, to re-study other cross-sectionally-based findings by means of longitudinal data, so that organizational theory can be put on a firmer causal footing. (Marsh and Mannari, 1989: 93)

Again the results of longitudinal research are contrasted invidiously with the findings from cross-sectional research.

Marsh and Mannari (1989) draw on the appealing distinction made by Cullen et al. (1986) between a theory of scale and a theory of structural change, with Blau's theory seen as a valid theory of scale but not of change. The notion is that a scale theory captures phenomena revealed in static cross-sectional studies, such as the negative relationship between size and administrative intensity, whereas the cross-sectional studies fail to capture the dynamics of change and causality which are the subject matter of a theory of structural change.

Yet a static picture is produced by causal dynamics and so the causal dynamics must operate in a manner consistent with the cross-sectional picture. The cross-sectional studies address associations between the levels of variables and utilize all the variation over the range of each variable, over the entire life of the organization. The dynamic changes are composed of incremental changes of portions of each variable over a period of some years. Yet these incremental changes must sum to the total level attained on each variable by each organization over its life to date. Thus the incremental dynamics becomes the cross-sectional picture. The cross-sectional picture is the result of the dynamic trajectories of the organizations from their birth up until today. Thus there are not two ontologically separate realms – the organization studied cross-sectionally and the organization studied longitudinally, for they are the *same* organization. Therefore patterns in one mode of analysis (such as longitudinal research) must be consistent with patterns derived from the other mode of analysis (cross-sectional research).

These theoretical reflections lead us to reject the notion that there is a scale phenomenon captured by scale theory and a change phenomenon captured by an antithetical theory. Thus the results of cross-sectional and longitudinal research must converge on the same theory. The question then becomes whether or not this theory is that of Blau.

Marsh and Mannari (1989) argue against Blau from their study of Japanese factories, finding that the causal model of Blau holds only to a degree and that it is crucially misspecified. Their approach is to show that as their successive analyses move away from static towards dynamic methods, so Blau's theory becomes increasingly questionable. They consider, in order, results from cross-sectional, longitudinal, panel and growers-versus-decliners analyses. We will consider their results in the same order.

Cross-sectional Analysis   Blau's (1970) theory holds that size positively causes structural differentiation which raises structural complexity that positively affects administrative intensity, but this indirect, positive effect of size on administrative intensity is overwhelmed by a direct negative effect of size on administrative intensity. Thus there are three variables connected by three causal arrows: size leads *positively* to structural differentiation that leads *positively* to administrative intensity and size also leads directly, *negatively* to administrative intensity. Marsh and Mannari (1989) mostly find that this pattern holds cross-sectionally for each year 1976 and 1983.

The only exception here is that for the 1976 cross-sectional study, the 'economies of scale' do not 'exceed the costs of complexity' (Marsh and Mannari, 1989: 88). Hence the negative direct effect of size on administrative intensity is not greater than the positive effect via structural differentiation (complexity). However, this argument by Marsh and Mannari (1989: 88) is based on the fact that magnitude of the positive path from complexity to administrative intensity, +.49, is greater than the negative path from size to administrative intensity, −.46. Yet, the cost of the structural complexity introduced by increasing size is the arc connecting size and administrative intensity via structural complexity which is $(+.71 \times +.49) = +.35$. This positive arc is numerically less than the negative direct effect of size on administrative intensity of −.46. Thus it is *not* the case that the 1976 data show an indirect positive arc which is greater than the direct effect of size on administrative intensity. The inference of Marsh and Mannari (1989) here is erroneous based on not examining the whole arc. Hence the 1976 cross-sectional results of Marsh and Mannari are not the opposite of that which would be expected from the Blau theory: they are, in fact, in the direction which the Blau theory would predict. The economies of scale exceed the costs of complexity in the 1976 cross-section. Thus the cross-sectional results for both 1976 and 1983 support Blau's theory.

Longitudinal Analysis A second, greater exception to the Blau pattern occurs in the longitudinal prediction of 1983 structure from 1976 size. Here neither path leading into administrative intensity, whether from size or structural differentiation complexity, is significantly different from zero. However, with a small sample size of 48 organizations, this may just reflect sampling error and the insensitivity of a small sample. It is noteworthy that the positive, indirect arc of size on administrative intensity via structural differentiation complexity is +.03, which is less than the direct path of size on administrative intensity of −.25, thus yielding a net effect which is negative – as Blau's theory predicts.

Throughout both the cross-sectional and the longitudinal analyses, the differences between the positive, indirect and the negative, direct paths are all consistently in the direction postulated by Blau; that is, the negative path is greater than the positive. The difference may or may not be statistically significant, but again in view of the small sample size this may not be an issue in this study.

Panel Analysis The major critical point made by Marsh and Mannari (1989: 89) is the deficiency of testing Blau's causal model by either cross-sectional or longitudinal design. Instead, Marsh and Mannari call for a panel design in which administrative intensity in 1983 is explained by a causal model not only of size in 1976 but also administrative intensity in 1976. Marsh and Mannari demonstrate that the addition of the administrative intensity in 1976 variable to the path model lowers the path from size in 1976 to administrative intensity in 1983, to −.13. This result is less than the longitudinal model, where it was −.25. In contrast, the path from administrative intensity in 1976 is positive and large at +.80. This leads Marsh and Mannari to charge that Blau misspecified his model by omitting prior administrative intensity, and that this variable is the real cause which Blau mistakenly attributed to size and complexity:

> Moreover, even the longitudinal test . . . is not *stricto sensu* a panel regression, since it does not include the lagged dependent variable – 1976 administrative intensity – in the model. When 1976 administrative intensity is held constant, size and structural complexity again have no significant net effect on 1983 administrative intensity . . . Thus, Blau's model is misspecified because it omits the lagged dependent variable, prior A/P ratio. When this is included in the model, we see that the causal effects Blau attributed to size and complexity are in fact due to the effect of earlier on later administrative intensity. (1989: 89)

Yet this is only to say that administrative intensity in 1983 is highly correlated with its value seven years earlier in 1976. This may be true statistically and numerically, but this sheds no light on what variables other than administrative intensity cause administrative intensity. This is not misspecification in the sense of adding another independent variable to explain the dependent variable, administrative intensity. This is no more than saying that the salaries of academics in 1989 are a correlate of their salaries in 1982; this is a fact, but not an explanation of academic salaries. The addition of prior administrative intensity to the causal model just pushes further back in time the search for the determinants of administrative intensity. Thus the addition of prior administrative intensity to the path analysis tells us little new, certainly not about some other important cause missed by Blau. Thus the panel analysis of Marsh and Mannari is not damaging evidence against Blau.

Analyses of Growers versus Decliners   The second major evidence adduced by Marsh and Mannari (1989: 89) against Blau is the result of splitting the sample into those organizations which grew in size and those which declined in size, a procedure reminiscent of Freeman and Hannan (1975). Marsh and Mannari (1989: 91) conclude that the pattern is different between growers and decliners, pointing to, in their view, a marked asymmetry in contrast to the symmetry expected from Blau's theory:

> Thus, Japanese factories are not immune to the ratchet effect. Growing size leads to growth and declining size results in decline in all personnel components. However, the changes in declining factories are not simply a mirror image of the growth of each personnel component in growing factories. Managers, supervisors and clerical personnel increase more rapidly in growing organizations than they decrease in organizations declining in size. Production and technical workers decrease more rapidly when size declines than they increase when size is growing. The basic situation is one of asymmetry, not the symmetry implied in theories such as Blau's.

For declining organizations the change in mean size of the managerial component is 15 per cent, which is about half the 29 per-cent change in mean size of the production workers (Marsh and Mannari, 1989: 91). This means that the ratio of managers to workers is increasing in declining organizations. However, Blau (1970) holds that a decrease in size will increase the A/P ratio, and this is what Marsh and Mannari find. They themselves (1989: 90) note in passing that 'The increasing A/P ratio in declining size factories supports what Blau's theory implicitly says.'

However, their ensuing discussion concentrates on the one part of their administrative intensity results which contradicts Blau, for as they state: 'The interesting finding then is that the A/P ratio increases in growing plants as well' (Marsh and Mannari, 1989: 90). This is a particular definition of what is interesting: a finding which challenges Blau. A finding on A/P in declining organizations which confirm Blau is not interesting. The implicit value judgement is that what is interesting is the evidence against the Blau theory, not that for the theory. Moreover, this occurs after Marsh and Mannari have reported that their results regarding changes in structural differentiation, for both growers and decliners, fit with the expectations from Blau's theory – namely, that organizations growing in size, on average, increase their structural differentiation, and organizations declining in size, on average, decrease their structural differentiation (1989: 90). Thus for three out of the four analyses of growers versus decliners the results conform to the theory of Blau. Yet it is the one out of the four results which runs counter to Blau's theory which is 'interesting.'

The anomalous result regarding administrative intensity in growing organizations is based on just 16 factories. The actual number of personnel in these growing organizations is not given, but for the total sample the median number of managers grows from 42.0 to 46.5 (Marsh and Mannari, 1989). Hence the growth in managers is of the order of five people; this suggests something about the small numbers involved and hence the potential for unreliability. The growth in administrative intensity of the growing organizations between 1976 and 1983 was from 18 per cent to 21 per cent – that is, only 3 per cent which is trivial, especially given any measurement error (1989: 90). Moreover, it may also be worth observing that the mean score on administrative intensity in 1976 of those organizations which grow in size is 18 per cent, which is less than the 1976 administrative intensity mean of the decliners, 26 per cent (1989: 90). Even when the growers had increased their administrative intensity by 1983 it was only 21 per cent which was less than the 1976 score of the decliners, 26 per cent, and even less than the 1983 score of the decliners, 32 per cent (1989: 90). Thus the growers might be undergoing some lagged move to equilibrium which causes them to grow trivially in administrative intensity between 1976 and 1983.

In conclusion, the Marsh and Mannari (1989) study mainly finds for the Blau model in its causal modelling analyses, which reveals paths of the sign Blau's theory predicts and economies of scale in administration. Similarly, the contingency analysis of structural change into growers and decliners overwhelmingly supports Blau's theory. The exception is the increase in administrative intensity of growing organizations. However, this is small in magnitude and based on too few organizations to be highly reliable. The arguments about asymmetry, misspecification and scale versus structural change theories are all unsatisfactory and mask the more fundamental support for

Blau's theory offered by these data. Once again, highly selective attention on an anomalous minority of the research data is combined with rhetorical argumentation to produce an interpretation contrary to Blau's theory, when a more straightforward interpretation of the results would be that they support the general theory of Blau. This, alas, is not 'interesting.' What is interesting is to find for the conventional wisdom about important differences between growth and decline in the manner of Freeman and Hannan (1975).

Review of Correlational Studies

In the theory and empirical findings of Blau (1970, 1972) and his colleagues, administrative personnel increase less than proportionately to production personnel as organizational size increases. Thus the correlation between size and administrative intensity is negative. Does this relationship hold generally across studies of size and administrative intensity?

Numerous studies have been conducted of the relationship between size and administrative intensity, and in order to try to clarify the relationship, a meta-analysis was conducted by Donaldson and Caulfield (1989). This examined studies of the relationship between organizational size and the proportion of employees who were managers. There were 17 studies which could be included in the meta-analysis; these studies are listed in Table 5.1. The studies were Al-Jibouri (1983); Ayoubi (1981); Blau et al. (1976); Blau and Schoenherr (1971); Child (1972b); Goldman (1973); Hickson et al. (1969); Hinings and Lee (1971); Holdaway et al. (1975); Marsh and Mannari (1981); Van de Ven and Ferry (1980) (some references report more than one study). Correlations were taken from the published studies, supplemented on occasion by information from the databank of Aston studies.

The total number of organizations was 2,128. The average correlation between organizational size and proportion of managers was negative, $r = -.45$. Thus the average result is as Blau's theory would predict. This supports economies of scale in administration as organizations grow in size.

There was, however, a considerable difference between public-sector and private-sector organizations. The average correlation between organizational size and proportion of managers, of the nine studies of 1,640 public-sector organizations, was $r = -.53$, which is significantly different from zero (at $p < 0.0005$). In contrast, the average correlation of the seven studies of 436 private-sector organizations was much lower at $r = -.18$, which is significantly different from zero (at $p < 0.0005$). The two correlations are significantly different from each other (at $p < 0.0005$). The result is that the size–administrative intensity relationship is negative in both the public sector and the private sector, but more strongly negative in the public sector.

In both public-sector and private-sector studies the relationship between size and administrative intensity is negative. The results from the correlational studies are consistent with the theory of Blau for both sectors, but more strongly for the public sector than for the private sector. Sector is a

Table 5.1   *Studies of relationship between organizational size and number of managers as percentage of employees*

Study*	n	Sector	r
Al-Jibouri, 1983	27	Private	.23
Ayoubi, 1981	34	Private	.30
Blau, Falbe, McKinley & Tracy, 1976	110	Private	−.28
Blau & Schoenherr, 1971 (local offices)	1201	Public	−.64
Blau & Schoenherr, 1971 (employment services)**	68	Public	−.38
Blau & Schoenherr, 1971 (unemployment insurance)**	71	Public	−.39
Blau & Schoenherr, 1971 (administrative services)**	67	Public	−.12
Blau & Schoenherr, 1971 (personnel & technical)**	77	Public	−.14
Blau & Schoenherr, 1971 (data processing)**	51	Public	−.18
Blau & Schoenherr, 1971 (legal services)**	53	Public	−.36
Child, 1972b	82	Private	−.11
Goldman, 1973	124	Private	−.54
Hickson, Pugh & Pheysey, 1969	52	Mixed	−.13
Hinings & Lee, 1971	9	Private	−.73
Holdaway et al., 1975	23	Public	.03
Marsh & Mannari, 1981	50	Private	.35
Van de Ven & Ferry, 1980	29	Public	−.13

* See Bibliography for full citation of studies.
**Headquarters divisions of the employment security agencies.

moderator of degree but not of sign. In neither sector is there diseconomy of scale in administration. There is not the disproportionate increase in managers and administrators relative to operation personnel of which Parkinson (1957) wrote. For both sectors there are economies of scale in administration.

Examining individual studies, we can see that 13 out of the 17 studies found the negative correlation which is consistent with the theory of scale economies in administration. Of the four studies that found a positive correlation, one was virtually zero (r = .03), so only three studies should be coded as nontrivially positive. Their average size was only 37 organizations, which is less than the average size of the 13 studies that found negative correlations, which was 154 organizations (66 if the largest study is excluded); thus small sample size may have introduced some error into the anomalous three studies, making their results less reliable. Overall, the 17 studies produce only limited support for Parkinson and argue instead for the existence of scale economies in administration.

Summary

Contrary to Parkinson (1957), Blau (1970) argued, in functionalist vein, that increasing organizational size led to economies of scale in administration – that is, to lower administrative intensity with increases in organizational size.

The correlational evidence advanced by Blau and others has been attacked by Freeman and Kronenfeld (1973) as being based on a tautology which would mask a true positive association between size and administrative intensity. However, there is no such problem of tautology in the administrative intensity topic. The reasoning of Freeman and Kronenfeld is based on flawed logic. For this reason their prescription about supposedly more adequate research procedures than those used by Blau fails to show any difference or superiority empirically in application to data (MacMillan and Daft, 1979). Thus the correlational evidence offered in support of Blau's theory is secure and not flawed by tautology, and the results regarding declines in administrative intensity with increasing size are genuine.

Nevertheless, such cross-sectional research designs have been seen as inferior to longitudinal research designs. The results from examinations of organizations which change their size have shown differences between growers and decliners. This has been widely interpreted as a deficiency in the theory and evidence of Blau and others, and as evidence supporting the view that the growth in administrators is organizationally dysfunctional, political and self-serving for management. However, the Blau theory states that there will be asymmetry between growers and decliners, with growers showing decreasing administrative intensity and decliners showing increasing administrative intensity. The idea of an economy of scale in administration implies that administrative intensity shrinks only for growers and that administrative intensity will rise for decliners – that is to say, less scale causes less economy in administration. The conclusions which Freeman and Hannan state from their research are congruent with Blau's theory. Their longitudinal research is consistent with the findings of cross-sectional enquiry, so there is no inherent deficiency in the methods used by Blau and others that generate findings supportive of the Blau theory.

Montanari and Adelman (1987) conclude in favour of politics and of a ratchet effect of size on the administrative component. This is on the basis of a simulation model in which the idea of the ratchet effect is in-built. Unsurprisingly, iteration of the model produces results consistent with the ratchet postulate. Montanari and Adelman (1987) conclude that political and cultural factors rather than size should be seen as driving the administrative component. Yet the model provides evidence only of size and not at all of politics as the cause.

Marsh and Mannari (1989) are also critical of Blau's theory, finding the empirical model to be misspecified, omitting a major cause of the administrative intensity, and again finding an asymmetry between growers and decliners which leads them to doubt Blau's theory as an explanation of structural change. However, the argument about misspecifications boils down to Marsh and Mannari (1989) wishing to insert into the empirical model the dependent variable measured at an earlier period of time. This adds nothing to the explanation. Further, in three out of four longitudinal analyses, the results of Marsh and Mannari (1989) support the structural theory of Blau. They chose to focus, however, on the one case which fails to support Blau's theory. This is that growing organizations show a small increase rather than the expected decline in administrative intensity. Given small sample size, the limitations in the reliability of the measures and the possibility of temporal lags in the causal system, this anomaly may not be very meaningful.

In contrast, the results of numerous correlational studies support the view that size and administrative intensity are related negatively. The relationship holds more strongly in the public sector than in the private sector. However, there is little empirical support for the theory of Parkinson (1957) of a tendency for administrative intensity to rise with increasing organizational size – namely, diseconomies of scale in administration.

Conclusions

Let us now draw our conclusions, considering the present and previous chapters together. Blau (1970, 1972) argues that the administrative intensity of organizations is positivist, being determined by size, and functionalist, in that economies of administration increase with scale. Parkinson (1957) and his followers argue, on the contrary, that administrative intensity of organizations is politically caused and so not amenable to positivist theory and is organizationally dysfunctional.

The results of research show that the administrative intensity of organizations is amenable to positivist explanation. The research results also support functionalism and contradict the political explanation. There are economies of scale in administration, with organizational size and administrative intensity being related negatively. There is very little support for the Parkinsonian idea of a positive relationship. The theory of increasing diseconomies of scale in administration as organizations grow in size, brought about by political processes of managerial self-interest at cost to the organization, is mainly false. The research tends to support the view of the administrative intensity of organizations as positivist and functionalist, rather than anti-positivist and political.

6

For Cartesianism: Against Organization Types and Quantum Jumps

Organizational typologies hold that there are just a few, starkly different types of organizations, each constituting a fit between the contingencies and organizational structure. Further, organizational typologies see fewer fits than structural contingency theory and see structural change as less frequent and more dramatic. Thus, instead of the more usual contingency view of organizations changing incrementally through many finely graded steps, organizational typologies see organizational change as discontinuous and occasional. These points of difference will be critically examined in this chapter and organizational typologies will be rejected in favour of a multivariate model of contingency–structure fits that is in keeping with the original structural contingency theory.

Organization theory often uses ideal-types, meaning abstract types, such as Weberian bureaucracy, that are so extreme as not to exist empirically, yet that serve as stark polarities against which actual organizations can be compared (Weber, 1968). The empirical organization lies at some intermediate point between any two ideal-types – for example, between full traditionalism and full bureaucracy. The line between any two ideal-types of organizational structure can be considered as a dimension of organizational structure. It is a continuum that can be measured quantitatively, so that organization A can be said to be more, say, formalized, than organization B, and so on. One of the achievements of pioneering structural contingency theory around the 1960s was to develop a set of variables of organizational structure (such as Pugh et al., 1968; Lawrence and Lorsch, 1967). This is a multivariate framework for the analysis of organizations. The multivariate framework provides a Cartesian model, in that the contingency and structural variables form a multidimensional space with an organization being defined analytically as a set of coordinates within that space.

Notwithstanding such scientific progress, in subsequent years there have been attempts to re-assert the concept of organizational typologies (Mintzberg, 1979; Miller, 1986; Meyer et al., 1993). The argument is that organizational attributes need to fit each other to be internally consistent in order to produce effectiveness. Thus the ideal-types are now claimed to be the only viable organizations. This is compatible with an ideationalist approach to organizations, in that there are a few Platonic ideal forms which are the manifestations of ideas into the world. This approach displays anti-positivist leanings.

Elsewhere we offered a short critical discussion of consistency theory. We argued that certain explanations of organizational structure offered by consistency theory could be as well accounted for by contingency theory (Donaldson, 1985). Now we critique the whole notion of approaching organizational structural analysis through typologies and seek to show the superiority of a Cartesian, multivariate framework.

Mintzberg (1979) and Miller (1986) have been leaders in the modern organizational typology movement. Their writings provide a clear, vivid set of organizational types or configurations and have been influential. Our argument is that the Mintzberg and Miller typologies are in error and that all such typologies are inherently unsound. A sounder approach is to consider organizational structure and contingency relationships as multidimensional with the contingency–structure fits as continua – that is, to take the Cartesian approach.

The Mintzberg Typology

In his widely used text-book, Mintzberg (1979) presents a typology of five different types of organizational structure. Typologies, because of their simplicity, may be useful as pedagogic devices for introducing students to the topic of organizational structure. However, they are of more limited use in research or prescription if the phenomena are really multidimensional with the types just being the extreme ends of the dimensions or ideal-types. If many of the actual organizations that exist are actually intermediate points between these extremes or ideal-types, then the organization is a combination of the typologies. To present types as the few congruent, internally consistent and therefore effective combinations of the underlying multiple dimensions is erroneous.

In his discussion of organizational structural designs Mintzberg (1979) abstracts five types, or configurations, from the previous theoretical literature: the simple structure, the machine bureaucracy, the professional bureaucracy, the divisionalized form and the adhocracy. Mintzberg develops as a cornerstone of his analysis the argument that there are several distinct modes of coordination within organizations (Thompson, 1967). He then holds that effectiveness results from internal consistency where the same coordination mode is used consistently within the one organization, thus producing the five distinct types: the simple structure coordinates through direct supervision; the machine bureaucracy coordinates through process standardization; the professional bureaucracy coordinates through skill standardization; the divisionalized form coordinates through output standardization; the adhocracy coordinates through mutual adjustment (Mintzberg, 1979). Hence, in order to be internally consistent, the same coordination device must be used throughout the organization, therefore mixing the organizational types produces ineffectiveness and so the types must be kept separate. Thus the ideal-types become distinct concrete types.

Yet the theoretical originator of the idea of separate coordination modes, Thompson (1967), held that some organizations have several different coordination modes within them. Indeed Thompson theorized about the relationship between different coordination modes within the same, effective organization. He argued that, within an organization, the lower-level work units would include mutual adjustment in their internal coordination mechanisms, that larger departmental groupings would use planning in their internal coordination mechanisms and that at the highest-level the divisions would be coordinated through standardization of procedures (Thompson, 1967). Many organizations of almost any degree of size and complexity contain several different coordination modes and yet are still effective (Van de Ven and Ferry, 1980). Different coordination modes exist within the same organization because they are required for effective operations (Thompson, 1967).

Having reduced organizational structures to five types, Mintzberg even sees one of these types, the divisionalized form, as problematic:

> The pure (conglomerate) Divisionalized Form emerges as a structural configuration symbolically perched on the edge of the cliff, at the end of a long path. Ahead, it is one step away from *dis*integration – breaking up into separate organizations on the rocks below. Behind it is the way back to a more stable integration, perhaps a hybrid structure with Machine Bureaucracy at some intermediate spot along the path. And ever hovering above is the eagle, attracted by its position on the edge of the cliff and waiting for the chance to pull the Divisionalized Form up to more centralized social control, on another, perhaps more dangerous, cliff. The edge of the cliff is an uncomfortable place to be – maybe even a temporary one that must inevitably lead to disintegration on the rocks below, a trip to that cliff above, or a return to a safer resting place on the path behind. (1979: 429)

This is despite evidence that multidivisional structures are effective in their appropriate context (namely, diversification) (Donaldson, 1987; Hamilton and Shergill, 1992; Hill et al., 1992), that the multidivisional structure has endured for many decades both in the population of organizations (Fligstein, 1985) and within individual organizations (Rumelt, 1974), and that the number of corporations in the world with multidivisional structure is increasing (Channon, 1973; Dyas and Thanheiser, 1976; Pavan, 1976; Suzuki, 1980).

At places in his discussion, Mintzberg (1979: 475–7) briefly allows that some organizations, 'hybrids', lie on intermediate points between any two of the five types. This is a step in the right direction towards a multidimensional treatment, though a completely multidimensional model would allow organizations to be anywhere between any of the five types. Moreover, a multidimensional model would explicate the dimensions (for example, centralization, formalization, professionalization and so on) which underlie the five types and use this as the framework on to which organizations are mapped. However, Mintzberg (1979) fails to develop such a multivariate model and so this aspect of his writing remains a suggestion, with the mainstay of the book propounding the view of a few types – the message for which the book has become known.

Organizational Configurations

Miller (1986) has offered a synthesis of research into strategy and structure. This uses the concept of organizational 'configurations' to produce a typology not only of organizational structure but also of strategy. Miller draws on earlier typological works (for instance, Mintzberg, 1979; Porter, 1980; Miles and Snow, 1978). In particular, he uses four of the five structural types of Mintzberg (1979) – the fifth of Mintzberg's structural types is omitted as not relevant for business corporations (Miller, 1986: 241). However, with the idea of configurations Miller (1986) pushes further with the concept of a typology than Mintzberg (1979). In the hands of Miller the five types from Mintzberg become four strategy–structure configurations, 'Gestalts' or types. To Miller these are the *only* viable combination of strategy and structure variables, though he cautions (1986: 233) that his list is not either 'final or exhaustive'.

Any deviations from the four configurations are ineffective for other strategy–structure combinations lack cohesion and internal harmony: 'the organization may be driven toward a common configuration to achieve internal harmony among its elements of strategy, structure and context. A central theme is pursued which marshals and orders the individual elements.' (1986: 236). Miller (1986: 236) exemplifies such a configuration by the machine bureaucracy. He lists several defining characteristics such as large size, standardization, formal communications and tight controls, operating in a stable and simple environment. He comments: 'Clearly many of these attributes are complementary and mutually reinforcing . . . Thus each element makes sense in terms of the whole – and together they form a cohesive system' (1986: 236).

Strategy–structure combinations that are deviations from the configurations lack this harmony and cohesion and are therefore temporary at best. Given the strengths of being a configuration and the frailty of deviations from the configurations, organizations are held by Miller (1986) seldom to change from their original configuration. When they do, it takes the form of a quantum jump from one type to another in order to avoid the disharmony and ineffectiveness of the intermediary strategy–structure combinations:

> Organizations tend to change their elements in a manner that either extends a given configuration, or moves it quickly to a new configuration that is preserved for a very long time. Piecemeal changes will often destroy the complementarities among many elements of configuration and will thus be avoided. Only when change is absolutely necessary or extremely advantageous will organizations be tempted to move concertedly and rapidly (to shorten the disruptive interval of transition) from one configuration to another that is broadly different. Such changes, because they are so expensive, will not be undertaken very frequently. Consequently organizations will adhere to their configurations for fairly long periods. (Miller, 1986: 236)

Miller (1986: 237) refers to this theory as the 'quantum view of change'. This is a model which denies viable intermediary forms or viable incremental change. It is a starkly simple model of stasis punctuated by occasional discontinuous change.

Because the Miller (1986) formulation is a strong assertion of the argument for types, we will give it the greatest attention. Miller's theoretical model is contradicted in many places by theory and evidence, as will be shown.

The idea of configurations is particularly likely to enjoy wide appeal since it builds on earlier, popular typologies. The idea that organization structure can be understood through five types (Mintzberg, 1979) has been widely received. Again, the notion that there are four types of strategy (Miles and Snow, 1978) has also been widely received.

The configuration theory (Miller, 1986) contains several damaging flaws and is inherently inadequate. The configurations themselves are too few and too simple. And the difficulties cannot readily be righted by modification of the existing configurations or by adding a few more configurations to the framework. Configurations run contrary to the trend within organization theory of complex, multidimensional models of fit between contingency and structure variables. The programme of configurations is therefore regressive rather than progressive. The configuration notion will hinder rather than help the tasks of theory-building, research, teaching and prescription.

The discussion of strategy–structure relationships by Miller (1986) offers an informative review of the literature and an attempt at synthesis. Both of these aspects are highly commendable. However, the particular synthesis which Miller (1986) proposes is in the form of configurations, and therein lie the problems. Miller postulates four such configurations (though noting that this is tentative and that some other viable configurations may exist). The four configurations are: the simple structure, the machine bureaucracy, the divisionalized conglomerate and the innovating adhocracy.

Configuration theory argues that there are only four combinations of values of contingency and structural variables which constitute fits (Miller, 1986). These configurations are dispersed at the edges of the space formed by the contingency–structural variables. (A visual depiction of such a space is offered by Mintzberg (1979: 470-1) as a pentagon with the fives configurations as its five points.) There are many intermediary combinations of contingency and structure values but none of these is viable, because they are misfits between contingency and structure. For instance, small size and little bureaucracy is one viable configuration (the simple structure) and large size and high level of bureaucracy is another viable configuration (the machine bureaucracy). However, there is no viable type – that is, configuration – offered for organizations of medium size with a medium level of bureaucratization. Thus the strategy–structure configurations are separated by considerable zones of nonviability and are often polar types which are discrete from one another. Accordingly, Miller (1986) argues that organizations make 'quantum' jumps from one configuration to another.

A Critique of the Concept of Strategy-Structure Configurations

The phrase 'strategy and structure' is often used in organization theory with a particular meaning derived from Chandler (1962) and Rumelt (1974). The word 'strategy' is often used to mean a sub-set of contingencies such as diversification and vertical integration. Similarly, the word 'structure' is used to refer just to the corporate structure at the apex of the corporation (for example, functional or divisional structures) (Chandler, 1962; Rumelt, 1974). In contrast, Miller (1986) uses the term 'strategy–structure relationship' to describe relationships between structural variables and numerous contingency variables such as diversification, size, technology and so on. Thus, what Miller terms 'strategy–structure relationships' might more conventionally in organization theory circles be termed 'contingency–structure relationships'. Likewise, Miller (1986) argues that the implications of strategy for structure extend to standardization, differentiation, integration and other aspects of the overall organizational structure. Thus the term 'strategy–structure' refers in Miller (1986) to virtually the entire set of contingency–structure relationships. Hence the terms 'strategy–structure' and 'contingency–structure' will be used interchangeably in this chapter.

Each configuration has a distinct profile of structure and environmental context. For example, the structure of machine bureaucracy is bureaucratized, extensively specialized, moderately differentiated and integrated by formal procedures, including developed cost controls and budgets. The machine bureaucracy arises in environments of low uncertainty and low change, high competition, slow growth and high industry concentration, using large scale as a barrier to entry. The stability and size promote bureaucratization and mass production, which facilitate a strategy of cost leadership. There are several links of mutual causation between size, stability, routine production, low-cost bureaucratization and strategy which reinforce one another (Miller, 1986). Pure price competition can be avoided through some market differentiation, such as branding, advertising, quality or forward vertical integration. Thus strategic options for the machine bureaucracy are cost leadership or market differentiation.

There is a problem in having only a few types such as the simple structure and machine bureaucracy configurations. How can the machine bureaucracy come into existence? How can an organization exist at all which is large in size if it has not been able to grow incrementally from the small, simple structure through medium size to large size?

In order to grow incrementally between simple structure and machine bureaucracy the organization would need to grow through a series of stages. For each stage to generate growth, that stage would have to be a fit so that the organization would perform adequately enough to produce new growth. This means that each stage would have to be a configuration. Hence there would need to be a large number of different fits – that is configurations in Miller's terms – one at each stage in the path of incremental growth. Each configuration would be adjacent to the next. Thus there would need to be viable fits or configurations between the two extreme configurations of simple structure and machine bureaucracy, and so there would need to be many viable fits or configurations. Yet configuration theory denies the existence of such intermediate fits. If that were the case, there would be many configurations rather than four. Moreover, the configurations would not just be extreme types, such as simple structure and machine bureaucracy. Thus configuration theory fails to explain the existence of the machine bureaucracy configuration. More generally, the notion of four configurations separated in structural space fails to account for the movement between organizational types that occurs through incremental change.

The failure to accommodate incremental growth makes the theory implausible. The only alternative origin for a large organization, apart from incremental growth, is that it was a large organization at the time of its creation, presumably spawned by a giant parent organization. Such a process may occur in cases such as a large subsidiary being created by a giant parent company, or where a large governmental organization is created by the state. However, many large organizations are not spawned from parental organizations in this way and grow incrementally from a small size and simple structure, (for example, Ford Motor Company, Hewlett-Packard, Matsushita Denki and so on). Hence the parent company explanation cannot hold for such cases. Many large commercial organizations, multinational corporations included, have shown substantial incremental growth over their lives. (Even the state government itself has grown.) Configuration theory is thus flawed because it cannot accommodate these cases of incremental growth.

Similarly, the postulate of no viability at intermediate positions between configurations seems implausible. For instance, many firms in the economy are at medium size; that is, they are intermediate between the simple structure and machine bureaucracies configurations and yet remain in being for many years, indicating that they are viable (Pugh and Hinings, 1976; Hannan and Freeman, 1989). Many empirical studies of organizations show that most organizations are at intermediate points on the various contingency and structural variables, rather than just at the extremes. Organizations are distributed along these variables so that there are many shades of grey and not just black and white. These continuous distributions are shown graphically for size and structural differentiation in Blau and Schoenherr (1971), for example. Again, studies of organizations conducted within the Aston programme and held in the Aston Databank show substantial variation in scores on the contingency and structural variables (see, for instance, Pugh et al., 1968, 1969a), rather than bunching at the extremes.

The whole approach of positing *few, discrete* strategy–structure combinations is rejected in our discussion here. There is a much larger number of viable strategy–structure combinations than four or half-a-dozen or so. The viable strategy–structural forms do not just exist at discrete points with wide separations of nonviable combinations.

A Critique of the Configurations

We will now critically examine in turn the divisionalized conglomerate, innovating adhocracy and machine bureaucracy configurations.

A Critique of the Divisionalized Conglomerate

One of the four Millerian configurations is the 'divisionalized conglomerate' (Miller, 1986: 246). A problem here is that most divisionalized corporations are not conglomerates (that is, unrelated product companies; see Rumelt, 1974).

Many divisionalized corporations are related product companies (Channon, 1973; Rumelt, 1974; Dyas and Thanheiser, 1976; Pavan, 1976; Suzuki, 1980). In fact, more divisionalized companies are related product companies than are unrelated product companies (Channon, 1973; Rumelt, 1974; Fligstein, 1991). The structures of related product companies differ from conglomerates, being more centralized (Channon, 1973; Rumelt, 1974).

Further, some divisionalized corporations are vertically integrated (Lorsch and Allen, 1973). Miller (1986) mentions vertical integration as one strategic option for divisionalized companies, but vertically integrated systems such as petro-chemical or forest products corporations are not 'conglomerates' (that is, pools of unrelated products). Such vertically integrated companies have internalized the value-added chain of a given extractive material such as oil or lumber (Rumelt, 1974). Moreover, their organization structures depart considerably from the divisional form of unrelated product corporations. Relative to conglomerates, the structure of vertically integrated corporations is more centralized and places less emphasis on divisional profitability as the performance criteria (Lorsch and Allen, 1973).

Thus there is not just one viable single form of divisional company, the conglomerate (pools of unrelated products), which is the only viable type of divisionalization. Both related-product divisionalized and vertically integrated divisionalized companies are viable.

There are many different sub-types of divisionalized company within the divisionalized type, each of which is a fit to its environment and strategy. There are degrees of difference in divisional structure on various dimensions, such as autonomy of divisions and divisional performance criteria (Allen, 1978; Hill, 1988). These structural differences reflect differences of degree in product diversity, vertical integration and so on (Allen, 1978; Hill, 1988).

Miller (1986: 247) holds that only the cost leadership and market differentiation strategies fit the divisionalized structure. He states that divisionalized corporations force their divisions to become somewhat bureaucratized and formalized so that they lose some flexibility, and that this 'precludes business-level strategies of differentiation through innovation' (1986: 247). (At one point Miller (1986: 246) observes that some divisions may have organic structures, which would seem to imply strategies of innovation, but he fails to integrate this insight into the subsequent theory statement.) However, many large, product innovative firms in industries such as electronics have multidivisional structures – for example, Philips, Plessey and so on. Product innovation is pursued within divisions and in central laboratories which cooperate with divisions (Pitts, 1976). While the argument may be made that large corporations are never as flexible and innovatory as small entrepreneurial firms, nevertheless there is substantial product innovation in the corporate sector of the economy and some large, divisionalized corporations pursue product innovation strategies (Rothwell, 1975). Thus the divisionalized conglomerate configuration masks the use of product innovation in divisionalized corporations.

Moreover, as Miller notes (1986: 247), divisions in the same corporation can vary in their strategies. By extension, some divisions in certain industries can pursue product innovation strategies while others pursue cost leadership strategies. Each division can be seen in structural contingency theory as an organization that may fit its environment. However, the configuration model of the organization as a single, pure type masks variations in product innovation within divisionalized corporations by restricting the assigned strategies to cost leadership and market differentiation.

Thus the configuration idea of internal consistency means that all divisionalized companies tend to be treated as the same as one another and as internally homogeneous, obscuring important differences.

A Critique of the Innovating Adhocracy Configuration

Another of the four configurations is the innovating adhocracy, as named by Miller (1986). This exists in an environment subject to high uncertainty, dynamism and growth. The required structure is organic, with an emphasis on expertise and flexible team-work. The innovating adhocracy is not coded as highly bureaucratic or standardized. As the name suggests, the description is of an organization not greatly characterized by formal structure. This seems valid as a description of a small hi-tech company with few employees.

However, some hi-tech companies are large in size with many employees. Like any organization of large size they require elaborate, extended hierarchy and extensive bureaucracy and standardization to administer large numbers of people (Weber, 1968). Quantitative studies show that large organizations in the hi-tech industries of electronics and pharmaceuticals are as bureaucratic as are organizations in low-tech industries such as confectionery (Child, 1973b). Qualitative case studies of large, hi-tech corporations reveal extensive, formalized systems for planning and for product development; for instance, the planning system at Texas Instruments and the new product development system at IBM (Corey and Star, 1971).

Organizations innovating products require organic structures among the jobs in contact with the task, such as designing a new computer, in contrast to the mechanistic systems of jobs close to the workflow in routine task systems, such as automobile assembly (Burns and Stalker, 1961; Woodward, 1965). But these differences between organic and mechanistic are very localized, reflecting the degree of uncertainty in the task being performed by that job or work unit. The overarching management structures of middle and senior management and staff functions such as accounting and personnel reflect the size of the corporation (Pugh et al., 1969a; Child, 1973b). Yet these bureaucratic aspects of large, innovatory organizations are absent from the innovatory adhocracy configuration. Thus the Millerian configuration framework fails to include the large, innovatory organization (Miller, 1986).

Innovatory organizations frequently show horizontal variations in their structure. Research and development units are organic in their internal structure; however, production or accounting departments are often more mechanistic (Lawrence and Lorsch, 1967). Once again, this reflects differences in the uncertainty of the task of each unit. The production departments of innovatory corporations are substantially mechanistic. Lawrence and Lorsch (1967) explicitly identified the internal heterogeneity – that is, differences in organizational structure from one department to another – in the innovatory firm by the term 'differentiation', noting that this is substantial for successful, innovatory firms. Thus while innovatory firms have some organic sections, to classify the whole firm as 'organic', as does Miller (1986), is too simplistic. In the large, innovatory organization there is the absence of a single organizing principle that provides internal consistency from one part to another. The notion of a configuration as a uniform structure whose effectiveness derives from uniformity is contradicted by research (Lawrence and Lorsch, 1967).

Thus Miller's concept of an innovatory adhocracy configuration has problems. There is no configuration of the large, innovatory corporation. Also, the configuration masks internal heterogeneity.

A Critique of the Machine Bureaucracy Configuration

The machine bureaucracy configuration (Miller, 1986) is a least-cost producer; however, the size required for a company to be a dominant, least-cost producer would surely vary by context. A machine bureaucracy viable in the automobile industry would be bigger than the dominant machine bureaucracy for dogs' collars. A dominant manufacturer in Australia is smaller than one in America (Capon et al., 1987). Thus the postulate that cost leaders need to be large and bureaucratic *relative to their competitors* does not lead to their all being of a singular machine bureaucracy type, equal in scale and bureaucracy level. Thus there would not be just one machine bureaucracy configuration, but rather a whole family of organizations, each large relative to its competitors, but differing in actual size across the family and therefore varying in degrees of bureaucratization of their organizational structure. The logic of the argument from low-cost production leads to recognition of situational factors of the particular industry and militates against the idea of one singular type or configuration.

Our discussion of three of the configurations (divisionalized conglomerate, innovating adhocracy and machine bureaucracy) has shown that they are not adequate. Each configuration has problems. In particular, each configuration seeks to impose uniformity on a whole set of related but differing sub-types. Overall, the four configurations fail to cover all the different types of viable business organizations. The four configurations considerably understate the range of viable strategy-structure combinations. They are too simplistic.

A Critique of General Arguments for Configurations

Miller (1986) advances three arguments in support of the general theory of organizational configurations. The first is that population-ecology theory states that there will be few viable strategies and structures in a particular environment. The second is that strategies and structures mutually reinforce each other to form a limited number of internally harmonious constellations of variables. The third argument is that organizational change is not incremental but rather quantum, organizations moving rapidly from one configuration to another. Each of the three component arguments will be examined in turn.

Lack of Basis in Population-ecology Theory

The first argument states that population-ecology theory tells us that there are few viable strategies and structures in a given environment (Miller, 1986). However, there is some doubt as to whether population-ecology theory does imply that there are so few viable strategies and structures and, more particularly, only four viable strategy–structure combinations. Population-ecology theory discusses abstract biological models and has been extended to postulate inertial phenomena in organizations (Hannan and Freeman, 1989). However, none of this implies four configurations. The heart of population-ecology is the idea of organizations needing to find a niche in the environment to support their continued existence or else suffer extinction (Hannan and Freeman, 1989). The concrete question is: how many niches are there in an environment as large and complex as, say, the US economy? Is it four, or 4,000? Two population ecologists, McKelvey and Aldrich (1983), argue that there are many different ecological niches in the American economy, such that each industry is a distinct niche; for instance, the airline industry is a niche within the transport industries, which is a set of niches. To be in fit each organization in that industry needs to develop the set of specific competences required by that niche. Hence there are many different fits. Thus population-ecology theory argues against the idea of just a few fits or configurations.

Thus the claim that configurations rest on population-ecology theory is open to question. Configuration theory cannot claim to have the backing of population-ecology theory. Thus the attempt at legitimation of configuration theory by seeking to borrow the authority of population ecology is herein rejected.

Problems with the Mutal Reinforcement Argument

The second argument in favour of configuration theory advanced by Miller (1986) is that organizational attributes mutually reinforce each other, resulting in the empirical configurations. Miller asserts that not only do contingencies cause structure, but structure causes increases in the contingency variables – in other words, there is reciprocal causation. Thus an initial increase in, say, the contingency variable leads to an increase in structure that feeds back, causing a further increase in contingency, so that the cycle repeats, driving the organization rapidly towards high levels of both contingency, and structure. This would be a way for an organization to make a quantum jump from, say, being low on size and bureaucracy (the simple structure configuration) to being high on both size and bureaucracy (the machine bureaucracy configuration). Thus reciprocal causation to produce explosive growth in contingency and structure is a mechanism that allows quantum jumps between configurations and is thus isomorphic with configuration theory.

In the area of strategy and structure, Miller (1986: 247) argues reciprocal causation in that diversification leads to divisionalization and divisionalization leads to diversification. However, empirical research has shown that diversification leads to divisionalization (Donaldson, 1987), but that divisionalization does *not* lead to diversification (Donaldson, 1982b). The causal connection between diversification and divisionalization is one way, *not* reciprocal. The diversification–divisionalization nexus is central to the strategy–structure configuration theory of Miller (1986). Accordingly, the lack of empirical support for reciprocal causation on this relationship should serve as a caution against assuming reciprocal causation in other relationships until they have been empirically confirmed.

Despite the theoretical isomorphism between configuration theory and reciprocal causation, there remains a problem with explosive growth. Organizations do not usually display explosive growth empirically. There is no sign in the economy that once firms grow a little in, say, size, they all continue growing unabated and all end up very large. Of those small organizations showing some initial growth, very few end up as giant corporations (Hannan et al., 1990). The mathematical structure of growth reveals considerable variation between organizations (Ijiri and Simon, 1977). Some companies persist for years with medium size and medium standardization.

The Lack of Quantum Jumps in Organizations

The third argument in favour of configuration theory by Miller is that organizational change is not incremental but quantum, a rapid shift from one configuration to another: 'piecemeal changes will often destroy the complementarities among many elements of configuration and will thus be avoided' (1986: 236). Miller (1986) cites evidence in favour of this view from his research (Miller and Friesen, 1980, 1982). However, published empirical evidence from other projects fails to support the quantum theory, and shows only incremental change.

Studies of strategy and structure show that for many corporations the adjustment of structure to changes in strategy – that is, divisionalization consequent upon diversification – takes decades (Channon, 1973; Rumelt, 1974; Dyas and Thanheiser, 1976; Donaldson, 1987). Similarly, firms do not rush towards machine bureaucracy from simple structure in quantum jumps. They typically grow incrementally in fits and starts, gradually climbing the scales of size and bureaucratization.

The postulate of quantum jumps holds that organizations make large jumps from one structure to another. This implies that, if structure is measured on a scale, the organization would move rapidly along that scale jumping from one structural value to a much greater or (much smaller) structural value. If organizational structure is not measured on a continuous scale, however, and is instead categorized into a few different types, or configurations, then there is no way of knowing how much difference there is between types. Hence an organization which shifts from one type to another could be said to be moving greatly, yet the magnitude of the change could not be verified. Thus, by using just types a plausible-sounding story could be constructed that every movement between two of the types was a quantum jump and a great structural change. However, empirical data of qualitative types do not allow empirical testing of the magnitude of structural movement. To test whether or not organizations make structural quantum jumps – that is, large changes in their structures in a short period – data of quantitative measures of organizational structure on the same organization at two or more points in time are required. Inkson et al. (1970) and Dewar and Hage (1978) present such diachronic data with quantitative structural scales.

Inkson et al. (1970) studied 14 diverse sorts of organizations in Birmingham, United Kingdom, over about a four-year period. Their data show a lack of change in the contingency variables (size, technology and dependence) and also in the structural scores: 'On the whole, the structural scores of the organization tended to be similar [to its score in the first study]' (1970: 322). Thus the overall pattern is of little change in either contingencies or structural variables over the four years, and not quantum jumps.

Let us look at their results more closely. The main structural scale was the structuring of activities scale; this represents the bureaucratic aspect of specialization and formalization (see Inkson et al., 1970). The structuring of activities scores mostly increased modestly over the period (1970: 322). In no case did the score double, though in one organization it increased greatly from 16 to 29. In one other organization the score increased from 10 to 16, and in another from 12 to 18. Thus there is only one organization which can be said to be changing structuring greatly over the period and two organizations which changed their structuring substantially. Thus only one out of the 14 organizations studied by Inkson et al. (1970) could even be considered as a candidate for the category of quantum jump in structuring. In the remaining 11 of the 14 organizations, the structuring changes were incremental, ranging from –6 per cent to +21 per cent only. Thus the organizations in this study were mostly changing structuring in an incremental way. The idea of the quantum jump fails the test of the empirical structuring data in the study of Inkson et al. (1970).

There is another way to look at such data. The quantum jump theory implies that sharp discontinuities would be present in data of structural change, as they are in quantum physics. An organization would either change or remain stationary – that is, make the quantum jump or not. Thus the rate of change of each organization would take only one of two possible values: zero or high. There would be no change scores at intermediary values – this is the essence of quantum theory. Thus the organizational structural change data would be bi-modal, with scores clustered at the zero and some high value, with no organizations in intermediary range. However, for the structuring change data in Inkson et al. (1970: 322), over the period of about four years, the 14 organizations showed the following distribution of percentage structuring changes: –6, 0, 3, 5, 6, 10, 14, 14, 16, 17, 21, 50, 60 and 81. This distribution is not bi-modal, clustering at zero and a single high value. The distribution is continuous, with organizations distributed at many different intermediary points between the highest and lowest values. The data fail to support the quantum jump model.

The study by Dewar and Hage (1978) examines 16 health and welfare organizations over two periods of about three years each. Two aspects of organizational structural differentiation were measured: horizontal and vertical differentiation (1978: 134). These kinds of structural scales, which are essentially single-item scales (1978: 134), are low in reliability and so structural change scores will be too unreliable. However, a third aspect of organizational structure was studied by Dewar and Hage (1978: 135), complexity, which is a count of the number of different occupational specialities which are present in each organization. This is measured by a 100-item scale (1978: 135), so the reliability would be expected to be high enough to allow examination of organizational structural change. The structural complexity data for the 16 organizations in the Dewar and Hage (1978) study, over the first three years, in percentages is: 0, 0, 0, 0, 0, 0, 0, 11, 14, 17, 17, 20, 26, 30, 59 and 66. This is not a bi-modal distribution. There is a mode at zero change, but no mode at the high end, and there are many organizations distributed at intermediate values between zero and the highest value. These data are not compatible with a quantum model.

Thus the examination of the evidence from the diachronic studies by Inkson et al. (1970) and by Dewar and Hage (1978) fails to support the theory that organizations make quantum jump changes in their structures. Most organizational structural change is incremental. In not one of the individual organizational structural changes which were reliable enough to be examined in these two studies was there a single case of an organization changing suddenly from the minimum value to the maximum value on the structural scale. Thus a consideration of evidence from empirical research which was conducted independent of the theory fails to support the quantum jump idea from configuration theory.

'Quantum' Divisionalization   Hoskisson and Galbraith (1985) have used the term 'quantum change' to distinguish those organizations which move rapidly and relatively completely from the functional to the multidivisional structure, and use the term 'incremental' to refer to slower, less complete divisionalization. While full, swift divisionalization is less incremental than slower, incomplete divisionalization, it is not truly quantum change. By measuring structure in a few categories or types, a complete move between types looks radical or quantum-like. However, if a fuller structural analytical framework were used, then the types of functional and multidivisional structures would be seen as two intermediary points on the more underlying structural dimensions such as centralization.

A divisionalized structure is only to *some degree* more decentralized than a functional structure (Chenhall, 1979). Thus the shift from functional to divisional only means a movement of some degree along the underlying centralization dimension. When a large corporation shifts from a functional to a divisional structure it is not a shift from zero to maximum decentralization. Over the life of the growing corporation, as it grew from small firm with a simple structure, to medium-sized functional firm, to large, functional corporation and then to large, diversified, divisionalized corporation, it would become progressively more decentralized at each step. Thus the decentralization changes would be gradual, each change being only incremental. And so the classification by Hoskisson and Galbraith (1985) of certain corporations as quantum structural change should not be seen as empirical support for the contention that organizational change is quantum-like, being either nil or a massive discontinuity.

Thus core aspects of the contingency–structure literature reveal structural change as incremental, not quantum. Size–structural differentiation (Dewar and Hage, 1978), size–bureaucracy (Inkson et al., 1970) and diversification-divisionalization (Rumelt, 1974) are not quantum change phenomena. Yet these relationships are central in the theory of configurations constructed by Miller (1986). Therefore the claim that organizational change is quantum, rather than incremental, is false.

The idea of a quantum change or jump is appealing, and the quantum idea and the quantum change phrase are in currency in organizational structural theory (Hoskisson and Galbraith, 1985). Doubtless this appeal is due in part to the way the name draws implicit authority from quantum theory in physics. However, the quantum theory of organizational structural change is unsupported by the data.

Most organizations, most of the time, are neither static nor changing greatly and rapidly. Yet quantum theory says these are the only possible two states. Most organizations most of the time are changing incrementally. Thus the idea of a quantum jump is empirically erroneous.

Hence all three arguments used by Miller (1986) to justify configuration theory are questionable. Configuration theory has no unique support from population-ecology theory and the existence of just four viable strategy–structure niches is undemonstrated; reciprocal causation, propelling organizations into the extreme polarities of the configuration is empirically unsupported; likewise, quantum change is not typical of several major contingency–structure relationships. Organizational change in structure is predominantly incremental.

The Distinction between Ideal-types and Types

A key issue is whether such typologies are ideal-types or empirical types. Weberian (1968) ideal-types are constructs, useful in comparing actual organization structures in their degrees of, say, traditionalism or bureaucracy. Ideal-types are extreme end-points of continua; they are poles of typologies. There may be no organizations actually at these end-points. Actual organizations are distributed along these continua. Ideal-types are not frequently found empirical types. Miller (1986), however, treats configurations as empirical types.

Miller offers justification of configuration theory by reference to the works of three theorists: Woodward (1965), Lawrence and Lorsch (1967) and Burns and Stalker (1961). Miller comments that 'all of [them] found integral structural configurations in their data' (1986: 237).

Burns and Stalker (1961: 122) use their concepts of organic and mechanistic as ideal-types; that is, polarities marking the ends of the structural continuum: 'the two forms of system represent a polarity, not a dichotomy; there are, as we have tried to show, intermediate stages between the extremities empirically known to us'. They did not argue that there are only two configurations that allow organizational effectiveness, an organic one and a mechanistic one; rather, effective organizational structures vary by degree according to the degree of technical and market change. Their conceptual framework deals with environment and structure as continua and the fit between the two is also a continuum varying across the range of environmental uncertainty (Burns and Stalker, 1961). Thus they are not offering discrete configurations in the manner of Miller (1986), but rather a contingency analysis expressed in continua (degree of environmental uncertainty requires a certain degree of organicness of structure).

Similarly, the thesis of Lawrence and Lorsch (1967) is expressed in concepts which are continua: environmental uncertainty, differentiation and integration. The three industries which they analyse (containers, processed food and plastics) happen to occur empirically at particular places on those continua, but they are not three configurations. They are not the only fits between environmental uncertainty and structure which are viable; rather, the three combinations are examples of a more general mode of analysis which, if applied to other industries, would yield other particular viable combinations of environmental uncertainty and structure (Lawrence and Lorsch, 1967).

Thus Burns and Stalker (1961) did not generate two configurations: organic and mechanistic. And Lawrence and Lorsch (1967) did not generate three configurations: container industry, processed food industry and the plastics industry. To make this interpretation is to reify the contributions of these authors; that is, to commit the fallacy of misplaced concreteness, mistaking an abstract type for a concrete thing. Burns and Stalker (1961) and Lawrence and Lorsch (1967) were offering contingency fit analysis which used concepts of contingencies and structure as continua. Later scholars who have sought to integrate these contributions with those of, say, size-bureaucracy theorists, have been forced to deal in multiple continua in multivariate models (for example, Khandwalla, 1977). Thus the configuration thesis is not a natural sequel to earlier structural research. Configuration theory is a particular and narrower formulation of rich multivariate concepts into a very limited number of discrete configurations.

Miller (1986: 237) goes on to note that there is 'considerable overlap between the structural and strategic typologies and taxonomies'. While this is true, it reflects the way different organization theorists all tend to draw from the same pool of ideas (Hickson, 1966; Lammers, 1981a, b). Thus it is the *ideas* that are few in number, not the types of organization.

Configurations versus Cartesianism

The idea that some combinations of strategy–structure are viable and others nonviable is common to many writers (Chandler, 1962; Khandwalla, 1977), including the present author (Donaldson, 1987). There are numerous contingency models of organization structure which postulate a fit between some contingency variable and some structural variable such that certain combinations lead to effective and some to ineffective organizations (Woodward, 1965; Lawrence and Lorsch, 1967; Thompson, 1967; Child, 1975). This idea of a fit is central to structural contingency theory (Drazin and Van de Ven, 1985) as it is to configuration theory. However, contingency research holds the view that contingency–structure fit relationships are a multivariate, multidimensional phenomenon. There are fits on several dimensions, and these can be combined in many ways yielding many different states of fit.

Thus organizations need to be analysed in terms of multiple variables which interact to form multiple fits. Most of the contingency factors are seen as variables, either continuous, such as size (that is, the number of employees) or as ordered categories such as diversification (single business, dominant business and so on). The underlying imagery is Cartesian: there are a number of continua and each organization is mapped by a series of coordinates into a particular location in an n-dimensional space. This Cartesian multivariatism in organization theory underlies many research programmes, for example, the Aston programme (Pugh et al., 1963, 1968, 1969a) and that of Hage and his colleagues (Hage, 1965; Hage and Aiken, 1967, 1969). Contingency factors such as size and diversity interact with structural factors such as specialization and divisionalization to produce a large number of fits.

Research shows that many aspects of organizations reveal differences of a continuous sort. Organizations vary in size continuously, the number of employees in organizations studied by researchers varies from a few dozen up to hundreds of thousands, with fine gradations in between: 500, 511, 520 and so on (Pugh et al., 1969a). Similarly, structural variables such as functional specialization, formalization and centralization have been studied in scales which make many finely graded differences (Pugh et al., 1968). Published tables and graphs document that organizations vary continuously on many context and structural variables and do not fall into a couple of discrete categories (Blau and Schoenherr, 1971; Child, 1973b).

Further, the fit between contingency and structure is also continuous, such as between size and functional specialization. The optimal degree of functional specialization varies continuously over the size range. There is a line of points of fit between size and functional specialization and between size and other aspects of organizational structure (see Child, 1975; Khandwalla, 1973). Thus the degree of specialization that fits an organization of 600 employees is a little greater than the degree of specialization that fits an organization of 550 employees, and so on. Reality is continuous and requires Cartesian, multidimensional coordinates. Organizations do not simply fall into two size categories of 'small' and 'large' and they are not either 'low' or 'extensive' in specialization. Yet these simple classifications are the building blocks used in the Millerian configurations of strategy–structure. This simple language and typology is not adequate for mapping organizational reality.

For example, a more adequate conceptual framework for discussing organization structure and innovation would distinguish several dimensions and use continua. The varying degree of uncertainty in each task gives rise to variations in degrees of organicness of structure (namely, loose role definitions, extent of lateral unscheduled communication and so on) between and within organizations (Burns and Stalker, 1961; Lawrence and Lorsch, 1967). The extent of hierarchy, bureaucratic structure and decentralization of authority vary with size (Pugh et al., 1969a; Child, 1973b; Miller, 1987; Blau, 1972). Thus both task uncertainty and size are continua requiring particular degrees of organicness and bureaucracy in the structural continua.

Therefore a multivariate framework is required; this will enable identification not just of large, noninnovatory organizations (machine bureaucracies) and small innovatory firms (innovating adhocracies), but also large innovatory firms, middle-sized innovatory firms, middle-sized, somewhat innovatory firms and so on. In short, the language becomes multidimensional and quantitative. The multivariate, contingency approach to organization structure has been evolving in this direction through theoretical and empirical work over the past two and a half decades (for example, Hall, 1963, 1977; Pugh et al., 1963, 1968, 1969a). There seems little point in abandoning this multivariate framework in favour of a too simplistic and confused set of configurations.

The Limited Complexity of Multivariatism

Miller (1986: 235) criticizes multivariate approaches as leading to too much complexity. Thus multivariate formulations have, in Miller's contention, the weakness of leading towards bewildering complexity so that coherent thinking is impaired and the analysis confuses more than clarifies. If valid, this is a damaging criticism indeed, for the aim of any research is to heighten understanding, and if research only creates confusion then the investigative work has been counter-productive.

The question is whether such potential complexity can be rendered more tractable. Can models be distilled of a limited number of causal paths between a limited number of variables? In the field of structural research there are signs of movement towards such a model.

The Aston programme produced some of the more complex research results between lists of variables. Yet the empirical results reveal that much of the complexity can be reduced because a few major factors of context and of structure can be abstracted from the morass of variables. It has been possible to capture much of the Aston programme results about bureaucratic structure in a few structural dimensions (structuring of activities and concentration of authority) and a few contextual dimensions (size and dependence) (Pugh et al., 1968, 1969a; Child, 1972b; Pugh and Hickson, 1976). This represents progress towards the establishment of Cartesian models of a few, underlying, independent dimensions of organizational structure and of contingencies (Pugh et al., 1968, 1969a; Child, 1972b; Pugh and Hickson, 1976). The Aston relationships have been distilled into relatively parsimonious models (Pugh et al., 1969a; Child, 1972b). Similarly the strategy–structure literature has been distilled into a small number of variables (diversification, vertical integration and divisionalization) and causal connections (Kotter et al., 1986; Donaldson, 1985).

As this process of study and distillation is repeated in other areas of the literature on organization research, these partial structural models can eventually be synthesized into a more complete model of organization structure. Such an overall model of organization structure is only moderately complex and not too complex for teaching or prescriptive use (for an example, see Child, 1984). The complexity of current multivariate structural research results presents a challenge to analysts to comprehend them and divine parsimonious, underlying theoretical models. Yet the task is not impossible and there are indications of a degree of progress towards that goal.

Nor do we believe that there is a ready alternative to continuing this programme. If phenomena inherently possess a degree of complexity, then their full comprehension may require a model of the same complexity (Beer, 1972). Certainly progress in medicine came only by identifying numerous diseases and the mechanisms and causes specific to each (Boorstin, 1983). Medicine was for a long time retarded by the simplistic theory that there are four humours of the body and that all disease is caused by their imbalance (Boorstin, 1983: 341).

Implications

The present chapter has documented the problems of configurations as a theoretical approach. As has been seen, configuration theory runs contrary to too much research to be valid.

For those seeking to build better theories of organization, typologies and configurations are inadequate. Progress comes in organizational structural research by mapping the degrees of variation between organizations and identifying the causal connections among variables. The Millerian simplifying configurations of strategy–structure are regressive intellectual moves in that, if influential, they lead to the replacement of more refined by less refined, less valid and less useful formulations.

Moreover, the point is not merely an academic one, for practical attempts at organizational design, diagnosis and prescription will falter if guided by configuration theory, as the framework is too simple to deal with the multiple forms and complexity of real organizations. For example, after diversifying, organizations will need to divisionalize and decentralize, but the exact form of divisional structure and degree of decentralization which are most appropriate depend on the degree of diversification. The structural requirements of related product diversification differ from those of unrelated product diversification (Pitts, 1976); geographic diversification requires different structures to product diversification (Channon, 1973). Yet the Millerian configurations allow for none of this fine gradation, asserting that larger organizations are either machine bureaucracies, innovating adhocracies or divisionalized conglomerates. This is too crude a set of categories to map the variations in structure already revealed by research. And those simple configurations are too crude to guide organizational design in large, complex organizations which are already typically somewhat divisionalized, decentralized to a degree, have some central functions but not others, have some standard procedures but not others, have some units which are organic and others which are mechanistic, and so on.

The configuration theory of organizational structural change is of quantum jumps. This is a dramatic imagery contradicted by empirical studies of organizational change. Through its use, academic discourse becomes over-dramatic and theatrical. Academics become less able to discuss with managers the reality of organizational change.

There is also reason to doubt that configuration models are useful in education. Few real organizations are simple structures or machine bureaucracies; almost all organizations lie somewhere in the middle. Students, be they MBA or executive, mostly come from organizations which have intermediary levels of size, standardization, organicness and so on. Managers are involved in managing change, usually of degree: some growth in size, a little more innovation, maturing of this product line but not that product line and so on. They need a framework on to which they can map their experience and which yields highly differentiated and gradated prescriptive advice. In configurations they find stark, but simplistic caricatures: simple structures, machine bureaucracy, innovating adhocracies. These models provide scant help.

Moreover, the simplicity of the configurations lends credence to a negative stereotype which some managers hold about management education – namely, that management professors only offer unrealistic 'theories' which are tricked out by gimmicks. Any realistic discussion of a manager's organization needs to move from the language of configurations to the underlying dimensional language of size, standardization, specialization, divisionalization, all expressed as matters of degree or quantities. Thus the substance of classroom discussion of organization structure and case analysis and prescription must use the multidimensional, multivariate contingency framework.

One further line of defence of the use of configuration theory might be that the concept will be used only in courses on business policy or corporate strategy – that is, capstone, synoptic courses in an MBA programme. Thus a person might say, 'All right, configurations are too simple to be acceptable to organization design specialists. But they're simple to understand and teach so they're OK in business policy courses which we all know are a gigantic simplification anyway and tend to be taught by generalists.' If organizational configurations are too simplistic to be useful in discussing organizational structure in courses such as organization design, it is hard to see how they become pertinent in a business policy course, especially if it is case based. Moreover, there is dubious educational merit in equipping students with precise frameworks early in the MBA course and then asking them to use a simplistic framework in the integrative course of their programme. Such a process pays scant regard to educational integrity or to the intellectual investments which students have been asked to make.

Business policy teachers will often be generalists and usually cannot be expected to be familiar with technical details of research in organization structure. Therefore they must be able to draw on synthetic, nontechnical models prepared by specialists in the organizational structure research field. Such synthetic models of multivariate, multidimensional strategy–structure fit relationships may be found in several sources (such as Kotter et al., 1986; Hage, 1980; Child, 1984; Donaldson, 1985). Syntheses of strategy–structure research, apart from the configurations framework, are available, and generalists might do well to avail themselves of these other contributions.

Configuration theory is a regressive concept for research, theory, teaching and prescribing. Moreover, there is a danger that despite the inherent shortcomings, configuration theory will come to be quite widely accepted. The very simplicity, which is its inadequacy, makes configuration theory easy to comprehend and transmit. Moreover, by drawing on widely accepted typologies, such as Mintzberg's (1979) typology of structure and Miles and Snow's (1978) typology of strategy, the acceptance of Miller's (1986) configuration theory is more likely as numerous people are already committed to component parts of the new theory. Thus the prospects for wide acceptance of configuration theory are quite promising. This increases the extent to which configuration theory endangers the rational analysis of strategy–structure relationships.

Our conclusion is that configuration theory in the field of strategy–structure relationships is a flawed approach. The continued existence of the present level of development of structural research, as well as future development of the subject, requires that configuration theory be rejected.

Conclusions

The five types of organizational structure offered by Mintzberg (1979), each based on a single coordination mode, are unhelpful. There is no need for an organization to contain only one coordination mode. As a result there are many more organizational fits than five. Similarly, there are considerably more viable strategy-structure combinations than the four configurations offered by Miller (1986). Moreover, viable strategy–structure combinations are not restricted to a few extreme polar types with no viable combinations in between. A synthesis of strategy–structure research has to recognize that fit can take continuous as well as discrete forms. Although previous researchers discern types, these are often ideal-types, analytic end-points of continua, not isolated polarities. Empirical research points to the organizational world as composed of variables and quantities interrelated multidimensionally, but with a degree of complexity which is intellectually manageable. While there may be some degree of reciprocal causation, this is theoretically unlikely to be strong, and empirical research supports the contention that at least some of the strategy–structure relationships are unidirectional. Organizational change is typically not quantum, but rather incremental. Although configuration theory is liable to enjoy popularity, the crudeness and lack of validity of the approach render configuration theory of little use in teaching, research or prescription. Thus configuration theory is a misconceived and regressive theoretical programme. It should be rejected in favour of persisting with the multivariate, Cartesian framework.

7

For Generalization in Positivist Organization Theory

Positivist organization theory holds that there are general relationships between contingency variables and organizational structure. A number of scholars have challenged this claim of generalization (McKelvey and Aldrich, 1983; Miller, 1986). In this chapter we counter these criticisms by showing that there are valid generalizations in positivist organization theory. The claims that general laws can be discovered and that major causes will be material factors are key parts of the positivist agenda in organization theory. We shall demonstrate that it is being fulfilled.

The relationships between contingency and organizational structure in structural contingency theory are presented as holding generally. Examples are the relationships between the contingency of strategy and the structure of divisionalization (Chandler, 1962; Rumelt, 1974), between size and bureaucratization (Child, 1973b) and between environmental uncertainty and organic structure (Burns and Stalker, 1961). Such relationships are seen in contingency theory as being highly general. All organizations everywhere are faced with the imperatives of these contingency factors and the need to adopt the structures that the contingency factors require. Hence the contingency–structure relationships are expected to hold across diverse settings of industry, nationality and so on. They are expected to be robust and not context- or situation-specific. However, this presumption of generalization has been challenged.

The Notion of Situational Moderators

Miller (1986: 235) rejects the idea that organizations can be understood by seeking to relate a contingency factor to a structural factor through a general relationship of the type of structural contingency theory. Instead, relationships are asserted to change radically depending upon context rather than generalizing across contexts:

> Statistical and real associations among variables are largely a function of the context in which they occur. . . . Relationships cannot, then, be divorced from their context. So the 'few variables at a time' alternative of relating strategy to structure would seem to be not only rather cumbersome and conceptually inelegant, but downright misleading as well. (Miller, 1986: 235)

Thus the approach of seeking general, bi-variate relationships between contingency and structure is eschewed by Miller as being inherently unsound.

The question is whether existing contingency theories understate the complexity of the relationships between contingency and organizational structure. Is the relationship between any one contingency and any one structural variable – for example, strategy and structure or size and bureaucracy – altered substantially from one context or situation to another? Is the relationship positive in one context or negative or nonexistent in another context so that a general statement such as 'strategy is positively related to structure' is false? If so, then generalization is undermined, for the only valid statements are limited to a specific context that must be identified – for example, 'strategy is positively related to structure only in America' or 'size is positively related to bureaucracy in manufacturing organizations but not in service organizations such as hospitals'. Thus the relationship between contingency and structure may be affected by a moderator variable, such as nationality or organizational type. Some suggest that some contingency–structure relationships are affected by multiple moderators, thus even more circumscribing their domain of validity (for instance, 'strategy leads to structure only in American manufacturing corporations'). This is the notion that contingency–structure relationships are themselves conditional upon still other contingencies – the view discussed earlier as 'hyper-contingency' (Bourgeois, 1984). By implication, the attempt by organization theorists from Weber (1968) onwards to offer general theories of organization is mistaken.

The Organizational Systematics Programme

McKelvey and Aldrich (1983) have argued against generalization across heterogeneous types of organization. They have asserted that this is an unwise and potentially fruitless endeavour, and suggest that a more illuminating approach to organization studies is to make studies of discrete homogeneous populations. Within such bounded populations, they argue, relationships will be uncovered which are specific to those populations. The resultant knowledge will take the form of a detailed taxonomy of different types of organizations with particular causal relationships in each. The approach of McKelvey and Aldrich (1983: 116) is termed 'organizational systematics'. This name will be used here to identify this school of thought. Freeman (1986), in an editorial essay in the *Administrative Science Quarterly*, provided authoritative support for this position and called for it to guide future research into organizations. The present discussion will draw out some implications of this position and consider its empirical validity.

Prior to the emergence of the organizational systematics approach, the approach to generalization was less cautious. Theorists such as Weber (1968) and Thompson (1967) asserted causal relationships (such as that between size and organization structure or uncertainty and organization structure) which were held to be general across organizations of different type, nation-

ality and other aspects of context. This led to attempts at empirical valida-
tions of such general theories, through samples of organizations. Some of the
classic attempts at empirical testing utilized samples of manufacturing organizations drawn from many industries (for example, Woodward, 1965) or even
of diverse work organizations, including manufacturing, retail and governmental organizations (Pugh et al., 1969a). The implicit justification for such
heterogeneous sampling is that the relationships under examination, such as
those connecting size or technology and structure, generalize across manufacturing industries and even across organizations of all types. They reflect a
belief in a general theory of organizations.

The generalization view has been challenged sharply by McKelvey and
Aldrich (1983). They argue that many important relationships are liable to be
specific to particular industries because of the unique environmental pressures shaping the survival requirements for, say, the airline industry as
opposed to the construction industry. Thus the more rewarding scientific
procedure is the study of homogeneous populations. This will allow us to
ascertain the relationships peculiar to each. From the comparison of the
results of such studies will emerge knowledge of which relationships differ
across certain populations and which relationships are common. Thus a
meaningful taxonomy of organizations can emerge which will reflect actual
similarities and differences in organizational relationships. This is to take the
form of a phylogenetic tree, as in biology. At its base will be the characteristics common across all organizations. As the taxonomy moves up the
phylogenetic tree, so the trunk divides and divides again into the classes and
sub-classes of organizations each of which shares certain common relationships, ultimately producing a finely differentiated taxonomy.

The programmatic implications of this position are daunting. Extensive
data collection, analysis and theory construction are required in each industry. Moreover, the boundaries of homogeneous populations are cast quite
narrowly. Thus knowledge creation will need massive human and financial
resources. Even if such resources are forthcoming for organizational research,
the process of study and eventual taxonomic synthesis is liable to take time.
The protagonists of the organizational systemics approach would argue that
no less a programme will be adequate to the task of knowledge creation.
However, for other scholars this sounds a pessimistic programmatic. The
returns on research investment in organization studies under such a scenario
may well make this enterprise look less inviting to sponsors than other areas
of social or natural scientific research whose programmatic statements offer
more hope about the prospects for generalization.

A further disconcerting element about the organizational systemics
approach is the implied escalation in the complexity of knowledge. Thirty
years ago the topic of organization design was conceived as composed of the
universally applicable, 'one best way' organization structures of the Classical
School of Management (Brech, 1957). In the 1960s this was disavowed by the
contingency approach, which argued that structures were contingent upon
their size, technology and uncertainty (Woodward, 1965; Pugh et al., 1969a;

Lawrence and Lorsch, 1967). The organizational systemics approach asserts that these contingency–structure relationships only hold in certain situations. Thus it is a contingency of contingencies or hyper-contingency approach. If contingency relationships are indeed contingent, then this is important knowledge and the organizational systemics approach will reveal such. However, unless the approach is a genuine advance in knowledge, complexity piled upon complexity is to be avoided. The parsimony preference in science states that theoretical frameworks should be no more complex than necessary.

The social reality facing organization studies, like all other curricula in schools of administration, is that there is considerable and perhaps mounting scepticism about the utility of the academic enterprise for students in educational programmes. There is a considerable popular groundswell of opinion in favour of getting back to basics (Peters and Waterman, 1982). Organizational scholars find much of this to be of dubious validity. However, if such movements are to be countered they require a clear articulation of the need for complex formulations and of the precise degree of complexity required. This again argues that the complexity implied by the organizational systemics approach deserves careful scrutiny.

There is further difficulty with the organizational systemics approach. There seems to be no way of stipulating a priori which relationships will hold in which populations. Moreover, there is no way of defining a priori the boundaries of a population. This is the reason for the preference for conducting studies in narrowly homogeneous populations and then discovering which populations are kindred and can be treated together as validly common. The process is inductive, emergent and grounded. This points to the atheoretical nature of the enterprise. Moderator variables are to be uncovered empirically, not deduced from theory (McKelvey and Aldrich, 1983).

Critique of Organizational Systematics

McKelvey and Aldrich (1983) illustrate their argument about the need for caution in generalizing, by arguing that one of the propositions of Blau (1970) needs to be moderated. They argue that the relationship between work volume and employee numbers asserted by Blau (1970) will be stronger in labour-intensive than in capital-intensive industries. This is indisputable. However, this conditional statement clearly flows from the logic of the general relationship itself. It is an example of general theory suggesting moderators. The process is one of deduction from a general idea, as will now be shown.

Capital and labour are jointly required to produce output. A labour-intensive industry is, by definition, an industry with a high ratio of labour to capital. Labour can be measured by the number of employees. If the industry is labour-intensive then, by definition, many more employees are needed to increase output than are needed in a capital-intensive industry to achieve the same increase in output. Work volume is the same concept as output. Thus, by definition, the relationship between work volume and employee numbers is stronger in labour-intensive than in capital-intensive industries. In capital-intensive industries the same increase in work volume can be achieved by adding fewer new employees because much of the work is performed by machines (namely, capital). Thus the strength of the relationship between work volume and employee numbers is greater for labour-intensive than for capital-intensive industries. The moderator idea here follows directly from the concepts and their definitions. It has not been generated inductively or emergently through considering homogeneous populations which each vary in their degree of capital intensity. Thus the McKelvey and Aldrich (1983) example of a moderator itself illustrates the way general relationships exist between organizational variables and the discovery of such relationships through a priori theoretical analysis rather than emerging through empirical search.

The foregoing are a series of reservations about the organizational systemics approach. It seems to lead to a slow, expensive, atheoretical programme which is justified by reference to the inherent complexity of the knowledge which will eventually be uncovered. But the complexity of knowledge is presumed a priori. The acid test of the organizational systemics as opposed to the general theory approach is whether empirical results to date point towards one or other as the more accurate reflection of organizational reality. Is there evidence supporting the claims of generality in organizational relationships or are relationships situationally specific? What does a quarter of a century of contingency research on organization structure have to say about generality?

The contention of this chapter is that research already conducted points unequivocally to the validity of generalization in contingency–structure relationships. A number of relationships between contingency and structure generalize across industries and across nations and other settings.

McKelvey and Aldrich (1983) point out that certain samples in structural contingency research, such as the Aston study (Pugh et al., 1969a), are heterogeneous. The samples are composed of different sorts of organizations (for example, manufacturing and service) from a diverse set of industries (Pugh et al., 1969a). McKelvey and Aldrich (1983) argue that the contingency–structure relationships found in such heterogeneous samples have not been demonstrated to hold in each separate industry. Whereas certain early research employed samples which mix across different manufacturing industries or diverse organizational types (Pugh et al., 1969a), later research has studied much more homogeneous samples of one industry (for instance, Donaldson and Warner, 1974a) or reported results analysed into industries (Child, 1973b). The following review will use these homogeneous studies to compare results across industries for studies of the same concept or aspect of organization structure.

Further, McKelvey and Aldrich (1983) note the research programme by Blau and his colleagues across samples of different types of organizations. However, they criticize the universal claims of the theory constructed from these empirical results, and state that the generalizations are really valid only for the organizational types actually studied. In any empirical science, a claim for general validity can never mean more than that the relationship has been replicated in a certain finite number of settings. The possibility always remains that a further sample or experiment may fail to replicate. Thus all claims to generalization are in some sense tentative (Popper, 1945). However, a relationship which has generalized to many settings, even if it does not subsequently generalize to all contexts, and is thus a limited or conditional generalization, is still an important piece of scientific knowledge. It constitutes a simple building block from which a more elaborate theory can be subsequently constructed. Thus, even allowing for the ultimately tentative nature of all scientific generalizations, generalization deserves encouragement, not castigation.

The Generality of Structural Contingency Theory

We will now make the argument for the generality of structural contingency theory by reviewing the evidence on a number of contingency-structure relationships and showing that they generalize. The review will focus on relationships studied in three areas: the research of Blau and his colleagues, the Aston programme and strategy–structure research. In each case there have been a wide set of studies allowing a test of generalization. We will examine in detail five contingency–structure relationships: size–vertical structural differentiation, size–functional specialization, size–standardization, size–formalization and strategy–divisionalization.

Generalization in the Blau Research

In the case of Blau and his colleagues, a number of their propositions have received support for their generality. Indeed, it is not apparent that research has yet discovered any settings in which certain relationships fail to hold. Thus at least some of the generalizations of Blau and his colleagues appear to have attained substantial generality. For instance, Blau (1970) argues that increasing organizational size leads to increasing structural differentiation along all dimensions of differentiation.

Vertical Structural Differentiation   Considering the vertical aspect of structural differentiation – that is, the number of levels in the hierarchy – general theory states that size and number of levels will be positively related (Blau, 1970). Blau and Schoenherr (1971) demonstrate that this size–hierarchy relationship generalizes across all the functional departments (for example, employment services, unemployment insurance) in the governmental employment security agency. As McKelvey and Aldrich (1983) grant, Blau (1972) further shows that this relationship generalizes to local branches of the employment security agencies, to city finance departments, department stores and universities. The relationship is also found in teaching hospitals (Blau, 1972). Other studies show that this same relationship holds in life insurance, labour unions, electrical engineering manufacturers, churches, savings and loans, health and welfare, federal government departments and commercial banks (Agarwal, 1979; Donaldson and Warner, 1974a; Grinyer and Yasai-Ardekani, 1981; Hinings et al., 1976, in Aston databank; Armandi and Mills, 1982; Dewar and Hage, 1978; Beyer and Trice, 1979; Wong and Birnbaum-More, 1994, respectively). Thus studies of homogeneous samples of organizations of one type or from one industry all find a positive relationship between size and hierarchy.

There are other studies that are of heterogeneous samples of diverse manufacturing organizations (Blau et al., 1976; Hickson et al., 1979; Reimann, 1973; Ayoubi, 1981; Marsh and Mannari, 1981; Hinings and Lee, 1971) or of a mixture of manufacturing and service organizations (Pugh and Hickson, 1976; Child, 1973b; Lincoln et al., 1981; Conaty et al., 1983); they also all find a positive relationship between size and hierarchy. This means that the relationship must hold in most of the settings which compose each study sample, otherwise the correlation in the total sample would not be positive. It argues against there being some large set of industries or types of organization where this relationship is negative or does not hold. Thus the study of a sample of heterogeneous organizations does not seem to lead to results different from the homogeneous samples. The method of studying heterogeneous samples is not erroneous.

In summary, out of 31 studies of the size–hierarchy relationship, all studies find a positive association (Donaldson and Robertson, 1986), as does a subsequent study (Wong and Birnbaum-More, 1994).

In a widely received critique of Blau's theory of structural differentiation and the associated empirical evidence, Argyris (1972) stated that the findings of Blau and Schoenherr (1971) reflected nothing more than the civil service regulations governing formal organizational structure. Because the organizations studied in Blau and Schoenherr (1971) are governmental organizations, employment security agencies and finance departments, they may well be subject to any civil service regulations regarding formal organizational structure. However, the positive relationship between size and vertical differentiation which was found in the studies of governmental organizations in Blau and Schoenherr (1971) is found also in studies of organizations outside the US government, and therefore is not dependent upon US civil service regulations. These include manufacturing organizations in the US (Reimann, 1977), business firms in the United Kingdom (Child, 1973b), labour unions in the United Kingdom (Donaldson and Warner, 1974a), electrical engineering manufacturers in the United Kingdom (Grinyer and Yasai-Ardekani, 1981), churches in the United Kingdom (Hinings et al., 1976, in Aston databank), manufacturing organizations in Germany (Child and Kieser, 1979), manufacturing organizations in Jordan (Ayoubi, 1981), manufacturing organizations in India (Shenoy, 1981) and manufacturing organizations in Poland (Kuc et al., 1981). Thus the positive connection between size and vertical differentiation is not caused by the US civil service regulations in those many organizations which show this pattern and which are not subject to these regulations. Accordingly, it is less likely that US civil service regulations are the cause of this relationship within the US government organizations studied by Blau and Schoenherr (1971). Thus the criticism of Argyris (1972) is contradicted by the evidence.

The relationship between size and vertical differentiation is not a result of some localized, idiosyncratic regulations; it is a genuine generalization reflecting a fundamental property of structures, and is a causal law. Increasing the number of people in an organization leads to an increase in the number of levels of the hierarchy because of the span of control limit at any one level in the hierarchy, and thus size leads to vertical differentiation (Blau, 1970).

Generalization in the Aston Research

The Theory of Size and Bureaucracy   Proponents of general theories of organization structure include those who have asserted the universality of bureaucratization. Weber (1968) argued that the bureaucratic structure of organizations is the solution to the problem of the effective administration of large numbers of people. Subsequent theorists such as Blau (1972) and Child (1973b) have offered formal models of the growth of structure in response to growth in size. In both cases they argue that increasing size leads to an increasing use of rules and documents to provide impersonal control of employees. Further, Child (1973b) posits that the degree of specialization by function increases with greater size. Thus, taken together, these theories of bureaucracy postulate that an increase in size leads (in terms of the Aston measures) to an increase in functional specialization (degree of administrative role specialization), overall standardization (extent of rules and procedures) and overall formalization (extent of documentation); for details of conceptual and operational definitions and origins, see Pugh and Hickson, 1976. The theory that size leads to bureaucratization implies that there will be positive correlations between size and each of these aspects of bureaucracy. A consistent set of correlations between size and each of these bureaucratic structural variables (functional specialization, standardization and formalization) would argue for generalization and against the organizational systematics approach.

Our review will consider the results from empirical studies of the relationships between organizational size and each of the three structural variables: functional specialization, overall standardization and overall formalization (for details of Aston scales, see Pugh et al., 1968). We will include in the review only those studies that use the full or long-form scales, as these are more reliable than the short-form scales and more conceptually comprehensive (Inkson et al., 1970). The studies are from both the published and unpublished literature, including studies held in the Aston databank (Richards, 1980). An earlier review by Miller (1987) found that the relationship between size and each of functional specialization and formalization enjoyed consistent support from empirical studies. The Miller (1987) review included studies using the short-form scales, but these will be excluded here since they are not so directly comparable. An earlier review by Donaldson (1986) also found that the relationship between size and each of functional specialization, standardization and formalization enjoyed consistent support from empirical studies. The review here will draw on a wider set of studies than the two earlier reviews (Donaldson, 1986; Miller, 1987), including later studies.

Size and Functional Specialization   The Aston scale of functional specialization measures the degree to which there is a division of labour in administration with organizational roles dealing with each facet of administration separately (see Pugh et al., 1963). General theory connects organizational size positively with the Aston concept of the degree of functional specialization (Blau, 1970; Child, 1973b).

Child (1973b) found this positive relationship between size and functional specialization in his study which mixes firms from manufacturing and service industries. However, he shows that this positive relationship is found also in the homogeneous sub-samples of each industry: pharmaceuticals, electronics, chocolates-and-confectionery, newspapers, advertising and insurance (1973b). Thus combining these organizations into a total sample of heterogeneous industries is not invalid, for the relationship holds in each industry.

The positive relationship between size and functional specialization has also been found in homogeneous studies of each of labour unions, electrical engineering manufacturers, textile firms, churches, community colleges, colleges, local government, hospitals and commercial banks (Donaldson and Warner, 1974a; Grinyer and Yasai-Ardekani, 1981; Clark, 1990; Hinings et al., 1976; Heron, unpublished, in Aston databank; Greenwood and Hinings, 1976; Glueck, unpublished, in Aston databank; Tauber, 1968; Wong and Birnbaum-More, 1994, respectively). Also the relationship has been found in numerous studies of samples of diverse manufacturing organizations (Hinings and Lee, 1971; Bryman et al., 1983; Child and Kieser, 1979; Hickson et al., 1974; Ayoubi, 1981; Zeffane, 1989; Shenoy, 1981; Reimann, 1977; Kuc et al., 1981; Azumi and McMillan, 1981; Payne and Mansfield, 1973; Blau et al., 1976) and in several studies which mix manufacturing and service organizations (Pugh and Hickson, 1976; Badran and Hinings, 1981; Conaty et al., 1983).

There are 40 studies of the relationship between size and functional specialization, and these are listed in Table 7.1. Every study finds a positive relationship between size and functional specialization (see Table 7.1). Twenty-five of the studies were of manufacturing organizations, eight of the studies were of service organizations and seven of the studies were of a mixture of manufacturing and service organizations. The positive relationship holds both in studies of manufacturing organizations and in studies of service organizations (see Table 7.1).

The studies were conducted in 16 different countries: Algeria, Canada, Egypt, Finland, France, Germany, Hong Kong, India, Iran, Japan, Jordan, Poland, Singapore, Sweden, the United Kingdom and the United States. The relationship between size and functional specialization generalizes across these 40 empirical studies, with their diverse organizational types and national settings.

Table 7.1 *Generality of size and functional specialization relationship*

Study*	Country	r	n
Manufacturing organizations			
Hinings and Lee (1971)	UK	.92	9
McMillan[†]	UK	.90	12
Pheysey[†]	UK	.86	10
Grinyer & Yasai-Ardekani (1981)	UK	.86	45
Child & Kieser (1979)	Germany	.83	51
Hickson et al. (1974)	USA	.82	21
Routamaa (1985)	Finland	.81	122
Hickson et al. (1974)	UK	.79	25
Ayoubi (1981)	Jordan	.78	34
Zeffane (1989)	France	.77	61
Zeffane (1989)	UK	.73	70
Shenoy (1981)	India	.73	35
Reimann (1977)	USA	.70	20
Clark (1990)	Canada	.70	47
Kuc et al. (1981)	Poland	.67	11
Tai (1987)	Singapore	.67	30
Tayeb (1987)	India	.66	7
Tayeb (1987)	UK	.56	7
Zeffane (1989)	Algeria	.50	50
Hickson et al. (1974)	Canada	.49	24
Azumi & McMillan (1981)	Japan	.42	51
Payne & Mansfield (1973)	UK	.34	14
Marsh and Mannari (1981)	Japan	.29	50
Horvath et al. (1981)	Sweden	.28	14
Blau et al. (1976)	USA	.25	110
Mixed: manufacturing and service organizations			
Bryman et al. (1983)	UK	.77	71
Aston (Pugh and Hickson, 1976)	UK	.67	46
National (Child & Mansfield, 1972)	UK	.61	82
Mansfield et al. (1980)**	UK	.55	78
Badran and Hinings (1981)	Egypt	.53	31
Conaty et al. (1983)	Iran	.47	64
Conaty et al. (1983)	USA	.36	65
Service organizations			
Community colleges (Heron[†])	Canada	.84	77
Churches (Hinings et al., 1976)	UK	.79	7
Labour unions (Donaldson & Warner, 1974a)	UK	.73	7
Commercial banks (Wong & Birnbaum-More, 1994)	Hong Kong	.62	39
Local government (Greenwood & Hinings, 1976)	UK	.59	84
Colleges (Holdaway et al., 1975)	Canada	.56	23
Hospitals (Glueck[†])	UK	.46	11
General and mental hospitals (Tauber, 1968)	UK	.41	6

Notes:
Size is transformed logarithmically for all studies except the three by Zeffane and the one by Tai (unknown for Shenoy); all logarithmic transformations are to base 10 except for studies by Routamaa, Marsh and Mannari and Wong and Birnbaum-More that use natural logarithms.
* See Bibliography for full citation of studies.
† Source is Aston databank.
**Revised scale fewer items, probably less reliable.
Information from published studies is occasionally supplemented from Aston databank.

Size and Standardization   Another Aston concept of structure is overall standardization, the extent of rules, standard procedures and organizational measurement practices (Pugh et al., 1968). General theory again relates organizational size and overall standardization positively (Child, 1973b).

This relationship between size and overall standardization has been found in each setting of advertising, chocolate-and-confectionery, daily newspapers, electronics, insurance, pharmaceuticals in the study by Child (1973b). It was also found in homogeneous studies of textile manufacturing, labour union and local governmental organizations (Clark, 1990; Donaldson and Warner, 1974a; Greenwood and Hinings, 1976; respectively). It was also found in samples of diverse manufacturing organizations (Hinings and Lee, 1971; Ayoubi, 1981) and in a mixed manufacturing and service organization sample (Pugh and Hickson, 1976). Again, no study reviewed has identified an industry in which the relationship is negative (Donaldson, 1986).

The review yielded six studies which gave the correlation between size and the overall standardization scale (Pugh et al., 1968), as shown in Table 7.2. The correlations between size and standardization were all positive. The organizational types studied span manufacturing firms (Hinings and Lee, 1971), local government organizations (Greenwood and Hinings, 1976) and labour unions (Donaldson and Warner, 1974a). The positive relationship holds both in studies of manufacturing organizations and in studies of service organizations (see Table 7.2). The studies cover only two countries, but include both a Western country (the United Kingdom) and a mid-eastern country (Jordan). The size–standardization relationship generalizes consistently across all studies and settings.

Table 7.2   *Generality of size and overall standardization relationship*

Study*	Country	r	n
Manufacturing organizations			
Hinings & Lee (1971)	UK	.94	9
Ayoubi (1981)†	Jordan	.57	34
Mixed: manufacturing and service organizations			
National (Child & Mansfield, 1972)	UK	.63	82
Aston (Pugh et al., 1969a)	UK	.56	46
Service organizations			
Labour unions (Donaldson & Warner, 1974a)	UK	.82	7
Local government (Greenwood & Hinings, 1976)	UK	.34	84

Notes:
Size expressed as a logarithm, unknown for Greenwood and Hinings.
* See Bibliography for full citation of studies.
† Revised scale, fewer items, probably less reliable.

Size and Formalization A further aspect of organizational structure is the degree of formalization. In Aston terms, formalization is the extent to which the organizational structure seeks to guide and regulate employee behaviour through written job definitions, manuals of procedure, written communications and written records of role performance (Pugh et al., 1968). Again theory states that there is a positive and general relationship between size and overall formalization (Child, 1973b).

The positive relationship between size and overall formalization is found in each setting of advertising, chocolate-and-confectionery, daily newspapers, electronics, insurance and pharmaceuticals (Child, 1973b). It is also found in homogeneous studies of textile manufacturers, community colleges, labour unions, colleges, government treasury departments, sanitation departments, educational and bank organizations (Clark, 1990; Heron, unpublished; Donaldson and Warner, 1974a; Mannheim and Moskovits, 1979; Wong and Birnbaum-More, 1994, respectively). It is also found in samples of diverse manufacturing organizations (Hinings and Lee, 1971; Ayoubi, 1981; Kuc et al., 1981; Azumi and McMillan, 1981; Shenoy, 1981) and in a sample of mixed manufacturing and service organizations (Pugh and Hickson, 1976).

There were 19 studies which gave the correlation between size and overall formalization (see Table 7.3). The studies ranged from manufacturing firms (Kuc et al., 1981) to commercial banks (Wong and Birnbaum-More, 1994) to community colleges (Heron, unpublished) to governmental treasuries (Mannheim and Moskovits, 1979). There were seven studies of manufacturing organizations, ten studies of service organizations and two studies of mixed organizations (see Table 7.3). The studies covered nine countries: Canada, Hong Kong, India, Israel, Japan, Jordan, Poland, Sweden and the United Kingdom. A positive correlation was found in 18 out of the 19 studies.

A negative relationship between size and overall formalization is found in only one study, that of Israeli welfare organizations (Mannheim and Moskovits, 1979). However, the other four types of Israeli organizations studied by Mannheim and Moskovits (1979) all produced a positive correlation, including studies of governmental organizations – for example, education (see Table 7.3). Thus the size–formalization relationship holds in many other Israeli organizations and so Israel is not a general exception. The sample size (n = 15) is small in the study of Israeli welfare organizations (Mannheim and Moskovits, 1979). Therefore the confidence intervals for the Israeli welfare correlation are –54 to +.48; this range includes the average correlation for the remaining service organizations, r = +.45. Thus the Israeli welfare result was not significantly different from the general pattern. It is an anomaly caused by small sample size. The result is consistent with the general, positive relationship. Given this re-interpretation of the single deviant finding, the association between size and formalization should be viewed as positive and consistent for all the 19 studies.

Summary of Size and Bureaucracy The review of studies reveals that for size–specialization and size–standardization, all the studies consistently

Table 7.3 *Generality of size and overall formalization relationship*

Study*	Country	r	n
Manufacturing organizations			
Hinings & Lee (1971)	UK	.92	9
Ayoubi (1981)**	Jordan	.73	34
Horvath et al. (1981)	Sweden	.68	11
Azumi & McMillan (1981)	Japan	.53	50
Shenoy (1981)†	India	.28	35
Kuc et al. (1981)	Poland	.26	11
Marsh and Mannari (1981)	Japan	.23	50
Service organizations			
Community colleges (Heron)††	Canada	.81	77
Labour unions (Donaldson & Warner, 1974a)	UK	.70	7
Education (Mannheim & Moskovits, 1979)†	Israel	.63	15
Treasuries (Mannheim & Moskovits, 1979)†	Israel	.59	15
Sanitation (Mannheim & Moskovits, 1979)†	Israel	.51	15
Colleges (Holdaway et al., 1976)†	Canada	.43	23
Commercial banks (Wong & Birnbaum-More, 1994)	Hong Kong	.25	39
Local government (Greenwood & Hinings, 1976)†	UK	.13	84
Banks (Mannheim & Moskovits, 1979)†	Israel	.09	19
Welfare (Mannheim & Moskovits, 1979)†	Israel	-.04	15
Mixed: manufacturing and service organizations			
National (Child & Mansfield, 1972)	UK	.58	82
Aston (Pugh et al., 1969a)	UK	.55	46

Notes:
Size is transformed logarithmically unless mentioned below.
* See Bibliography for full citation of studies.
† Study does not report whether size logarithmically transformed.
** Revised scale fewer items, probably less reliable.
†† Source is Aston databank.

showed positive correlations. The review of the studies of size–formalization shows that all except one study found the theoretically expected correlation. The anomalous study for size–formalization was shown to be consistent with the theoretically expected findings. Thus the relationship between size and three major aspects of bureaucratic structure (functional specialization, standardization and formalization) generalizes.

The foregoing examines some fairly central relationships within the neo-Weberian programmatic of a general theory connecting size and bureaucracy (Weber, 1968; Blau, 1970; Child, 1973b). Some empirical studies, although they are based upon reviews which attempt to be comprehensive, may have been omitted unwittingly and some of these may contain deviant findings. However, enough evidence has accumulated to indicate support for generalization across many different industries and types of organization. These results argue against the idea that generalization cannot be established and that the approach of the organizational systematics is required.

Having established the generality of the relationship between size and bureaucratic structure, let us now turn to another aspect of organizational structure – namely, divisionalization – and review its relationship with the contingency factor of strategy.

Generalization in the Strategy-Structure Research

Whereas the above section has reviewed studies which have considered the neo-Weberian analyses of organization structure, in this section we turn to a second major stream of organization structure studies, those that have flowed from the work of Chandler on divisionalization. In his seminal writing, Chandler (1962) argued that the adoption of the divisional form of organization structure was prompted by the strategic diversification of the corporation. A number of empirical studies have been conducted to assess the extent to which the shift from a functional to a divisional structure is related to strategy – namely, degree of diversification. In this section these studies will be reviewed to examine the consistency of their findings and thus to establish the generality of the relationships between strategy and divisionalization. Because empirical studies have been conducted in several advanced industrial countries – Australia, France, Germany, Japan and New Zealand as well as in the United States and United Kingdom – the generality of these relationships beyond the Anglo-American traditional centres of management can be tested. In this way we can check whether there is any Atlantic ethnocentrism in the theories of divisionalization.

This branch of the organization structure literature is concerned with the organization structure of the apex of a business corporation. A functional structure is one where the major sub-units of the corporation are each specialized functions, such as manufacturing, marketing, research and so on, each of which reports directly to top management; that is, the head of each function reports directly to the CEO. The CEO has to coordinate the functions, and the profit centre is the entire business firm. The functional form is a centralized structure in terms of decision-making authority relative to the multidivisional form (Chenhall, 1979). In the multidivisional structure the major sub-units of the business corporations are divisions, each of which is self-contained to a degree, having their own functions of manufacturing, marketing, research and so on. Each division is usually a separate profit centre. The head of a division coordinates the functions within their division. Each divisional head reports directly to the corporate office – that is, to the CEO and their staff. The corporate level has limited involvement in operational decision-making, which is taken, to a degree, autonomously by each division. Thus the multidivisional structure (or divisional for short) is more decentralized than the functional structure.

In the theory of Chandler (1962), divisionalization connects with the strategy contingency, in that although a functional structure is adequate to manage a simple, undiversified company, diversification into several products or areas produces greater complexity of the managerial task and requires a decentralized, divisionalized structure for effective operations, in order to simplify the coordination around each separate product or area. Thus strategy leads to structure.

In order to ensure comparability, the analysis is restricted to studies which use similar definitions of the variables (strategy and divisionalization) and provide a quantitative assessment of the degree of association between strategy and divisional structure. There were eight studies and they covered seven countries: Australia (Chenhall, 1979), France, Germany (Dyas and Thanheiser, 1976), Japan (Suzuki, 1980), New Zealand (Hamilton and Shergill, 1993) and the United States (Rumelt, 1974), and two studies of the United Kingdom (Channon, 1973; Grinyer and Yasai-Ardekani, 1981).

A number of other studies also provide assessments of the associations between these variables. For example, in addition to Rumelt (1974) there are other studies of the largest US corporations (Palmer et al., 1987; Mahoney, 1992), and in addition to Channon (1973) there are other studies of large UK corporations (Grinyer et al., 1980; Hill and Pickering, 1986). However, there is a degree of overlap between the corporations in these studies and those already included in the studies in our analysis, so these latter studies were excluded to avoid double-counting (which would produce a spurious impression of consistency). In the case of the United Kingdom, the study by Channon (1973) is of large corporations, whereas the study by Grinyer and Yasai-Ardekani (1981) is of small and medium-sized companies and so the companies are different and hence both studies are included. The objective of the present enquiry is to test for generality across countries and so the key is to have a study from every country possible while avoiding duplication.

The correlation between diversification strategy and divisionalization for each of the eight studies is shown in Table 7.4. The study correlations between strategy and structure were all positive. This is consistent with the theory of Chandler (1962). The relationship generalizes across countries, including not only the United Kingdom and the United States but also continental Europe (France and Germany), Asia (Japan) and Oceania (Australia and New Zealand). It generalizes across studies of large corporations (Rumelt, 1974) and medium-sized corporations (Grinyer and Yasai-Ardekani, 1981; Hamilton and Shergill, 1993).

Summary of Reviews

We have reviewed empirical studies of core relationships from the theoretical traditions aligned with Blau, Weber and Chandler. The relationships generalize for each of size–vertical differentiation, size–functional specialization, size–standardization, size–formalization and strategy–divisionalization. In each case, the correlations from the studies were shown to be overwhelmingly consistent with the theoretically expected general pattern. Thus all the contingency–structure relationships examined here generalize. Each holds despite the different types of organizations and their being drawn from around the globe.

Table 7.4   *Generality of the relationship between strategy[a] and divisionalization[b]*

Study*	Country	n	r
Dyas & Thanheiser (1976)	Germany	52	.80
Hamilton & Shergill (1993)	NZ	91	.68
Dyas & Thanheiser (1976)	France	47	.53
Chenhall (1979)	Australia	218	.52
Grinyer & Yasai-Ardekani (1981)	UK	40	.49
Suzuki (1980)	Japan	82	.48
Channon (1973)	UK	62	.46
Rumelt (1974)	USA	172	.43

Notes:
a Strategy is degree of diversification by product.
b Divisionalization is the distinction between functional and divisional structure.
* See Bibliography for full citation of studies.

Discussion

The success at generalizing about core organizational structural theory relationships between contingency and structure proves that simple, generalizing approaches yield fruit. The organizational systematics approach is unnecessary.

These studies do not support the Miller (1986) theory of a lack of generality of contingency–structure relationships. Indeed, these studies provide a major challenge to it. For the five contingency–structure relationships considered here, all studies are consistent. For these relationships context does not emerge as a crucial moderator of these bi-variate relationships. Thus the claim that bi-variate relationships 'are largely a function of the context in which they occur' (Miller, 1986: 235) is invalid for these contingency–structure relationships. These relationships include those such as strategy–structure and size–standardization which are central to the typology or configuration theory of Miller (1986).

Conclusions

The organizational systemics approach to the study of organizational structure, although novel, offers an approach fraught with difficulties. The proposed organizational systematics programmatic is lengthy, resource-expensive and pessimistic about the possibilities of immediate achievement. It implies a process which is inductive, emergent and tending to be atheoretical. The presumption is that knowledge about organizations must be more complex than the contingency approach posits.

However, happily, organizational research to date reveals that generalization of contingency–structure relationships is possible. These relationships are quite robust. This generalization of contingency–structure relationships was demonstrated here in three topic areas: size–structural differentiation, size–bureaucracy and strategy–structure. Organizational size was shown to relate to various aspects of vertical differentiation and bureaucratization (functional specialization, standardization and formalization) with a high degree of generality across widely differing contexts. Similarly, the relationship between strategy and divisional structure was shown to generalize across countries.

The programme of generalizing research has proved fruitful. The agenda of positivist organization theory of explaining organizations by material factors such as size in simple general theories is being fulfilled. Research should eschew the complication and pessimism of the organizational systematics approach and continue with the generalizing contingency theory approach, extending it to other areas of organizational life. Structural contingency theory yields generalizations that are valid globally. They are general relationships on which the sun never sets.

8

For Generalization of Organizational Size

Positivist organization theory explains many aspects of organizational structure by the contingency of the size of the organization. However, the idea of a general concept of organizational size has been attacked. Once again, robust general statements are criticized in favour of a more cautious, specific approach (Hopkins, 1988; Lioukas and Xerokostas, 1982). Even the straightforward idea that we can meaningfully talk of a variable called 'organizational size' is called into question. Size is, so to speak, deconstructed into a morass. This assault on a pillar of positivism gives succour to the anti-positivist cause, yet it is done in a way that deploys positivist methods, making it more serious for positivism. In this chapter we consider this critique and show that there is a generalizable concept of organizational size.

Structural contingency theory assigns a major role to organizational size as one of the main contingency variables shaping organization structure, including structural differentiation, bureaucratization, decentralization and divisionalization (Blau, 1970: Pugh et al., 1969a; Williamson, 1970). Thus organizational size is widely used in structural contingency theory and research. However, even the idea that organizational size is a meaningful and homogeneous concept is challenged. The assumption is disputed that different aspects of size, such as numbers of employees, amount of assets, sales dollars and so on, go together, so that one can talk about 'size' (Hopkins, 1988; Lioukas and Xerokostas, 1982). The argument is made that these different variables each form distinct dimensions, uncorrelated with one another, so that there is no unitary dimension of size. The lesson taken is that organization studies should cease to talk about size, and, rather, use more specific concepts such as employees, assets or sales and so on, in organizational theory and research. Clearly this critique strikes a purportedly damaging blow against structural contingency theory and existing research (see, for example, Blau, 1970; Pugh et al., 1969a). The denial of generality and appeal for a much more specific approach is in that sense consistent with the organizational systematics movements (see Chapter 7). Again we shall argue that a generalizing approach is sound and that size can be considered a unitary dimension for most purposes in organization theory and research.

The Generality of Size .

The centrality of size as a contingency variable in contingency analysis has generated a critical discussion about whether or not size is a unitary dimension

(Hopkins, 1988; Lioukas and Xerokostas, 1982). Many writers on contin-gency theory and many structural contingency researchers utilize size as a general concept and then measure size by a variety of operational variables including numbers of employees, sales, assets and so on (see, for instance, Blau, 1970; Pugh et al., 1969a; Grinyer et al., 1980). This diversity of opera-tional measures has in turn provoked the challenge that these differing variables tap distinct dimensions, that size is not unidimensional and that therefore employees, sales, assets and so on are not interchangeable opera-tionalizations of a singular concept. If these measures are not interchangeable then it calls into question present practices of writing theories about 'size' as a singular construct (see, for example, Blau, 1970) or of cumulating across empirical studies with diverse measures of size.

The implication is that, if size is a multidimensional construct, then theory and research will need to reflect this diversity, with separate theory and research being required for each dimension of size. Integration across the differing size dimensions would become a new task in structural contingency theory, and a difficult one. It would require an articulated theory of how the differing size dimensions (such as assets and employees) interrelate. The dif-fering structural effects of each different size dimension need to be specified. Empirical research would need to be conducted and cumulated in a way sen-sitive to the multidimensionality of size. More pessimistically, size might turn out to be multidimensional in a haphazard and unpredictable sort of way, with correlations among different aspects of organizational size varying widely and according to no rational format. This would reflect a host of var-iegated situational factors which only reveal themselves incrementally through lengthy empirical researches in the manner of organizational sys-tematics.

The Hopkins Study

Hopkins (1988) has examined empirically the issue of the interchangeability of measures of size – in particular, of assets and number of employees. He concludes:

> The results of this study create doubt as to the interchangeability of assets and employees as a measure of firm size in all cases. Apparently, a high degree of inter-changeability only exists within certain situations, i.e., either within certain industries or among small asset firms. Interchangeability cannot be assumed *a pri-ori* in all cases. . . .
> If interchangeability cannot be assumed, then either the theoretical concept of firm size should be discarded or the measures must be refined. In the former case, researchers could use an alternative construct such as organizational resources; in the latter case, researchers could utilize a multidimensional measure of size includ-ing both assets and employment.
> Future research should consider these refinements as well as testing the validity of other size measures such as sales, equity, market value, capacity, etc. In any case, future researchers utilizing the concept of size should recognize the limitations associated with using any measurement approach. (Hopkins, 1988: 100)

Thus employees and assets are correlated with each other to a high degree only among smaller firms and in certain industries. For example, Hopkins (1988) finds a high correlation between assets and employees in the electric utility industry of +.96 but a low correlation of only +.27 in the banking industry. He extends his observation about industry specificity to argue that homogeneous samples will yield higher intercorrelation among size measures than will heterogeneous samples. He suggests that

> Furthermore, it is important to recognize, as shown by Child (1973[b]) how the results reported in size studies vary depending on the nature of the sample, i.e., homogeneous vs. heterogeneous. In cases where the researcher assumes interchangeability, results may be flawed. Inconsistencies may be generated when researchers examining the same dependent variable use different measures of size with a heterogeneous sample. (1988: 100)

The article by Hopkins therefore strikes a cautionary note about the interchangeability of size measures, warning that interchangeability cannot be assumed and that more complex approaches will often be needed in future research.

Each of the four conclusions of Hopkins (1988) about the interchangeability of size measures of firms will be critically examined in turn: that they are not interchangeable, that interchangeability is limited to certain industries, that interchangeability is problematical for large firms and that interchangeability is problematical for heterogeneous samples. We will argue that Hopkins overstates the problems in his data and that there is more generalizability of the size construct therein than he states.

Interchangeability of Size Measures

Hopkins (1988: 97) found that, for a sample which combines firms across several industries, the correlation between organizational assets and employees was only +.38. However, Hopkins (1988: 99, Table 2) also transformed both assets and employees logarithmically and then the correlation was +.73. He comments that this log transformation reduces the variance of the distributions, makes them more normal and deals with curvilinearity (1988: 97). However, he treats the logarithmic results as merely corroborating the raw variable results and fails to bring out the significance of the assets-employees being higher after log transformation.

Normality is desirable in analysis using the correlation coefficient as the normal distribution fits the assumptions underlying the tests of significance. Further, size distributions are typically highly skewed with many smaller and fewer larger firms, because there are more smaller than larger organizations in the world. The few large firms readily become outliers having a disproportionate effect on the correlation coefficient, which is sensitive to values far distant from the means of the variables being correlated. Logarithmic transformation typically reduces the effects of outliers, giving a more robust estimate of the correlation. Thus normalization of the distributions of assets and employees through the logarithmic transformation yields a more reliable and valid correlation coefficient on which tests of statistical significance can be more validly performed.

Thus the results of the intercorrelation of log assets and log employees is a more reliable guide about the interchangeability of these two size measures than are the results from correlating untransformed raw assets and raw employees. Moreover, since studies relating structure to size often take the log of size (for example, Blau and Schoenherr, 1971; Blau, 1972; Pugh and Hinings, 1976), the issue of interchangeability in size measures in such studies is better addressed by the examination of the correlations between log assets and log employees.

Hopkins (1988: 100) notes that correlations are improved, for several industries, by the log transform. He comments that this reflects the curvilinearity of the relationship. Where a variable has a curvilinear relationship with another variable, as in the relationship of size and vertical differentiation (Blau and Schoenherr, 1971), then a logarithmic transformation, on occasions, will linearize the relationship and increase the correlation coefficient. However, when *both* variables are logarithmically transformed, as are assets and employees in this study (Hopkins, 1988), then there is no necessary curvilinearity in the relationship between assets and employees and it may be linear. The rise in correlation between the log and raw size measures is more likely to reflect the normalization of both size measures. Thus we interpret the rise in correlation after the log transformation of the asset–employee correlations as a more valid representation of the true, *linear* relationship between assets and employees.

Since the correlations between logarithmically transformed variables offer more reliable estimates of the relationship between assets and employees, they will be utilized here in preference to the correlations between the raw size variables. As has been seen, when both assets and employees were logarithmically transformed, they correlated +.73, indicating a substantial degree of interchangeability. Thus the main result of Hopkins' study is really to *affirm* the interchangeability of these two size measures.

Size Interrelations as Industry-specific

Hopkins (1988: 97) concludes that the magnitude of the asset–employee correlation varies markedly by industry. However, when the correlations between log assets and log employees for each industry are examined, the correlations are, in descending order: +.97, +.94, +.90, +.89, +.89, +.86 and +.33 (see Table 8.1). For three out of seven industries the correlations are +.90 or better and for all but one industry the correlations are +.86 or better. The level of interchangeability of log assets and log employees is high in general, with the exception of banking. Thus, although there is some variation in correlation across industries, it is not typically large. All industries save one (banking) conform to the generalization that assets and employees are closely correlated.

Moreover, an examination of the industries is instructive. Since banks are

Table 8.1 *Correlations of two size dimensions: assets and employees*[1]

	Heterogeneous across industry[2]	Homogeneous industries						
		Electric utility	Apparel	Retail food	Dept stores	Textiles	Oil and gas	Banks
Total	.73* (238)	.97* (62)	.94* (50)	.90* (38)	.89* (42)	.89* (44)	.86* (44)	.33* (136)
Large[3] assets	.30 (119)	.83 (31)	.88 (25)	.65 (19)	.60 (21)	.57 (22)	.79 (22)	–.04 (68)
Small assets	.45 (119)	.97† (31)	.88 (25)	.66 (19)	.89° (21)	.86° (22)	.52 (22)	.71† (68)

Notes:

1 Both assets and employees transformed logarithmically.

2 Firms drawn from 14 industries randomly chosen from Compustat. Each large firm (assets >$200m) matched with small firm (assets < $200m) from same industry.

3 Large firm is assets >$200m for across-industry; for within-industry analysis sample is split at median assets and therefore varies by industry.
   Numbers in parentheses are number of observations.
   Data are drawn from Compustat for fiscal year end 1978.

* Means correlation significantly different from zero at p<.05

† Means correlation for small asset firms significantly different from correlation for large asset firms at p<.01

° Means correlation for small asset firms significantly different from correlation for large asset firms at p<.05

Source: Hopkins (1988: 99, Table 2)

in the retail service industry it might be thought that service or retail industries, being labour-intensive, are different in their asset–employee correlations than heavy industry, such as, in this study, oil and gas and electric utilities. Yet other retail service industries display high correlations. Department stores have a log correlation of +.89 and retail food companies have a log correlation of +.90. There does not seem to be a moderator variable here of manufacturing versus service, nor of capital-intensive versus labour-intensive, nor of geographically concentrated versus retail branch networks. Banking may conceivably be part of a larger class of exceptions bounded by some classification such as the financial service industry. However, only further research can tell.

The conclusion is robust that assets and employees are interchangeable across six widely differing types of industry – except banking. Thus an interpretation of Hopkins' results is to state that generally assets and employees are interchangeable, though banking is an exception. Assets and employees are therefore generally interchangeable size measures in most industries, though there may be some exceptional industries, such as banking, where the correlation is markedly lower.

Size Interrelations in Large Firms

Let us now examine the finding of Hopkins that assets and employees are highly correlated only in samples of small firms. He finds that the correlation among small firms is statistically significantly greater than that among larger firms in two out of the seven industries he examined and also in an across-industry sample (matched for industry) (1988: 97).

In the correlations between log assets and log employees, there is no statistically significant difference between larger firms' and smaller firms' sub-samples for the across-industry sample. However, in the within-industry analyses, smaller firms have significantly larger asset–employee correlations than larger firms in four of seven industries (departmental stores, electric utilities, banks and textiles). Thus, while one can state that there is a size moderator in certain industries, one can state that for the more general, across-industry sample there is no size moderator. Thus the asset–employees correlation is greater for smaller than for larger organizations only in some situations and does not hold in general.

The magnitude of the moderating effect of firm size on the assets–employees correlation is, mostly, not large. For log assets and log employees, the difference in correlation is .29 for department stores, .14 for electric utilities and .29 for textiles – only for banks is the magnitude greater and there it is very large, .75. For the three industries of stores, utilities and textiles, among their large organizations, the log asset–log employees correlations are +.60, +.83 and +.57, respectively; that is, they are considerable. Thus once again, when the anomalous banking industry is excepted, one can state, that for samples of firms, even if all of large size, the interchangeability between assets and employees is always (in this study) substantial. Thus the qualification introduced by a size moderator is not large enough in magnitude to alter greatly the conclusion of interchangeability.

The banks show an abnormally low asset–employee correlation of +.33. The correlation in small banks is +.71, which is quite typical relative to the small firms in the other industries (which vary from +.52 to +.97). The anomaly is confined to the very low correlation of –.04 in the large banks. This sub-sample in turn depresses the correlation for the overall banks sample, producing the low correlation of +.33. Thus in the data of Hopkins, the only industry sub-sample to show a positive correlation between assets and employees of less than +.52 is this large banks sub-sample. The question therefore arises as to whether this discrepant correlation in large banks is due to some instability inherent in the data analysis exercise that on a chance basis happens to have produced an anomaly in one out of the 14 industry sub-samples.

There may be purely technical reasons why size sometimes moderates the asset–employee correlation. If the asset and employee data in this study are skewed, as is usually the case with size data, then the log transformation reduces this skew but usually does not eliminate it. The firms will be bunched towards the small size end and the tail of the distribution takes the form of a long tail at the large firm size end – that is, a few very large firms. These very large firms would be expected to be the outliers in the scatterplot of assets on employees and greatly affect the correlation coefficient. Dichotomizing a sample on the size variable will mean that the smaller organizations will be more bunched together in size than will the larger organizations. There will be more variance among the larger organizations' sub-sample than among the smaller organizations' sub-sample. This gives any outliers more weight; that is, organizations can lie further out. Thus any correlation involving size will be more reliable in the smaller organizations' sub-sample than in the larger organizations' sub-sample. In the larger organizations' sub-sample, the few largest organizations could constitute weighty outliers which would swing the correlation around.

The problem of outliers is worse in samples of fewer numbers of organizations, for in samples of many organizations the effect of a few outliers is diluted. In samples of fewer organizations, however, even one or two outliers will have a great effect on the correlation. The dichotomization of the sample into small versus large organizations also reduces the sample size.

Thus we are suggesting that the lower asset–employee correlation in large rather than small organizations may be influenced by the interaction of two purely technical problems (heteroskedasticity and small samples). It is possible that the problem of small sample size may compound the outliers' problem, producing by chance an anomaly such as the large banks correlation (–.04) that is without real meaning.

If this scenario were to hold in the data of Hopkins (which is unknown until the data are inspected), then we would expect that the samples of larger organizations would show a higher spread of correlations from industry to industry than would the samples of.smaller organizations. The results of Hopkins (1988) conform to this expectation. For the log-transformed correlations, they vary more across the industries for the large firms (from –.04 to +.88) than for the small size firms (from +.52 to +.97). Thus the wide variation in correlations across industry sub-samples of larger firms may be due to purely technical problems and not be substantive.

Therefore organizational size is not a major moderator of the asset–employees correlation. Differences between smaller and larger organizations' sub-samples are probably technical rather than reflecting a real difference in the relationship. The banks anomaly is restricted to large banks and is probably technical in origin.

Size Interrelations in Heterogeneous Samples

Hopkins (1988) argues that interchangeability of size measures is especially problematic when the sample is heterogeneous rather than homogeneous; that is, multi-industry rather than from a single industry. This may be examined in his study by comparing the correlation in the heterogeneous case (the across-industry sample) with the average result from the homogeneous samples (the mean, sample-weighted correlation of the seven industry samples). The log asset–log employee correlation for the heterogeneous case was +.73, whereas the average correlation for the homogeneous case was +.72, which is to say, no different. Thus taking a homogeneous sample is not necessarily superior to taking a heterogeneous sample.

Some of the variation in correlations between the seven homogeneous industry samples is actually due to their small sample size (59 on average). The averaging of the correlations across the seven industries takes out much of this artefactual variation. The sample size of the seven homogeneous industries combined is 416 organizations, which is large, like the sample size of the heterogeneous, across-industry sample, 238 organizations. Research which restricts sampling to one setting (that is, a single industry) in an effort to avoid heterogeneity will often, as a result, tend to yield smaller samples than the more inclusive multi-setting, more heterogeneous samples. But a homogeneous sample of smaller size will make a less reliable estimation than a heterogeneous sample of larger size.

While there may be some real variation in correlation from industry to industry, the range here of +.86 to +.97 (the banks anomaly aside) is minor and inflated by small sample size error, so that real range is even smaller. This suggests that the real between-industry variation is trivial and of no theoretical consequence.

Thus the injunction by Hopkins to study size effects in homogeneous rather than heterogeneous samples is overstated. There is little difference in the estimated correlation between large samples of homogeneous and heterogeneous organizations, in his study. General relationships involving size will be better estimated from heterogeneous than from homogeneous samples. If studying only homogeneous samples led to smaller sample size, this would produce a greater error of estimation. Thus the injunction to study homogeneous samples is unnecessary and potentially unhelpful.

The belief of Hopkins that homogeneous samples are superior to hetero-geneous samples echoes the strictures of McKelvey and Aldrich (1983) about the folly of studying contingency structure relations in heterogeneous sam-ples, yet the belief is not well founded. The two measures of size which Hopkins examines – assets and employees – are highly positively correlated. The appearance of differences across industries and across size ranges is to a degree illusory, reflecting lack of normalization and small sample size. When such artefacts are controlled, much of the differences in correlation between industry and size categories falls away. There remains an anomaly in the large banks sub-sample but this may be due to the chance cumulation of artefacts. Typically, assets and employees correlate highly and positively and with suf-ficient robustness for them often to be interchangeable indices of a general concept of size. The idea of a general concept of size is supported.

The Denial of Generalization

Thus the study by Hopkins mostly yields conclusions which are the opposite of his interpretation. It would appear that approaching the data with the mental set that size is not interchangeable and that homogeneous samples are superior to heterogeneous samples leads to a subjective perception that the data support these contentions when objectively the opposite is truer. Yet the story told by Hopkins reflects the current conventional wisdom in much of the field of organization studies as advocated by eminent American authori-ties such as McKelvey and Aldrich (1983) and Freeman (1986). Yet again we have seen that an examination of the actual data does not support their the-sis. Thus on matters of interchangeability and heterogeneity, sub-components of the wider issue of generalization in organization studies, we see that the field is under the influence of a hegemonic doctrine which denies generaliz-ability and yet is in error.

The more truly representative the sample, the higher the correlation which will be observed and hence the greater the degree of interchangeability between the organizational size measures in the sample. As we have seen in the Hopkins study, the degree of positive association within his sample was considerable, being typically +.86 or better within six out of seven of the homogeneous industry samples (with banking as the anomaly), and even for the heterogeneous sample the correlation was +.73. These sorts of figures show that employees and assets are quite highly correlated in the population. Thus there are grounds for doubting that in the population of organizations the true correlation departs that much from a high correlation and that employees and assets are in any meaningful sense each separate dimensions of organizational size as a construct which is multidimensional. Hopkins' (1988) article would thus be better read as showing that employees and assets are strongly related. It also provides a useful cautionary tale on how this rela-tionship may be obscured by failing to normalize the data (through not making the logarithmic transformation) and by small sample size.

The Lioukas and Xerokostas Study

As discussed earlier (in Chapter 4), Lioukas and Xerokostas (1982) investigated the relationship between size and structure in a comparison of geographic divisions in the Greek retail electricity distribution organization. They preface their analysis with cautions from the literature about the possible multidimensionality of the size construct, referring to Kimberly (1976) and other writers. They deal with the multidimensionality of size by gathering data on several different size aspects and empirically analysing their interrelationship. Lioukas and Xerokostas (1982: 860) show that 14 different aspects of size (number of production workers, number of consumers, sales, length of network and so on) produce five different orthogonal factors (that is, uncorrelated factors) in a factor analysis. Thus they conclude that size is not a unidimensional construct and cannot be treated as such in their data. However, as will now be seen, a closer examination reveals that their five factors really reflect a single underlying factor of size. Therefore their study should be seen as supporting the generality of size.

Of the five orthogonal factors, one factor split is the difference between low- and medium-voltage (on consumers, sales and networks) (Lioukas and Xerokostas, 1982: 862, Table 3). Many organizational studies would probably combine total sales or total number of consumers which would eliminate this dimensional difference. Certainly, the split of data by voltage may be a distinction made within this industry but seems to have no theoretical basis for organization theory. It is idiosyncratic to the study setting and carries no general implications for organizational studies. Thus factors one and two are really the same factor.

Similarly, factor three is loaded on network and transformer capacity of the electrical system (Lioukas and Xerokostas, 1982: 862, Table 3), which again seems industry-, or study-, specific and not of relevance to general organization theory. Thus factor three is really part of factor one.

Again, factor four is composed of high loadings on two variables with no apparent conceptual connection (Lioukas and Xerokostas, 1982: 862, Table 3). The first is geographic area, which actually loads more highly on factor one than factor four (1982: 862, Table 3), so there seems no reason to view this as other than an aspect of factor one. The second variable is an unusual one, the market potential represented by the number of nonelectrified customers. This variable loads more highly on factor two than on factor four (1982: 862, Table 3). Since we have already argued above that factor two should be combined with factor one, factor four collapses into factor one. It means that bigger electricity districts also have fewer nonelectrified customers. Thus not even a mechanical application of factor analysis would lead conclusively to the idea that there is really a fourth independent dimension in these data.

Finally, the fifth factor is a small one, explaining only 4 per cent of the variance. Lioukas and Xerokostas (1982: 860) comment that it has 'no clear meaning'. This may be disregarded as trivial.

Hence the five factors in Lioukas and Xerokostas (1982) constitute no real evidence for the multidimensionality of size in their data.

Our overall interpretation is that there are no real, separate, orthogonal factors – that is no separate dimensions – once the data are assembled into the usual forms of total sales and total consumers. Indeed, these variables of sales, consumers and transformer capacity (that is, assets) are all positively highly correlated with one another and with production workers. Their range of intercorrelations is +.58 to +.97 and the average correlation is +.83. This is a high and consistent level of intercorrelation, especially when one recalls that there will be some lowering of correlation through measurement error. Thus all of these key variables of sales, consumers, assets and production workers show high intercorrelation constituting a single, unidimensional variable of size. Hence the study by Lioukas and Xerokostas(1982) should actually be coded as supporting the unidimensionality of size.

The Lioukas and Xerokostas (1982) study, like the Hopkins (1988) study, supports the unidimensionality of size and the interchangeability of the various aspects of size, such as sales, employees and assets.

The Generality of the Relationship between Different Size Aspects and Structure

The question of whether two size variables are interchangeable in organizational research ultimately hinges on whether the correlation between a structural variable of interest and a size variable is markedly altered if one index of size is used in place of another. The question is whether each different indicator of organizational size shows the same degree of correlation with structure or whether some size indicators have positive correlations and other size indicators have negligible or negative correlations.

For instance, in Grinyer et al. (1980: 198) the correlation between sales and structure was +.29 and between employee and structure was +.33, and so the difference in the two correlations was only .04 in the correlation coefficient. Hence the difference introduced by using sales rather than employees as the measure of size is trivial in this study. Different size indicators often yield similar estimates of size–structure relationships in structural contingency research.

Technically speaking, small differences in correlations may sometimes be sufficient to make the difference between a finding of significant or non-significant on a statistical significance test, depending on the sample size. But this, in a way, is just an illustration of the hazards of relying upon statistical significance tests within samples of small size.

Size is not a multidimensional construct. Different aspects of size go together empirically. Size is better thought of as a bundle of related aspects of size (employees, assets, sales and so on) which are positively associated with one another, but not perfectly so. The present enquiry suggests that they may be used to a degree interchangeably as explanatory variables of organizational structure in examinations of theories that size causes structure. The pitfalls in such analysis are not in any inherent multi-dimensionality of organizational size but rather in the usual social science problems of the hazards of small samples, outliers and statistical significance tests.

Conclusions

Even the relatively simple issue of how we think about the variable of organizational size is subject to critical scrutiny. The idea that organizational size can be measured by different variables which can be used interchangeably has come under attack. It is asserted that the organizational world is complex rather than simple, that generalization is erroneous, and that there is a need for research to proceed incrementally and cautiously under the doctrine that everything is highly situationally specific in ways which cannot be known a priori through general theory. This chimes well with the influential views of the organizational systematicists.

In the event, data interpreted in this fashion are, when examined more closely, revealed to give support to the robustness of organizational size as a construct and to the interchangeability of its indices in structural contingency research. Errors in analysis will arise more from overlooking basic methodological points regarding normalization, sample size and significance testing. Organizational size is a unidimensional construct for many purposes – in particular for the explanation of organizational structure by the size contingency. Thus organizational size remains viable as a concept and can continue to play its role as one of the main pillars of positivist organization theory – that is, as a major material cause of aspects of organizational structure in general laws.

9

Conclusions

In this volume we have argued for positivist organization theory. We have argued that this theory is cogent and empirically valid. We have shown that it is superior to the various other organization theories considered here.

Structural contingency theory is positivist and functionalist. Critics have expressed doubts about both of these attributes and have striven to develop analyses of organizations that are anti-positivist or anti-functionalist. These theories include strategic choice theory, political theory, typology theory and organizational systematics. However, none of these anti-positivist or anti-functionalist theories that have been considered here are sustainable. They suffer damaging problems at either the theoretical or empirical levels – and frequently at both levels.

Anti-positivism has fared poorly. The attempt to remove determinism has foundered, devolving into a critique that cannot be accepted and that is undermined by the increasing success of determinist models. Similarly, the attempt to use typologies or configurations of organizations is unsatisfactory given the abundant evidence supporting multivariate models connecting contingencies and organizational structure. Again, the attempt to replace the generalizing approach of positivism by the far more localized programme of organizational systematics assumes a lack of generalization in the research connecting contingencies and organizational structure that is demonstrably false.

Anti-functionalism has also fared poorly. The attempt to replace functional by political explanations has not been successful on the topic of the growth of administrators in organizations – despite repeated attempts to assert a political analysis. The power-political model suffers inherent problems and fails to be substantiated in empirical research. The political approach has led into complex interpretations as part of the anti-positivist agenda. However, in the topic of the growth of administrators a deeper analysis has revealed strong, clear, simple causation by the material factor of organizational size. Thus positivist organization theory has again been vindicated. And the patterns revealed display economies of scale in administration, in keeping with functionalist theory. The attempts to construct organization theory in a more anti-positivist and anti-functionalist direction have sought to follow wider fashions, but are unsound.

Let us now briefly summarize our reservations about each of the theories that have been considered here: strategic choice, the political explanation of organizational structure, organizational typologies and organizational systematics.

Strategic Choice

Strategic choice theory (Child, 1972a; Bourgeois, 1984) argued against the idea that structure is determined by contingencies. It asserted a large scope for choice by managers and other organizational actors. A large role is seen for the ideational, perceptual, political and ideological factors that are held to influence the structure that is selected.

The argument for strategic choice and free will, in the topic of organizational structure, is a critique of the research, seeking to show that the connection between contingencies and structure is weak. However, the true correlation between contingency and structure variables has been shown here to be strong with little variance unexplained, especially after allowing for a time lag in the adjustment of structure to contingency. The timing of transition out of misfit of structure to contingency into fit, through adjustment of structure to contingency, is related to the occurrence of a deterioration in performance which is partially caused by the misfit and partially caused by exogenous factors. Thus contingency determines structure through an intervening process which involves objective corporate performance. Once performance is entered along with contingency–structure misfit, the specification of the causal systems driving structure is more complete. There would be less unexplained variance which could possibly reflect processes of power, politics, values, ideologies, beliefs, perceptions and so on of the actors.

Fit is attained through structural adjustment to match the given contingency variable. There is little attainment of fit through adjusting the contingency to fit the structure. There is no generally available alternative route to fit through contingency adjustment. Once a particular value of the contingency variable has been adopted, there is an imperative to adopt a particular structure in order to regain fit and performance. The notion that organizations escape from structural adaptation by making a contingency adaptation and thereby finding a zone of choice is not supported.

The empirical evidence presented herein bears out the traditional view in structural contingency theory that there is a causal path which runs from contingency to structure and that there is little indeterminacy in the system. Specifically, there appears to be little scope for the effect of contingency on structure to be mediated by cognitive or political or other social processes. Managers choose the new structure and this involves cognition, perception and problem-solving. But these are mainly intervening variables between contingency and structure; that is, the decision processes seem to be largely determined by the contingency and other objective, situational factors. Once the contingency changes and produces a misfit, then problems ensue and problem-solving initiated by the managers results in a recommended new structure. This recommendation becomes accepted when the problems grow into increasingly poor performance. The structure which emerges is predetermined by the objective contingency, misfit and performance variables. Once the contingency changes, organizations adapt their structure in highly predictable ways. Organizational structural change moves according to laws which are deterministic. This accords with positivistic organization theory. Moreover, organizations in misfit tend to adopt a new structure which is better adapted. Organizational structural change is thus also functional.

There is some evidence that certain attributes of managers, such as CEO functional background or personality, have some influence on organizational structure, especially in smaller organizations, but this is determinism, albeit by career or psychological make-up, rather than evidence of free choice.

Managers play a key role in the process of structural change. They make the diagnosis of the source of the problems in the existing structure and select the new structure, influenced by their knowledge gained through education. And they usually pick a better-fitting structure. Thus there is a high degree of organizational rationality in managerial action. This is especially so given that there has been little research-based, objective knowledge about which structures are best fitting over most of this century.

Thus the strategic choice thesis and free-will critiques of structural contingency theory are in error. Structures are produced by the contingency in deterministic fashion with very little mediation by variations in managerial values.

The Political Explanation of Organizational Structure

The political model of organization holds that organizations are structured not so as to maximize their effectiveness but rather to serve the interests of their members and therefore reflect the power of dominant individuals and groups. One of the most extreme statements of this view is offered by Parkinson (1957). Not even the satiric nature of his writings has deterred serious organizational scholars from advocating his cynical views. However, there are considerable problems with Parkinson's thesis – although it was probably never intended to be taken so seriously. The academic followers of Parkinson have advanced complex theoretical interpretations of their own data that are contradicted by the simpler patterns therein and which are problematic also in terms of theoretical consistency. Simple positivist models of determination by size work much better and enjoy robust generalization across nations. Their evidence actually shows a functionality in the way organizations add administrators as they grow in size. Similarly, attempts to refute the functionalist theory of Blau largely fail to stand up to critical scrutiny. The topic of the growth of administrators shows the way managers make benign, pro-organizational decisions about this aspect of organizational structure.

Organizational Typologies

Within organization theory some theorists have rejected the positivist notion that the dimensions of contingency and structure constitute a continuous multi-dimensional space in the Cartesian manner. Instead, they propose that there are just a few viable organizational types – say, four or five (Mintzberg,

1979; Miller, 1986). The argument is buttressed by pointing out that there are numerous typologies of organization structure which feature just a few types in each typology, and moreover, that it is the same or similar types in each typology. This, however, proves nothing about the real world and is more a comment about typologizers. It shows rather that typologizers tend to be parsimonious in their mental constructs so that successive typologies have been derivative of earlier typologies.

Typologies of organization structure which speak of a few vividly juxta-posed types are easy to communicate and enjoy a certain appeal. However, they postulate that organizations are located at the ends of underlying con-ceptual continua with the middle ranges of the continua being mainly empty of organizations. Yet surveys of organizations show that organizations are widely distributed along underlying structural dimensions such as structural differentiation (Blau and Schoenherr, 1971), functional specialization, for-malization and decentralization of authority (Pugh et al., 1968). The stark bi-modal world of organizations clustered at the ends of continua is a myth.

Similarly, typologies hold that organizations are clustered at the ends of the continua because these are the only viable types – that is, the only fits which produce effectiveness. Yet the fit of structural continua to contingency con-tinua is itself a continuum, as exemplified by the fit of bureaucratic structure to size which is a continuous line through the size–structure two-dimensional space (Child, 1975). Again typologies hold that since only the end-points of the continua are viable, organizations jump across from one end-point to another. Yet organizations almost never jump from the low to the high end-point of structural scales; they move incrementally along the scales, making modest changes over many years. A small automobile assembler cannot sim-ply jump across to become General Motors, otherwise many small firms would levitate up to become large industry majors. Firms grow slowly and with difficulty up through the stages of 10 employees, 100 employees, 1,000 employees, 10,000 employees, 100,000 employees and so on, which is why firms vary widely in size and structure, with many firms being at neither end of the size continuum – that is, neither very small nor very large.

The typologizing or configuration theory is empirically false and theoreti-cally naïve. It illustrates the problem of reifying constructs – that is, of constructing a few ideal-types as points of contrast, giving the ideal-types names, and then making the error of thinking that these ideal-types exist and compose the whole world.

The existence of so few viable types has been explained by positing that each structure must be organized to reflect just one of a limited number of coordinating devices (Mintzberg, 1979). However, many organizations con-tain more than one coordinating device (Thompson, 1967), and the existence of a coordinating device in an organization which also uses other coordinat-ing devices does not preclude these coordinating devices from functioning effectively (Van de Ven et al., 1976).

The typological or configurational theory of organizations is a theory which is empirically false. It is regressive in that it seeks to replace the view of organization structures and contingencies as a set of multidimensional continua; that is, a rich view, with a too simple view. Whatever the attractions of typologies as introductory, expository devices, they create problems when researchers and theorists seek to use them, and when managers seek to use them to diagnose and redesign their structures. Typologies and configuration models are best abandoned in the field of organization structure. They are the equivalent of the flat Earth model in astronomy, a simple, understandable model which people found attractive but which precluded true understanding of reality. We should rather recognize that real organizations vary within a multidimensional, Cartesian space.

Organizational Systematics

Organizational systematics is another attempt to replace structural contingency theory as the guiding framework. This draws upon population-ecology theory to argue that successful organizations are adapted to an ecological niche. Organizational systematics argues that since each niche is different, each organization in the set of successful organizations within a particular niche must have developed a unique set of competences tailored to that niche, and therefore the configurations of organizational and environmental characteristics will be specific to each niche. Thus they assert that there are unlikely to be general relationships between context and organization structure. They call instead for a programme of research which works inductively from the specific to the general, from sub-industry to industry to sector to economy as a whole. The research programme would identify environment–organizational relations for each 'species' and only latterly and emergently identify general organizational–environmental relationships. The implied research programme is monumental in scale, scope and time period, and a science of organization might take centuries to materialize.

Fortunately no such programme is needed, since relationships between context and structure do exist which generalize validly. Our discussions documented a number of such context–structure relationships which hold very generally across organizations of different types and settings. Thus the organizational systematics approach is a grandiose and lengthy programme which is pessimistic about the prospects for early achievements by organizational science. However, the results to date of empirical studies are sufficient to show that the organizational systematics ideas about uniqueness and niche-specificity are, in the matter of organization structure, false. Generalization is possible in organizational science. The positivist ambition of constructing robust general theories is being attained. The long and difficult programme of organizational systematics is not needed.

A Lesson for Organization Studies

There is a lesson to be learnt from our discussion. Organizational research may fare better if it adopts this precept: *sound theorizing is not wishful thinking*. A pervasive problem in organization theory is that theories are constructed that are simply a statement of how people might like the world to be; in other words, the theories are value-driven. Yet the role of theory is to explain the world as it is. Only by clearly seeing the world as it really is can we make informed choices about how we wish to act. Value-driven theories that are appealing but false only serve to mislead us. Action predicated upon false theory will be ineffectual and we end up frustrated or having made the situation worse.

Strategic choice theory is a clear case of a theory that is popular because it is appealing. Many people wish to believe in a large scope of managerial choice, because they are educators or consultants or moralists or radical reformers. Thus ideology propels them towards strategic choice theory because it goes with their world-view. Again, the typology or configuration theory is popular because it is easy to grasp. And political explanations are perennially popular, because they are also easy to grasp, as they attribute causality to persons who are more tangible than contingency factors; moreover, political explanations are also attractive because they chime with the cynicism many of us feel as we look at our fellow organizational inhabitants. Yet for progress to occur in human organization, ideologies, wishful thinking and simplistic explanations have to be replaced by scientific knowledge that accurately captures reality. Only valid knowledge allows us to identify feasible courses of action with beneficial consequences. Knowledge is like psychotherapy in that we 'salvage bits of reality', and with more realistic aspirations we empower ourselves to act in the real world.

The influence of ideologies shows the way that ideas have their effect. Ideas affect other ideas. A believer in an ideology consciously or unconsciously seeks out ideas that buttress that ideology. Thus it is in the world of human discourse that we see ideas having effect. In the world of practical action ideas have little effect. Action is shaped by the material situation. Repeated behaviour is moulded by the experience of failure and success in practical acts. The further one moves away from the practical world into the symbolic world of language, the more influential ideas become to organize perception. Academic theory is particularly distant from the practical world and so here ideas and ideologies have a strong effect. Therefore academic discourse is perennially prey to the baleful influence of erroneous ideas.

The main antidote to fanciful theorizing is empirical testing. For this reason academic literatures in social science emphasize putting theoretical hypotheses to the test through confrontation with empirical data. In organization studies this means using field data from real organizations. Only in this way can veracity be attained. Happily, in modern organization studies there is now a great deal of empirical data available from the diligent efforts of many primary researchers. When fondly held but erroneous theories are tested against actual reality, falsification occurs, opening the door to theories that better capture reality (Popper, 1945).

The Positivist Theory of Organizational Structure

Our theory is positivist in that it is determinist, deals in general relationships and sees the causes of organizational structure as residing in material factors such as organizational size. The theory is also functionalist in that it explains why organizations adopt their particular structures in terms of the consequences of those structures. Specifically, organizations tend to adopt the structures that are the more effective. Which structure is effective depends upon the contingency factors of size, strategy and so on. Thus structures are seen as resulting from functional adaptation to the contingency factors.

The theory is determinist in that the organizational structure is shaped by the need to fit the contingencies. Therefore the organizational structure is determined by the contingencies. There is little or no scope of choice in that the organization will need to adopt the organizational structure that fits the contingencies, in order to avoid performance loss. This deterministic model that underlies most of the pioneering structural contingency theories has been formalized into the Structural Adaption to Regain Fit (SARFIT) model (Donaldson, 1987). This holds that there is a cycle of adaptive change. The organization is initially in fit between structure and contingency and, in consequence, has high performance. If the organization now changes the value of its contingency factor, it moves from fit into misfit as the new contingency value no longer fits the old organizational structure. The misfit causes operating problems and reduces the organizational performance. This in turn leads the organization to re-organize and adopt a new organizational structure that better fits the new contingency value. Thus the organization regains fit and performance. This is the series of changes that occurs as the organization adapts its structure to changes in the contingency. This is the more accurate meaning of the short-hand proposition that contingency determines structure.

Structural contingency theory is multivariate in the sense that many contingency and structural factors are continuous variables. The fit between a structural value and a contingency value is also a continuous line connecting each point of fit. There are a number of such fit lines between each of the pairs of contingency and structural variables. Thus fit is a curve that connects all of these fit lines within the multidimensional space formed by all the contingency and structural variables. Hence there are very many points of fit in this space. And any one point of fit connects with the next points of fit in each direction, so that the organization can move from one fit to another. This allows the organization to change greatly over time by a series of incremental steps. Growth from small business to large multinational corporation is made possible in this way.

Structural contingency theory deals in general relationships between contingency and structural variables. These relationships hold across many different settings. Some of the more important contingencies of organizational structure are size, strategy and public accountability. Some of the more fundamental aspects of organizational structure are structural differentiation, bureaucratization and decentralization of authority. We will now outline the main relationships between contingencies and organizational structure.

Several major relationships are between the size contingency and different aspects of organizational structure. Organizational size can be considered to be a unitary dimension that embraces different aspects of organizational scale, such as employees, output, assets and so on, for these different aspects tend to be highly correlated.

Let us first consider those aspects of organizational structure that make up the organization chart. Structural differentiation is the extent to which the organizational structure is composed of different pieces. Vertical differentiation is the number of levels in the hierarchy. Horizontal differentiation is the number of divisions, departments per division, span of control at each hierarchical level and the division of labour into specialized roles. As organizational size increases this causes an increase in the structural differentiation of all structural aspects, both vertically and horizontally (Blau, 1970). Thus large organizations, relative to smaller organizations, have taller hierarchies, more divisions, more departments per division, larger spans of control and greater division of labour (Blau, 1972; Blau and Schoenherr, 1971).

Larger size leads to greater separation of production from administrative work and greater specialization of roles within both production and administration (Blau, 1970). Greater specialization promotes productiveness and reduces the training and remuneration costs of employees (Blau, 1972). The specialization also increases the homogeneity of work-groups, which in turn increases the effective span of control and thereby helps to reduce the growth of managers that larger size creates through growth in hierarchy (Blau, 1970).

Growth in size leads also to bureaucratization in that there is more use of administrative specialists, standard procedures and documents (namely formalization) (Pugh et al., 1969a; Child, 1973b; Donaldson, 1986; Miller, 1987). This increases predictability and speed of decision-making, thus reducing the load on line management. This in turn helps reduce the growth in management and in administrators as the organization grows in size (Blau, 1970).

Size growth leads to greater decentralization of decision-making authority down the hierarchy (Pugh et al., 1969a; Child, 1973b; Donaldson, 1986). Greater size leads to greater complexity and more decisions to be made. Top managers are more remote from events down the line and the hierarchy acts to some extent as a communications barrier. Moreover, the increasing number of managerial levels as the organization grows in size means that there are more managers to share the decision-making load (Pugh et al., 1969a; Blau and Schoenherr, 1971). Therefore higher management delegates increasingly more decision-making authority down the hierarchy as organizational size increases.

Public accountability retards the delegation of authority that would otherwise occur as size increases (Pugh et al., 1969a). Private organizations, such as firms or corporations, delegate authority down to middle managers, who are then monitored in terms of profit performance. In contrast, in public organizations (such as the government), the organization is held accountable to the public at large over a much wider set of issues – for example, EEO, pollution, preference for national suppliers, or conformance with governmental policy. In this way, these public organizations are kept under governmental, and in the democratic countries, under democratic control. Essentially, the goal set for these organizations by their 'owners', the public, is not maximum task effectiveness narrowly defined but, rather, compliance with the will of the people broadly defined.

Strategy is also a contingency that affects organizational structure. When strategic plans are realized, the set of activities in the organization changes, with diversification in products or services, or shifts in geographic coverage of operations or vertical integration. Increases in diversification increase the internal complexity and the complexity of the external environment of the organization. This overloads a functional structure (that is, a structure in which the managers reporting to the CEO are each responsible for a function such as manufacturing, marketing, research and so on). The organization therefore adopts a multidivisional structure in which each division handles a separate product or service (Chandler, 1962). The divisions exercise an enhanced degree of autonomy, providing an extra degree of decentralization (Chenhall, 1979). The greater the difference across the diversified set of products or services, the more the autonomy of the divisions (Lorsch and Allen, 1973). Similarly, if the organization diversifies geographically, replicating itself in different geographic regions, each of which operates self-sufficiently, then the organization will adopt a geographic division structure (Channon, 1973). If the organization diversifies both in products or services and geographically, then a matrix structure may become appropriate (Davis and Lawrence, 1977; for a fuller specification see Donaldson, 1985). Strategy is the major determinant of divisionalization, but size has a secondary role in that there is a need to keep the size of any one division within certain limits (Jaques, 1976).

Task uncertainty affects organizational structure. The pursuit of innovation raises the uncertainty of organizational tasks. This requires the employment of more highly educated workers who work according to their professional training (Hage and Aiken, 1967, 1969). There is less use of narrowly defined roles, standard procedures and managerially given job definitions (Gerwin, 1979). There is more use of initiative, participation in decision-making, respect for expertise and definition of roles through mutual discussion (Hage and Aiken, 1967, 1969). Thus the organizational structure of roles involved in innovation and uncertain tasks is organic rather than mechanistic (Burns and Stalker, 1961). However, within the same organization there can be wide differences from department to department, section to section or job to job. For example, the production department may be quite mechanistic, reflecting routines of repetitive production, whereas the research department may be more organic, reflecting the lack of repetition in innovation (Lawrence and Lorsch, 1967).

Thus the task uncertainty-organicness connection is best thought of as working at the micro-level (that is, a single job or work-group). The macro-structure of a large, innovative corporation will need to feature substantial bureaucratization in administrative specialization, formalization, hierarchy and planning, as Child (1973b) shows. The difference in sub-cultures (organic versus mechanistic) across departments that nevertheless depend on each other (for example, production depends on research for new products) will lead to a requirement for careful integration involving integrator roles and a problem-solving approach (Lawrence and Lorsch, 1967).

Thus, as organizations grow in size they create more elaborately differentiated and bureaucratized structures that are increasingly decentralized. The other contingency factors add to this skeleton. Public accountability retards decentralization. Strategic diversification alters the nature of the major organizational sub-units from functional departments to divisions and matrices. Task uncertainty and innovation rate required alter the nature of the employees and the way their jobs and their work-groups are structured in a more fine-grained sense.

This in outline is the model that emerges from structural contingency theory and is supported by research. There are minor details that are added to appreciate the complete model, but the above captures the main points. It is a model of only moderate complexity. And it is one of contingency, structure and contingency–structure fits as continua in a multidimensional space. It provides an internally consistent account of how organizations grow and come to be so different in their organizational structures one from another – for instance, IBM from a small firm. The structural contingency theory model is valid, enjoying considerable support from many empirical studies. It also enjoys a high degree of generality across organizations of many different types and spans the globe.

The Coherence of Positivist Organization Theory

The positivist organization theory has the attraction of being a coherent theory. The functionalism, incrementalism and positivism hang together. These different characteristics of the theory each match the other, producing an internally congruent account of organizational structure and structural change.

Any theory has to provide a causal explanation. The sociological theory of structural functionalism does this by explaining the structure in terms of its outcomes. Applied to organizations, functionalism holds that the organization adopts the structure required in order to perform effectively. Thus the consequence of the structure is its cause. An issue for all functionalist theories is how this is accomplished. Given that the structure follows in time after the creation of the structure, how can it have brought that structure into being in the first place? The teleological answer is that 'destiny' brought the required structures into being, but this approach is rightly rejected in modern science as metaphysical (Isajiw, 1968). The population-ecology answer is that functionalist structures are in existence because they have survived the culling process out of a pool of different structures created through random processes (Hannan and Freeman, 1989). However, we reject this view, as structures are not generated at random, and those which remain are not simply the result of culling; there is a great deal of positive adaptiveness by individual organizations changing their structures (see Donaldson, 1995). Etzioni (1968) answers the problem through the capacity of elites to see the structures that will be required in the future and then bring them into being.

The answer offered here differs from all of these. Organizations adopt structures that better fit their contingencies as a result of a process of *incremental adaptation*. They move out of misfit into better fit by changing their structures a little, but sufficiently to attain fit. The new fit allows effectiveness to rise and thereby generate the additional resources necessary to grow a little more. This changes the contingencies incrementally and induces more misfit, that again requires a further incremental change in the structure to gain another new fit. In this way the organization grows incrementally both in its structure and in its contingencies. Over time, this series of growth spurts allows an organization (if the environment permits) to change considerably growing from, say, a small firm to a large, diversified corporation.

In order for large changes in growth to occur over the life of an organization it is necessary that the organization be able to grow incrementally through a series of steps. This means that there have to be many fits in existence between the beginning and end points of the growth career, not just the two end-points themselves. Only if there are intervening fits in a path of fits next to one another can the organization grow incrementally from one to the other. This Cartesianism of the structural contingency theory model is thus an important component that makes it coherent, especially consistent with incrementalism.

An organization that changes gradually, in a series of small steps through incremental adaptation, can accomplish this through problemistic adaptation (Simon, 1965). The managers of the organization can see that there is a problem when the organizational performance declines as a result of the misfit. They find a solution that satisfices – namely, a solution that improves performance without necessarily being the optimal one. All that is required is a solution that raises performance enough to constitute an approximation to a fit and allows another growth spurt. Moreover, the managers can find such a satisficing solution close to the *status quo* in that all that is required is a little structural change, such as a little more specialization or decentralization. Thus the problem-solving process attributed to managers under the theory of incremental adaptation is feasible and consistent with Simon's work about managerial behaviour as problemistic and satisficing. Managers do not require a vision of a future structure radically different from their present one.

In contrast, theories of organizational change, including structural change, of a major, discontinuous and radical kind, always have the difficulty of explaining how managers know that there is such a different structure. Such theories often invoke a guiding idea to influence the manager. This involves new cognitions and sufficiently strong belief to motivate a discontinuous break with the *status quo*. Hence the idea of radical change as being a paradigm change, a switch in psychological Gestalts, a revolution in thought, frame-breaking or inspired by vision. At the extreme, quasi-religious processes are invoked, such as visionary, charismatic leaders of the organization. Thus theories of organizational structural change that deal in big, discontinuous changes often give a large role to ideas, in order to explain how a bold change is charted. Since the organization must break with its past, such structural changes theories may also posit a process of intervention from outside the organization by a parent organization, a national charismatic leader, the state or central planners. This may involve use of power over the organization and its members to overcome resistance to the visionary changes. Change comes from outside and 'above'.

The incremental adaptation theory sees structural change less dramatically. Each change is a small step. It requires little overcoming of internal resistance. It does not need to be guided by a vision or master plan. It is more a question of doing a little more of what is already being done. There is extrapolation from successes in the past. The learning is within the organization rather than depending on comparison with radically different organizations somewhere else. There is no requirement for great ideas. Nor is there a need for strong external inspiration. Little commitment is required. It is more a case of business almost as usual, but with a slight addition.

It may be objected that some organizational change is radical and discontinuous and is driven by charismatic leaders with missions that depart radically from those of the present. Although some organizational change might be of this type, positivism holds that change is typically incremental and driven by problemistic adaptation. Positivism maintains a healthy scepticism about whether many of the organizational changes glibly described as transformational are really so. There is drama and novelty in describing a change as radical. A CEO classified as charismatic or transformational thereby takes on a heroic cast. This is the language favoured by journalists and the mass media. Positivism would wish to see measurements on variables that demonstrate that a particular organizational change was in fact radical. Many changes so labelled are the result of no measurement or inadequate measurement (see Chapter 6).

Similarly, some organizational changes attributed to a transformational CEO infused with a messianic mission are probably better understood in more mundane ways. For example, Jack Welch at GE is often described as a transformational leader driven by a visionary mission. Tichy and Sherman (1993) write of him in these terms, yet a close reading of their case history of GE makes it clear that the mission, far from being a bold plan that guided the change, emerged incrementally over the years. The philosophies of 'reality and candour' and 'integrated diversity' came only several years into Welch's time as CEO, as a result of his experiences with the change process (Tichy and Sherman, 1993). The case history reveals a manager dealing with a series of problems rather than a messianic visionary who enters knowing the answers in a grand philosophy that has only to be implemented.

Some organizations make big changes, such as selling off some of their divisions, but these changes are usually forced upon them by disastrously poor organizational performance, which leads them to liquidate assets in order to keep the corporation afloat. Such moves are thus problem-driven. And they are readily guided by problemistic decision-making: cash is urgently needed and so major assets are turned into cash. Some big changes are mergers, and these are often impelled by competition, such as needing to attain scale to be able to keep up with the industry leader or in response to a merger by competitors. Thus the theory of positivistic theory of organizational change as being caused through problemistic adaptation applies also to changes that are larger than incremental.

Whereas theories that see organizational change as radical or discontinuous frequently also see the need for strong intervention from outside the organization, the theory of incremental adaptation holds that the incremental changes can be made by the organizational managers so that there is no need for outside intervention. In fact, outside intervention may be quite dysfunctional, in that outsiders lack appreciation of the particular set of contingent circumstances facing the organization and lack the learning-by-doing that enables management to identify the required next step. Chandler (1962) gives several cases of large corporations successfully devising a new structure through the problem-solving efforts of their managers studying their own corporation in its situation. The exception is the corporation that engaged an outside consultant whose recommended structure, based on the structures used in other companies, proved unworkable in practice (Chandler, 1962). This incrementalism is compatible with a liberal theory of society in which societal effectiveness is achieved by the autonomous decision-making of many diverse organizations rather than by direction of central government.

Thus ideas are not important in the explanation of incremental structural adaptation. It is a positivist phenomenon in that the push comes from the exigencies of the situation. These are composed of material factors, such as organizational size and the task. This holds even for the contingency of strategy. It is not the ideational aspects of strategy, such as the plan for the future, but rather the present, material exigency, such as the product diversity or geographic spread of operations that is the cause of the organizational structure. The problems caused by misfit between the organizational structure and the contingencies bear down upon managerial decision-making and force the adoption of a better-fitting structure. In particular, the lower performance that results from misfit creates an imperative to change.

It might be objected that task uncertainty has been included among the contingency factors and that this is the perception of managers (and other organizational members), so cannot be called a positivist material factor. Clearly uncertainty refers primarily to a perception in the minds of managers that they are not sure what to do next because of lack of knowledge or lack of information. But this mental state has its origins in the material world – that is, in the task inside the organization or in the environment of the organization.

High task uncertainty in organization theory often originates in innovation. The organization is trying to do something it has not done before, such as invent a new product or implement a new process. The uncertainty inheres in the lack of knowledge about that product or process; that is, the novelty of the technology means that nobody knows enough about it to make sound predictions that allow for planning. For example, Galbraith (1973) gives the example of the engineers at Boeing struggling to invent the 747 and not being able to predict which aspects of the design specification will be feasible and when they will be attained, thus making coordination by plan impossible. Thus the uncertainty in their jobs stems from uncertainty in the material world: will it fly? Where knowledge or information already exists so that the task in the organization could be rendered less uncertain, then organization theory holds that the organization will avail itself through the hiring of experts and so on (Hage, 1965). Thus, where task uncertainty exists it is because of the lack of human knowledge about the material world. It is, so to speak, the intransigence and mystery of nature. So task uncertainty is produced by states of nature and therefore by material causes. Uncertainty is a mental condition but its roots are positivist.

As a positivist theory of human behaviour, the key to the explanation of organizational structure does not lie in the consciousness of the organizational inhabitants. The structure that eventuates over time may not at all be a structure that they foresaw, intended or strove to bring about. Some members of organizations may even be quite unable to comprehend the exact nature of the present organizational structure. Their preferred form of structure may be contrary to the present organizational structure or to the structure that their present actions will eventually bring into being.

Large organizations have complex structures. Some large organizations have sets of organization charts that cover over 100 pages. But these kinds of structures do not typically come about because some person planned them with some grand design. The organizational structures become gradually more complex over the years as the organization grows in size and diversifies. At each step the managers solve their immediate problems by adding a new rule here or a new department there. Often this is done by managers who personally dislike bureaucracy and will readily state that their personal philosophy is to prevent the organization from becoming a bureaucracy. Thus organization structures incrementally come into being from managers being forced by material circumstances to adopt more elaborate structures that may be quite opposed to their preferences or ideologies.

Organizations add more bureaucratic elements of structure for each additional employee when they are small than when they are large (Blau, 1970; Child, 1972b). This empirically well-established paradox shows that structuring decisions are not driven by managerial preferences and ideologies. It means that small businesses actually bureaucratize at a faster rate than large corporations. This is despite the fact that small businesses are typically run by owner-managers who abhor bureaucracy, while many large corporations are run by professional managers with business degrees, who have been trained to venerate sophisticated administrative devices. Moreover, owner-managers have strong financial incentives not to add any unnecessary administrative costs as they reduce their profits. Further, owner-managers typically dislike the loss of power that bureaucratization entails, as decisions become rule-governed, impersonal and decentralized. Likewise, the professional managers who control large corporations but own only little of them are under strong incentives to empire-build by proliferating unnecessary bureaucracy (it boosts their status and pay) (Williamson, 1970). Despite the presence of these psychological and financial motivations the owner-managers of small businesses actually bureaucratize faster than the professional managers of large corporations. This shows that bureaucratization is not caused by these personal motivations and preferences and occurs despite them. The owner-managers bureaucratize rapidly because they are forced to, because their personal control of the business becomes ineffective and outmoded as the business expands beyond a small size.

This is similar to markets in economics. The price of a good emerges through the interactions of many buyers and sellers rather than being created by plan. The economic actor may have little understanding of the market and how it operates and came about. Nevertheless, he or she can function well through adaptive behaviour based on limited information; for example, prices, that assist him or her in local problem-solving. This locally focused action rebounds to the common good; it results in maximum wealth creation. Thus there is an underlying similarity between the concepts of economics and positivist organization theory. Both are rooted in a positivist world-view that sees human structures as emerging spontaneously from human interactions as they struggle to deal with the material world. Both are liberal philosophies that eschew dictatorship by government and messianic religious suasion.

Modern positivism eschews totalizing formulas – that is, the final solutions that will solve all problems for all time. The twentieth century has witnessed no lack of such totalizing theories, such as Communism, Nazism and Pol-Potism – at present we have the spectre of Islamic fundamentalism. Each offers a supposedly complete solution to the human condition, through radical transformation. This is to be accomplished through revolution from above – that is, by state violence and indoctrination. Thus the totalizing theory becomes a totalitarian practice. Much human misery has resulted therefrom.

Liberal theories, by contrast, stress that the world is constantly changing so that no solution is truly final. Therefore adaptation today will become maladaptation later on and further adaptations will be needed. People best proceed by incremental change, by making adaptations to particular circumstances that work here and now but not there and then. Therefore human beings will need to go on being flexible and adaptive. For such reasons Popper

(1945) has stressed the role of adaptive problem-solving through piecemeal social engineering, and warned against the grand vision as so often misguided and dangerous. In the matter of organizational structure, the structures that exist today in our large organizations were not foreseen by those who founded them as fledgling companies in the last century. For ideationalists this is unpalatable; for positivists it is a fact one can welcome. Thus positivism in organization theory is a morally and ethically valid position.

In these ways the functionalism, incrementalism and positivism of the positivist theory of organizations go together, forming an intellectually coherent whole.

The Future of Positivist Organization Theory

There is much future work to be done in extending, refining and consolidating positivist organization theory. Much of this involves working on detailed problems within the body of literature. Such an agenda has been provided elsewhere (Donaldson, 1995). However, there is a major lacuna in the theory that bears mentioning here.

Positivist organization theory is now quite good at specifying the major contingencies that shape many of the major aspects of organizational structure. The mechanism of adaptation is the organization moving from misfit into fit by adopting a new structure that fits the new level of the contingency variable. The trigger for structural adaptation is low organizational performance. While the role of low performance, indeed of a performance crisis, is widely acknowledged theoretically (Child, 1972a; Williamson, 1970) and empirically (Chandler, 1962; Donaldson, 1987), the existing discussions are limited. Therefore there is scope for a systematic theory of the role of performance in organizational adaptation. This is a major task of theory construction for the future. This will help us to understand more fully this material cause of organizational structure that so affects the occurrence of change. And it will assuredly be a positivist theoretical development, furthering the explanatory power of positivist organization theory.

Bibliography

Agarwal, Naresh C. (1979) 'Nature of size–structure relationship: Some further evidence', *Human Relations*, 32 (6): 441–50.

Al-Jibouri, Sadia Jabouri Joudi (1983) 'Size, technology, and organizational structure in the manufacturing industry of a developing country: Iraq'. Unpublished doctoral dissertation, Mississippi State University.

Allen, Stephen A. (1978) 'Organizational choices and general management influence networks in divisionalized companies', *Academy of Management Journal*, 21 (3): 341–65.

Anderson, Carl R. and Paine, Frank T. (1975) 'Managerial perceptions and strategic behavior', *Academy of Management Journal*, 18 (4): 811–23.

Argyris, Chris (1972) *The Applicability of Organizational Sociology.* London: Cambridge University Press.

Armandi, Barry R. and Mills, Edgar W., Jr (1982) 'Organizational size, structure, and efficiency: A test of a Blau-Hage model', *American Journal of Economics and Sociology*, 41 (1): 43–60.

Astley, W.G. and Van de Ven, Andrew H. (1983) 'Central perspectives and debates in organization theory', *Administrative Science Quarterly,* 28 (2): 245–73.

At-Twaijri, Mohamed Ibrahim Ahmad and Montanari, John R. (1987) 'The impact of context and choice on the boundary-spanning process: An empirical extension', *Human Relations*, 40 (12): 783–98.

Ayoubi, Z.M. (1981) 'Technology, size and organization structure in a developing country: Jordan', Chap. 6 in D.J. Hickson and C.J. McMillan (eds), *Organization and Nation: the Aston Programme IV*. Farnborough, Hants: Gower.

Azumi, K. and McMillan, C.J. (1981) 'Management strategy and organization structure: A Japanese comparative study', Chap. 9 in D.J. Hickson and C.J. McMillan (eds), *Organization and Nation: the Aston Programme IV*. Farnborough, Hants: Gower.

Badran, M. and Hinings, C.R. (1981) 'Strategies of administrative control and contextual constraints in a less developed country: The case of Egyptian public enterprise', Chap. 7 in D.J. Hickson and C.J. McMillan (eds), *Organization and Nation: the Aston Programme IV*. Farnborough, Hants: Gower.

Bain, George Sayers (1970) *The Growth of White-Collar Unionism*. Oxford: Oxford University Press.

Bedeian, A.G. (1990) 'Choice and determinism: A comment', *Strategic Management Journal*, 11 (7): 571–3.

Bedeian, A.G. and Zammuto, R.F. (1991) *Organization Theory and Design*. Chicago: The Dryden Press.

Beer, S. (1972) *Brain of the Firm*. London: Penguin.

Behling, O. (1980) 'The case for the natural science model for research in organizational behavior and organization theory', *Academy of Management Review*, 5 (4): 483–90.

Benson, J. Kenneth (1977) 'Organisations: A dialectical view', *Administrative Science Quarterly,* 22 (1): 1–21.

Beyer, J.M. and Trice, H.M. (1979) 'A reexamination of the relations between size and various components of organizational complexity', *Administrative Science Quarterly*, 24 (1): 48–64.

Blalock, H.M. (1961) *Causal Inferences in Nonexperimental Research*. Chapel Hill, NC: University of North Carolina Press.

Blau, Peter M. (1970) 'A formal theory of differentiation in organizations', *American Sociological Review,* 35 (2): 201–18.

Blau, Peter M. (1972) 'Interdependence and hierarchy in organizations', *Social Science Research,* 1: 1–24.

Blau, Peter M. and Schoenherr, P.A. (1971) *The Structure of Organizations.* New York: Basic Books.

Blau, Peter M., Falbe, Cecilia McHugh, McKinley, William and Phelps, Tracy K. (1976) 'Technology and organization in manufacturing', *Administrative Science Quarterly,* 21 (1): 21–40.

Bobbitt, H.R., Jr and Ford, J.D. (1980) 'Decision-maker choice as a determinant of organizational structure', *Academy of Management Review,* 5 (1): 13–23.

Boorstin, Daniel J. (1983) *The Discoverers.* New York: Random House.

Bourgeois, L.J., III (1984) 'Strategic management and determinism', *Academy of Management Review,* 9 (4): 586–96.

Brech, E.F.L. (1957) *Organisation: The Framework of Management.* London: Longmans, Green.

Bryman, A., Beardsworth, A.D., Keil, E.T. and Ford, J. (1983) 'Research note: Organizational size and specialization', *Organization Studies,* 4 (3): 271–7.

Burns, Tom and Stalker, G.M. (1961) *The Management of Innovation.* London: Tavistock.

Burrell, Gibson and Morgan, Gareth (1979) *Sociological Paradigms and Organisational Analysis: Elements of the Sociology of Corporate Life.* London: Heinemann.

Capon, N., Christodolou, C., Farley, J.U. and Hubert, J.M. (1987) 'A comparative analysis of the strategy and structure of United States and Australian corporations', *Journal of International Business Studies,* 18 (Spring): 51–74.

Chandler, Alfred D., Jr (1962) *Strategy and Structure: Chapters in the History of the American Industrial Enterprise.* Cambridge, MA: MIT Press.

Chandler, Alfred D., Jr (1977) *The Visible Hand: The Managerial Revolution in American Business.* Cambridge, MA: Harvard University, Belknap Press.

Channon, Derek F. (1973) *The Strategy and Structure of British Enterprise.* London: Macmillan.

Chenhall, Robert H. (1979) 'Some elements of organizational control in Australian divisionalized firms', *Australian Journal of Management,* Supplement to 4 (1) (April): 1–36.

Child, John (1972a) 'Organizational structure, environment and performance: The role of strategic choice', *Sociology,* 6: 1–22.

Child, John (1972b) 'Organization structure and strategies of control: A replication of the Aston Study', *Administrative Science Quarterly,* 17: 163–77.

Child, John (1973a) 'Parkinson's progress: Accounting for the number of specialists in organizations', *Administrative Science Quarterly,* 18 (3): 328–48.

Child, John (1973b) 'Predicting and understanding organization structure', *Administrative Science Quarterly,* 18 (2): 168–85.

Child, John (1975) 'Managerial and organizational factors associated with company performance, Part 2: A contingency analysis', *Journal of Management Studies,* 12: 12–27.

Child, John (1984) *Organization: A guide to problems and practice.* 2nd edn, London: Harper and Row.

Child, John and Kieser, Alfred (1979) 'Organizational and managerial roles in British and West German companies: An examination of the culture-free thesis', Chap. 13 in C.J. Lammers and D.J. Hickson (eds), *Organizations Alike and Unlike.* London: Routledge and Kegan Paul.

Child, John and Mansfield, Roger (1972) 'Technology, size and organization structure', *Sociology,* 6 (3): 369–93.

Christensen, C. Roland, Andrews, Kenneth R. and Bower, Joseph L. (1978) *Business Policy: Text and Cases.* 4th edn, Homewood, IL: Richard D. Irwin.

Clark, P. (1990) *Aston Programme: Describing and Explaining the Structure of Canadian Textile Firms.* Aston University: Aston Programme Press. Birmingham.

Clegg, Stewart and Dunkerley, David (1977) (eds) *Critical Issues in Organizations.* London: Routledge and Kegan Paul.

Clegg, Stewart and Dunkerley, David (1980) *Organization, Class and Control.* London: Routledge and Kegan Paul.

Conaty, J., Mahmoudi, H., and Miller, G.A. (1983) 'Social structure and bureaucracy: A comparison of organizations in the United States and prerevolutionary Iran', *Organization Studies,* 4 (2): 105–28.

Cook, Thomas D. and Campbell, Donald T. (1979) *Quasi-experimentation: Design and Analysis Issues for Field Settings.* Chicago: Rand McNally College Publishing.

Corey, Raymond and Star, Steven H. (1971) *Organization Strategy: A Marketing Approach.* Boston: Division of Research, Graduate School of Business Administration, Harvard University.

Crozier, Michel (1964) *The Bureaucratic Phenomenon.* London, Tavistock Publishers.

Cullen J. B., Anderson K.S. and Baker D.D. (1986) 'Blau's theory of structural differentiation revisited: A theory of structural change or scale', *Academy of Management Journal,* 29 (2): 203–29.

Daft, Richard L. (1986) *Organization Theory and Design.* 2nd edn, St Paul, MN: West Publishing.

Davis, Stanley M. and Lawrence, Paul R. (1977) *Matrix.* Reading, MA: Addison-Wesley.

Davis, Gerald F. and Stout, Suzanne K. (1992) 'Organization theory and the market for corporate control: A dynamic analysis of the characteristics of large takeover targets, 1980–1990', *Administrative Science Quarterly,* 37 (4): 605–33.

Dewar, Robert and Hage, Jerald (1978) 'Size, technology, complexity, and structural differentiation: Toward a theoretical synthesis', *Administrative Science Quarterly,* 23 (1): 111–36.

Donaldson, Lex (1982a) 'Comments on "Contingency and choice in organization theory"', *Organization Studies,* 3 (1): 65–72.

Donaldson, Lex (1982b) 'Divisionalization and diversification: A longitudinal study', *Academy of Management Journal,* 25 (4): 909–14.

Donaldson, Lex (1983) 'Explaining structural change in organizations'. Unpublished paper, Australian Graduate School of Management, Kensington, NSW.

Donaldson, Lex (1985) *In Defence of Organization Theory: A Reply to the Critics.* Cambridge: Cambridge University Press.

Donaldson, Lex (1986) 'Size and bureaucracy in East and West: A preliminary meta analysis', in S.R. Clegg, D. Dunphy and S.G. Redding (eds), *The Enterprise and Management in East Asia.* Hong Kong: University of Hong Kong Press.

Donaldson, Lex (1987) 'Strategy and structural adjustment to regain fit and performance: In defence of contingency theory', *Journal of Management Studies,* 24 (1): 1–24.

Donaldson, Lex (1995) *American Anti-management Theories of Organization: A Critique of Paradigm Proliferation.* Cambridge: Cambridge University Press.

Donaldson, Lex and Caulfield, Clyde C. (1989) 'Economics of scale in public and private administration: Is market discipline mythic?', Sydney, NSW: Australian Graduate School of Management in the University of New South Wales (Working Paper, 89-003).

Donaldson, Lex and Robertson, J. Angus (1986) 'A meta-analysis of size and hierarchy: Universal generalization moderated by routineness and managerial capitalism', Sydney, NSW: Australian Graduate School of Management in the University of New South Wales (Working Paper 86-012).

Donaldson, Lex and Warner, Malcolm (1974a) 'Structure of organizations in occupational interest associations', *Human Relations,* 27 (8): 721–38.

Donaldson, Lex and Warner, Malcolm (1974b) 'Bureaucratic and electoral control in occupational interest associations', *Sociology,* 8 (1): 47–57.

Drazin, Robert and Van de Ven, Andrew H. (1985) 'Alternative forms of fit in contingency theory', *Administrative Science Quarterly,* 30 (4): 514–39.

Dyas, Gareth P. and Thanheiser, Heinz T. (1976) *The Emerging European Enterprise: Strategy and Structure in French and German Industry.* London: Macmillan.

Etzioni, Amitai (1968) *The Active Society: A Theory of Societal and Political Processes.* London: Collier-Macmillan; New York: Free Press.

Feyerabend, P. K. (1975) *Against Method: Outline of an Anarchistic Theory of Knowledge.* London: New Left Books.

Fligstein, Neil (1985) 'The spread of the multidivisional form among large firms, 1919–1979', *American Sociological Review,* 50, 377–91.

Fligstein, Neil (1990) *The Transformation of Corporate Control.* Cambridge, MA: Harvard University Press.

Fligstein, Neil (1991) 'The structural transformation of American industry: An institutional account of the causes of diversification in the largest firms, 1919–1979', in Walter W. Powell and Paul J. DiMaggio (eds), *The New Institutionalism in Organizational Analysis*. Chicago: University of Chicago Press.

Ford, Jeffrey D. (1980) 'The administrative component in growing and declining organizations: A longitudinal analysis', *Academy of Management Journal*, 23 (4): 615–30.

Franko, Lawrence G. (1974) 'The move toward a multidivisional structure in European organizations', *Administrative Science Quarterly*, 19 (4): 493–506.

Freeman, John H. (1986) 'Data quality and the development of organizational social science: An editorial essay', *Administrative Science Quarterly*, 31 (2): 298–303.

Freeman, John H. and Hannan, M.T. (1975) 'Growth and decline processes in organizations', *American Sociological Review*, 40: 215–28.

Freeman, John H. and Kronenfeld, Jerrold E. (1973) 'Problems of definitional dependency: The case of administrative intensity', *Social Forces*, 52: 108–21.

Galbraith, Jay R. (1973) *Designing Complex Organizations*. Reading, MA: Addison-Wesley.

Galtung, J. (1967) *Theory and Methods of Social Research*. London: George Allen and Unwin.

Gerwin, Donald (1979) 'Relationships between structure and technology at the organizational and job levels', *Journal of Management Studies*, 16 (1): 70–9.

Goldman, P. (1973) 'Size and differentiation in organizations: A test of a theory', *Pacific Sociological Review*, 16 (1): 89–105.

Gouldner, Alvin W. (1954) *Patterns of Industrial Bureaucracy*. Glencoe, IL: Free Press.

Greenwood, R. and Hinings, C.R. (1976) 'Contingency theory and public bureaucracies', in D.S. Pugh and C.R. Hinings (eds) *Organizational Structure: Extensions and Replications: the Aston Programme II*. Farnborough, Hants: Saxon House.

Grinyer, Peter H. and Yasai-Ardekani, Masoud (1981) 'Strategy, structure, size and bureaucracy', *Academy of Management Journal*, 24 (3): 471–86.

Grinyer, Peter H., Yasai-Ardekani, Masoud and Al-Bazzaz, Shawki (1980) 'Strategy, structure, the environment, and financial performance in 48 United Kingdom companies', *Academy of Management Journal*, 23 (2): 193–220.

Hage, Jerald (1965) 'An axiomatic theory of organizations', *Administrative Science Quarterly*, 10 (4): 289–320.

Hage, Jerald (1980) *Theories of Organization: Form, Process and Transformation*. New York: Wiley.

Hage, Jerald and Aiken, Michael (1967) 'Program change and organizational properties: A comparative analysis', *American Journal of Sociology*, 72: 503–19.

Hage, Jerald and Aiken, Michael (1969) 'Routine technology, social structure and organizational goals', *Administrative Science Quarterly*, 14 (3): 366–76.

Hall, D.J. and Saias, M.D. (1980) 'Strategy follows structure!' *Strategic Management Journal*, 1: 149–63.

Hall, Richard H. (1963) 'The concept of bureaucracy: An empirical assessment', *American Journal of Sociology*, 69: 32–40.

Hall, Richard H. (1977) *Organizations: Structure and Process*, 1st edn, 1972; 2nd edn, Englewood Cliffs, New Jersey: Prentice-Hall.

Hamilton, R.T. and Shergill, G.S. (1992) 'The relationship between strategy–structure fit and financial performance in New Zealand: Evidence of generality and validity with enhanced controls', *Journal of Management Studies*, 29 (1): 95–113.

Hamilton, R.T. and Shergill, G.S. (1993) *The Logic of New Zealand Business: Strategy, Structure, and Performance*. Auckland, New Zealand: Oxford University Press.

Hannan, Michael T. and Freeman, John (1989) *Organizational Ecology*. Cambridge, MA: Harvard University Press.

Hannan, Michael T., Ranger-Moore, J. and Banaszak-Holl, J. (1990) 'Competition and the evolution of organizational size distributions', Chap. 11 in J.V. Singh (ed.), *Organizational Evolution: New Directions*. Newbury Park, CA: Sage.

Hickson, David J. (1966) 'A convergence in organization theory', *Administrative Science Quarterly*, 11 (2): 225–37.

Hickson, David J., Pugh, D.S. and Pheysey, Diana G. (1969) 'Operations technology and organization structure: An empirical reappraisal', *Administrative Science Quarterly,* 14 (3): 378–97.

Hickson, David J., Hinings, C.R., Lee, C.A., Schneck, R.E. and Pennings, J.M. (1971) 'A strategic contingencies' theory of intraorganizational power', *Administrative Science Quarterly,* 16 (2): 216–29.

Hickson, David J., Hinings, C.R., McMillan, C.J. and Schwitter, J.P. (1974) 'The culture-free context of organization structure: A tri-national comparison', *Sociology,* 8 (1): 59–80. Also as chap. 1 in D.J. Hickson and C.J. McMillan (eds) (1981) *Organization and Nation: The Aston Programme IV.* Farnborough, Hants: Gower.

Hickson, David J., McMillan, C.J., Azumi, K. and Horvath D. (1979) 'Grounds for comparative organization theory: Quicksands or hard core?' Chap. 2 in C.J. Lammers and D.J. Hickson (eds), *Organizations Alike and Unlike: International and Interinstitutional Studies in the Sociology of Organizations.* London: Routledge and Kegan Paul.

Hill, Charles W.L. (1988) 'Corporate control type, strategy, size and financial performance', *Journal of Management Studies,* 25 (5): 403–17.

Hill, Charles W.L. and Pickering, J.F. (1986) 'Divisionalization, decentralization and performance of large United Kingdom companies', *Journal of Management Studies,* 23 (1): 26–50.

Hill, Charles W.L., Hitt, Michael A. and Hoskisson, Robert E. (1992) 'Cooperative versus competitive structures in related and unrelated diversified firms', *Organization Science* 3 (4): 501–21.

Hinings, C.R. and Lee, Gloria (1971) 'Dimensions of organization structure and their context: A replication', *Sociology,* 5: 83–93.

Hinings, C.R., Hickson, D.J., Pennings, J.M. and Schneck, R.E. (1974) 'Structural conditions of intraorganizational power', *Administrative Science Quarterly,* 19 (1): 22–44.

Hinings, C.R., Ranson, S. and Bryman, A. (1976) 'Churches as organizations: Structure and context', in D.S. Pugh and C.R. Hinings (eds), *Organizational Structure: Extensions and Replications: The Aston Programme II.* Farnborough, Hants: Saxon House.

Hirsch, Paul (1975) 'Organizational effectiveness and the institutional environment', *Administrative Science Quarterly,* 20 (3): 327–44.

Holdaway, Edward A., Newberry, John F., Hickson, David J. and Heron, R. Peter (1975) 'Dimensions of organizations in complex societies: The educational sector', *Administrative Science Quarterly,* 20 (1): 37–58.

Hopkins, H. Donald (1988) 'Firm size: The interchangeability of measures', *Human Relations,* 41 (2): 91–102.

Horvath, D., McMillan, C.J., Azumi, K. and Hickson, D.J. (1976) 'The cultural context of organizational control: An international comparison', *International Studies of Management and Organization,* 6 (3): 60–86. Also as chap. 10 in D.J. Hickson and C.J. McMillan (eds) (1981) *Organization and Nation: The Aston Programme IV.* Farnborough, Hants: Gower.

Hoskisson, R.E. and Galbraith, C.S. (1985) 'The effect of quantum versus incremental M-form reorganization on performance: A time-series exploration of intervention dynamics', *Journal of Management,* 11 (3): 55–70.

Hrebiniak, Lawrence G. and Joyce, William F. (1985) 'Organizational adaptation: Strategic choice and enviromental determinism', *Administrative Science Quarterly,* 30 (3): 336–49.

Hunter, John E., Schmidt, Frank L. and Jackson, Gregg B. (1982) *Meta-analysis: Cumulating Research Findings Across Studies.* Beverly Hills, CA: Sage.

Ijiri, Yuji and Simon, Herbert A. (1977) *Skew Distributions and the Sizes of Business Firms.* Amsterdam: North-Holland .

Inkson, J.H.K., Pugh, D.S. and Hickson, D.J. (1970) 'Organization context and structure: An abbreviated replication', *Administrative Science Quarterly,* 15 (3): 318–29.

Isajiw, Wsevolod W. (1968) *Causation and Functionalism in Sociology.* London: Routledge and Kegan Paul.

Jaques, Elliott (1976) *A General Theory of Bureaucracy.* London, Heinemann.

Jensen, Michael C. (1989) 'Eclipse of the public corporation', *Harvard Business Review,* (September–October): 61–74.

Jensen, Michael C. and Meckling, William H. (1976) 'Theory of the firm: Managerial behavior, agency costs and ownership structure', *Journal of Financial Economics,* 3 (4): 305–60.

Khandwalla, Pradip N. (1973) 'Viable and effective organizational designs of firms', *Academy of Management Journal,* 16 (3): 481–95.

Khandwalla, Pradip N. (1977) *The Design of Organizations.* New York: Harcourt Brace Jovanovich.

Kimberly, John R. (1976) 'Organizational size and the structuralist perspective: A review, critique and proposal', *Administrative Science Quarterly,* 21 (4): 571–97.

Kosnik, Rita D. (1987) 'Greenmail: A study of board performance in corporate governance', *Administrative Science Quarterly,* 32 (2): 163–85.

Kotter, John P., Schlesinger, Leonard A. and Sathe, Vijay (1986) *Organization: Text, cases and readings on the management of organizational design and change.* 2nd edn, Homewood, IL: Irwin.

Kuc, B., Hickson, D. J. and McMillan, C.J. (1981) 'Centrally planned development: A comparison of Polish factories with equivalents in Britain, Japan and Sweden', Chap. 5 in D.J. Hickson and C.J. McMillan (eds), *Organization and Nation: The Aston Programme IV.* Farnborough, Hants: Gower.

Lammers, Cornelis J. (1981a) 'Contributions of organizational sociology: Part 1: Contributions to sociology – a liberal view', *Organization Studies,* 2 (3): 267–86.

Lammers, Cornelis J. (1981b) 'Contributions of organizational sociology: Part II: Contributions to organizational theory and practice – a liberal view', *Organization Studies,* 2 (4): 361–76.

Lawless, Michael W. and Finch, Linda K. (1989) 'Choice and determinism: A test of Hrebiniak and Joyce's framework on strategy–environment fit', *Strategic Management Journal,* 10 (4): 351–65.

Lawless, M.W. and Tegarden, L.K.F. (1990) 'Choice and determinism: A reply', *Strategic Management Journal,* 11 (7): 571–77.

Lawrence, Paul R. and Dyer, D. (1983) *Renewing American Industry: Organizing for Efficiency and Innovation.* New York: The Free Press.

Lawrence, Paul R. and Lorsch, Jay W. (1967) *Organization and Environment: Managing Differentiation and Integration.* Boston: Division of Research, Graduate School of Business Administration, Harvard University.

Lenz, R.T. (1980) 'Environment, strategy, organization structure and performance: Patterns in one industry', *Strategic Management Journal,* 1: 209–26.

Lincoln, J.R., Hanada, M. and Olson, J. (1981) 'Cultural orientations and individual reactions to organizations: A study of employees of Japanese-owned firms', *Administrative Science Quarterly,* 26 (1): 93–115.

Lioukas, S.K. and Xerokostas, D.A. (1982) 'Size and administrative intensity in organizational divisions', *Management Science,* 28 (8): 854–68.

Lorsch, Jay W. and Allen, Stephen A. (1973) *Managing Diversity and Inter-dependence: An Organizational Study of Multidivisional Firms.* Boston: Division of Research, Graduate School of Administration, Harvard University.

McCloskey, Donald N. (1983) 'The rhetoric of economics', *Journal of Economic Literature,* 21: 481–517.

McKelvey, Bill and Aldrich, Howard (1983) 'Populations, natural selection and applied organizational science', *Administrative Science Quarterly* 28 (1): 101–28.

MacMillan, Alexander and Daft, Richard L. (1979) 'Administrative intensity and ratio variables: The case against definitional dependency', *Social Forces,* 58 (1): 228–48.

MacMillan, Alexander and Daft, Richard L. (1984) 'Inferences about economics of scale DO depend on the form of statistical analysis: A reconciliation', *Social Forces,* 62 (4): 1059–67.

McNeill, W. H. (1982) *The Pursuit of Power: Technology, Armed Force, and Society since A.D. 1000.* Chicago: Chicago University Press.

Mahoney, Joseph T. (1992) 'The adoption of the multidivisional form of organization: A contingency model', *Journal of Management Studies,* 29 (1): 49–72.

Mahoney, Joseph T. (1993) 'Strategic management and determinism: Sustaining the conversation', *Journal of Management Studies,* 30 (1): 173–91.

Mannheim, B.F. and Moskovits, N. (1979) 'Contextual variables and bureaucratic types of Israeli service organizations', Chap. 9 in C.J. Lammers, and D.J. Hickson, (eds), *Organizations Alike and Unlike: International and Interinstitutional Studies in the Sociology of Organizations.* London: Routlege and Kegan Paul.

Mansfield, Roger, Todd, Dave and Wheeler, Jo (1980) 'Structural implications of the company–customer interface', *Journal of Management Studies*, 17 (1): 19–33.

Marsh, Robert M. and Mannari, Hiroshi (1981) 'Technology and size as determinants of the organizational structure of Japanese factories', *Administrative Science Quarterly*, 26 (1): 33–57.

Marsh, Robert M. and Mannari, Hiroshi (1989) 'The size imperative? Longitudinal tests', *Organization Studies*, 10 (1): 83–95.

Merton, R.K. (1957) *Social Theory and Social Structure*. Rev. edn. Glencoe, IL: Free Press.

Meyer, Alan D., Tsui, Anne S. and Hinings, C.R. (1993) 'Configurational approaches to organizational analysis', *Academy of Management Journal*, 36 (6): 1175–95.

Meyer, John W. and Scott, W. Richard with the assistance of B. Rowan and T.E. Deal (1983) *Organizational Environments: Ritual and Rationality*. Beverly Hills, CA: Sage.

Meyer, Marshall W. (1979) *Change in Public Bureaucracies*. Cambridge: Cambridge University Press.

Miles, Raymond E. and Snow, Charles C. (1978) *Organizational Strategy, Structure, and Process*. New York: McGraw-Hill.

Miller, Danny (1986) 'Configurations of strategy and structure: Towards a synthesis', *Strategic Management Journal*, 7: 233–49.

Miller, Danny and Droge, Cornelia (1986) 'Psychological and traditional determinants of structure', *Administrative Science Quarterly*, 31 (4): 539–60.

Miller, Danny, Droge, Cornelia and Toulouse, Jean-Marie (1988) 'Strategic process and content as mediators between organizational context and structure', *Academy of Management Journal*, 31 (3): 544–69.

Miller, Danny and Friesen, P.H. (1980) 'Momentum and revolution in organizational adaptation', *Academy of Management Journal*, 23 (4): 591–-14.

Miller, Danny and Friesen, P.H. (1982) 'Structural change and performance: Quantum vs. piecemeal–incremental approaches', *Academy of Management Journal*, 25 (4): 867–92.

Miller, Danny and Toulouse, Jean-Marie (1986) 'Chief executive personality and corporate strategy and structure in small firms', *Management Science*, 32 (11): 1389–409.

Miller, George A. (1987) 'Meta-analysis and the culture-free hypothesis', *Organization Studies*, 8 (4): 309–26.

Mintzberg, Henry (1979) *The Structuring of Organizations: A Synthesis of the Research*. Englewood Cliffs, NJ: Prentice Hall.

Montanari, John R. (1979) 'Strategic choice: A theoretical analysis', *Journal of Management Studies*, 16 (2): 202–21.

Montanari, John R. and Adelman, Philip J. (1987) 'The administrative component of organizations and the ratchet effect: A critique of cross-sectional studies', *Journal of Management Studies*, 24 (2): 113–23.

Nunnally, J.C. (1978) *Psychometric Theory*. 2nd edn. New York: McGraw-Hill.

Palmer, D., Friedland, R., Jennings, P.D. and Powers, M.E. (1987) 'The economics and politics of structure: The multidivisional form and the large US corporation', *Administrative Science Quarterly*, 32 (1): 25–48.

Palmer, D., Jennings, P.D. and Zhou, Xueguang (1993) 'Late adoption of the multidivisional form by large US corporations: Institutional, political, and economic accounts', *Administrative Science Quarterly*, 38 (1): 100–31.

Parkinson, C. Northcote (1957) *Parkinson's Law and Other Studies in Administration*. Boston: Houghton Mifflin.

Pavan, Robert J. (1976) 'Strategy and structure: The Italian experience', *Journal of Economics and Business*, 28 (3): 254–60.

Payne, Roy L. and Mansfield, Roger (1973) 'Relationships of perceptions of organizational climate to organizational structure, context, and hierarchical position', *Administrative Science Quarterly*, 18: 515–26.

Perrow, C. (1979) *Complex Organizations: A Critical Essay*. 2nd edn (1st edn, 1972), Glenview, IL: Scott, Foresman & Co.

Peters, Thomas J. and Waterman, Robert H., Jr (1982) *In Search of Excellence: Lessons from America's Best-Run Companies*. New York: Harper and Row.

Pfeffer, Jeffrey and Salancik, Gerald R. (1978) *The External Control of Organizations: A Resource Dependence Perspective*. New York: Harper and Row.

Pitts, Robert A. (1976) 'Diversification strategies and organizational policies of large diversified firms', *Journal of Economics and Business*, 28 (3): 181–88.

Popper, K.R. (1945) *The Open Society and its Enemies, vol. 2, The High Tide of Prophecy: Hegel, Marx and the Aftermath*. London: Routledge and Kegan Paul.

Porter, M.E. (1980) *Competitive Strategy*. New York: Free Press.

Powell, Walter W. and DiMaggio, Paul J. (1991) *The New Institutionalism in Organizational Analysis*. Chicago: University of Chicago Press.

Price, James L. and Mueller, C.W. (1986) *Handbook of Organizational Measurement*. Marshfield, MA: Pitman.

Pugh, D.S. and Hickson, D.J. (eds) (1976) *Organizational Structure in its Context: The Aston Programme I*. Farnborough, Hants: Saxon House.

Pugh, D.S., Hickson, D. J., Hinings, C.R., Macdonald, K.M., Turner, C. and Lupton, T. (1963) 'A conceptual scheme for organizational analysis', *Administrative Science Quarterly*, 8 (3): 289–315.

Pugh, D.S., Hickson, D.J., Hinings, C.R. and Turner, C. (1968) 'Dimensions of organization structure', *Administrative Science Quarterly*, 13 (1): 65–105.

Pugh, D.S., Hickson, D.J., Hinings, C.R. and Turner, C. (1969a) 'The context of organization structures', *Administrative Science Quarterly*, 14 (1): 91–114.

Pugh, D.S., Hickson, D.J. and Hinings, C.R. (1969b) 'An empirical taxonomy of structures of work organizations', *Administrative Science Quarterly*, 14 (1): 115–26.

Pugh, D.S. and Hinings, C.R. (eds) (1976) *Organizational Structure: Extensions and Replications: The Aston Programme II*. Farnborough, Hants: Saxon House.

Reimann, Bernard C. (1973) 'On the dimensions of bureaucratic structure: An empirical reappraisal', *Administrative Science Quarterly*, 18 (4): 462–76.

Reimann, Bernard C. (1977) 'Dimensions of organizational technology and structure: An exploratory study', *Human Relations*, 30 (6): 545–66.

Reimann, Bernard C. (1979) 'Parkinson revisited: A component analysis of the use of staff specialists in manufacturing organizations', *Human Relations*, 32 (7): 625–41.

Reimann, Bernard C. and Inzerilli, Giorgio (1979) 'A comparative analysis of empirical research on technology and structure', *Journal of Management*, 5 (2): 167–92.

Richards, V. G. (1980) Research Note: 'The Aston databank'. *Organization Studies*, 1 (3): 271–78.

Rothwell, Roy (1975) 'Intracorporate entrepreneurs', *Management Decision*, 13 (3): 142–54.

Routamaa, Vesa (1985) 'Organizational structuring: An empirical analysis of the relationships and dimensions of structures in certain Finnish companies', *Journal of Management Studies*, 22 (5): 498–522.

Roy, William G. (1990) 'Functional and historical logics in explaining the rise of the American Industrial Corporation', in Craig Calhoun (ed.), *Comparative Social Research, A Research Annual: Business Institutions (Vol. 12)*. Greenwich, CT: JAI Press, 19–44.

Rumelt, Richard P. (1974) *Strategy, Structure and Economic Performance*. Boston, MA: Division of Research, Graduate School of Business Administration, Harvard University.

Schreyögg, Georg (1980) 'Contingency and choice in organization theory', *Organization Studies*, 1 (4): 305–26.

Schreyögg, Georg (1982) 'Some comments about comments: A reply to Donaldson', *Organization Studies*, 3 (1): 73–8.

Scott, Bruce R. (1971) *Stages of Corporate Development*. Boston, MA: Harvard Business School.

Shenoy, S. (1981) 'Organization structure and context: A replication of the Aston study in India', Chap. 8 in D.J. Hickson and C.J. McMillan (eds), *Organization and Nation: the Aston Programme IV*, Farnborough, Hants: Gower.

Silverman, David (1970) *The Theory of Organizations*. London: Heinemann.

Simon, Herbert A. (1965) *Administrative Behaviour: A Study of Decision-making Processes on Administrative Organization*. 2nd edn, New York: Free Press.

Smith, M.R. (1978) 'Profits and administrative intensity: A longitudinal analysis', *Sociology,* 12 (3): 509–21.

Suzuki, Y. (1980) 'The strategy and structure of top 100 Japanese industrial enterprises 1950–1970', *Strategic Management Journal,* 1 (3): 265–91.

Tai, Elizabeth (1987) 'Adaptability and organisational effectiveness: A study of thirty manufacturing firms in Singapore'. Unpublished PhD thesis, University of New South Wales, Sydney, Australia.

Tauber, I. (1968). 'A Yardstick of Hospital Organization'. Diploma thesis, University of Aston, Birmingham, England.

Tayeb, Monir (1987) 'Contingency theory and culture: A study of matched English and Indian manufacturing firms', *Organization Studies,* 8 (3): 241–61.

Thompson, James D. (1967) *Organizations in Action.* New York: McGraw-Hill.

Tichy, Noel M. and Sherman, Stratford (1993) *Control Your Destiny or Someone Else Will: How Jack Welch is Making General Electric the World's Most Competitive Corporation.* New York: Currency Doubleday.

Tricker, R.I. (1984) *Corporate Governance: Practices, Procedures and Powers in British Companies and their Boards of Directors.* Aldershot, Hants: Gower.

Van de Ven, Andrew H., Delbecq, A.L. and Koenig, R., Jr (1976) 'Determinants of coordination modes within organizations', *American Sociological Review,* 41: 322–38.

Van de Ven, Andrew and Ferry, Diane L. (1980) *Measuring and Assessing Organizations.* New York: Wiley.

Warner, M. (ed.) (1977) *Organizational Choice and Constraint: Approaches to the Sociology of Enterprise Behaviour.* Farnborough: Saxon House.

Weber, Max (1968) *Economy and Society: An Outline of Interpretive Sociology,* ed. Guenther Roth and Claus Wittich. New York: Bedminster Press.

Weick, Karl E. (1987) 'Perspectives on action in organizations', Chap. 2 in Jay W. Lorsch (ed.), *Handbook of Organizational Behavior.* Englewood Cliffs, NJ: Prentice Hall.

Whitley, R.D. (1977) 'Concepts of organization and power in the study of organizations', *Personnel Review,* 6 (1): 54–9.

Whittington, R. (1988) 'Environmental structure and theories of strategic choice', *Journal of Management Studies,* 25 (6): 521–36.

Whittington, R. (1989) *Corporate Strategies in Recession and Recovery: Social Structure and Strategic Choice.* London: Unwin Hyman.

Williamson, Oliver E. (1970) *Corporate Control and Business Behavior: An Inquiry into the Effects of Organization Form on Enterprise Behavior.* Englewood Cliffs, NJ: Prentice Hall.

Williamson, Oliver E. (1971) 'Managerial discretion, organization form, and the multidivison hypothesis', in Robin Marris and Adrian Woods (eds), *The Corporate Economy: Growth, Competition and Innovative Potential.* Cambridge, MA: Harvard University Press.

Williamson, Oliver E. (1985) *The Economic Institutions of Capitalism: Firms, Markets, Relational Contracting.* New York: Free Press.

Wong, Gilbert Y.Y. and Birnbaum-More, Philip H. (1994) 'Culture, context and structure: A test on Hong Kong banks', *Organization Studies,* 15 (1): 99–123.

Woodward, Joan (1965) *Industrial Organization: Theory and Practice.* London: Oxford University Press.

Zeffane, Rachid M. (1989) 'Organization structures and contingencies in different nations: Algeria, Britain, and France', *Social Science Research,* 18: 331–69.

Index